W9-BQY-454

Reaching the Unreached

The Old-New Challenge

Edited by

Harvie M. Conn

Presbyterian and Reformed Publishing Company
Phillipsburg, New Jersey

LINCOLN CHRISTIAN COLLEGE

Copyright © 1984
Presbyterian and Reformed Publishing Company

All rights reserved. No part of this book may be reproduced in any form or by any means, except for brief quotations for the purpose of review, comment, or scholarship, without written permission from the publisher, Presbyterian and Reformed Publishing Company, Box 817, Phillipsburg, New Jersey 08865.

PRINTED IN THE UNITED STATES OF AMERICA

Library of Congress Cataloging in Publication Data
Main entry under title:

Reaching the unreached.

Bibliography: p. 169
1. Evangelistic work—Congresses.   2. Missions—Theory
—Congresses.   I. Conn, Harvie M.
BV3755.R4   1984   266'.5   84–3347
ISBN 0-87552-209-2

"That which is of first
importance is the carrying of
the message to those who have never heard."
—Robert A. Jaffray

Bookstore

S 47

6 Jan. 86

71818

Contents

Foreword

John Murray, the Reformed theologian, in an essay on "The Church and Mission," speaks of "the appalling spectacle that confronts us in the sphere of mission." It is the failure on the part of men and women to understand and discharge responsibility and buy up opportunity. "Our remissness," he continues, "springs from our lack of concern for the salvation of perishing souls, our lack of love, our lack of zeal for the claims of Christ and of his body the church, and finally our lack of jealousy for the glory of God. If fervour of spirit and the service of the Lord animate our hearts, then with the apostles we cannot but speak the things which we have seen and heard. And we may not be dismayed by the odds of unbelieving opposition and indifference. The gospel is the power of God unto salvation and his Word will not return unto him void. And he has put this treasure in earthen vessels that the excellency of the power may be of God and not of us" (Murray 1976:252).

In the last decade especially a concept has arisen within evangelical circles to remind us in a fresh way of that unfinished task—unreached people groups. As a technical category, it has been shaped out of the need for strategy planning to reach three-fourths of the world's population who do not know Christ in a saving way. At least a billion people can be evangelized by local churches. But there are at least another two billion who can only be reached by cross-cultural missionaries. The "unreached people" emphasis is one approach to the task.

Who and where are the unreached? What new methods and updated resources are available for reaching them? How can we avoid past mistakes in this undertaking? What must be done to restructure mission boards, to mobilize theological seminaries and churches for the work?

From March 16 to 18, 1983, 48 participants gathered at Westminster Theological Seminary, Philadelphia, to join in seeking answers to these questions. Missionaries and pastors, men and women, mission board representatives, Third World church leaders and mission instructors, they came together on an unofficial basis to interact, to stir the fire, to recapture the "zeal for God's house" (Ps. 69:2; John 2:17).

A fivefold purpose dominated the sessions. We sought (1) to focus, in as practical a way as possible, on the need for reaching the unreached peoples; (2) to define the terms used in recent discussions and trace their usage over the last decade; (3) to offer suggestions for avoiding past mistakes in the task and for developing new methods for the future; (4) to offer concrete suggestions to mission boards, seminaries, and churches for mobilizing the church to reach the unreached; (5) to challenge the world Reformed community to build new structures to finish the task.

How far we succeeded we must leave to the reader to decide. Those looking for a heavy concentration on theoretical discussions will be disappointed. We deliberately sought to minimize these and to concentrate on questions of strategy. Not that theoretical questions are unimportant. Gathered as a Reformed Missions Consultation and, in most cases, representing Reformed institutions and Calvinistic theological convictions, we did not expect strategy presuppositions to go unexamined!

Our concerns this time were different from those of the six previous consultations. And, without much prior planning, they emerged repeatedly in all the papers. "Why have we as a church been so slow to fulfill our dynamic mandate of the kingdom of Jesus Christ?" Robert Recker asked on our behalf. "Will 'unreached peoples' become another missiological fad if the church remains preoccupied with its own edification and doctrinal purity?" underlines Roger Greenway. "Will our built-in potential for drifting off course once more divert our resources from the primary goal of making disciples of Jesus Christ among the peoples of the world?" agonizes Paul Long. Addison Soltau, speaking from his heart, and ours, chides the seminaries that train us as "static and isolationist." "Consistent pressure," he calls, "must be brought to bear to undermine the age-long concept that the routine business of church is unrelated to mission, and the church's missionary outreach is limited to specialists." The affirmation was clear throughout the consultation: let us join with our brothers and sisters everywhere and get the job done.

When the time was over, we left with renewed vision and a new set of questions emerging from our discussions. How could we get our message to the churches? How could highly trained mission specialists work with all of God's people to avoid creating a divorce between a potential "mission elite" and the grassroots in the churches? What steps had to be taken to bring the message of unreached peoples to our constituencies? Our frustrations at being an unofficial study group emerged strongly at this point.

How could we help our constituencies see the invisible, unreached peoples of the West? Is our traditional language of "home" and "foreign" missions still too geographically oriented to find the unevangelized frontiers of our Jerusalem neighborhoods? What of the marginal peoples in our North American cities, and the parochial boundaries of our largely suburban churches that do not cross over into the Hispanic, the Black, the Asian Samarias?

How can we find better ways to receive more input from Third World church leaders? Our consultation saw itself as a microcosm of the larger problem. A limitation of available funds inhibited us from inviting a significant number of Third World people. One board had graciously provided travel expenses for a Central American churchman to attend the consultation. And his was a rich contribution to us all. Others came who were studying in the United States. But the papers were prepared by Westerners. And because of that our orientation remained Western. What sacrifices must be made to internationalize the task? Paul Schrotenboer reflected the sentiments of many when he proposed ''that this conference, recognizing the inadequacy of missiologists, mission secretaries, or even churches of the West to undertake the vast challenge of reaching the unreached alone, take the necessary initial steps to arrange for a consultation/workshop of Reformed and evangelical churches from the West and the Third World to implement jointly the objective of effective interdependence in reaching the unreached.'' Again the unofficial character of the consultation left us with few official strings to pull. But all of us hoped our concern would be heard.

How can we bring the theologians who dominate our schools and our doctrinal developments into the discussion? As long as the unreached peoples remain a concern only of professional missiologists in our schools and the secretaries of our boards, our understanding of ecclesiology will continue to reduce itself to introverted churchliness. There was disappointment and anger and frustration. Reformed church people have had a long tradition of listening carefully to its theologians. And no one at the consultation was proposing a change in that healthy respect. But we yearned for the hour when theologians would listen to the concerns of this gathering. One sensed our theologians were seen as placing the church as the goal of missions. The stress was on her isolated piety and liturgy, her inner riches. Where was the vision of the church ''inside out,'' in exodus to the world and as a sign of the kingdom of God?

These were the kinds of questions we verbalized as we went through the process. There were others we did not. And as I write this foreword, I could wish also to write an afterword. The questions on my silent agenda would include many emerging for me from Paul Schrotenboer's panoramic vision of chapters six and seven.

What effect does Western wealth and ready access to technology have on reaching the unreached? Have we become so blinded by our resources that we cannot see the dangers those resources represent to the unreached poor of the earth? What is the evangelistic role played by the church's call for justice among the oppressed of the world's cultures? How does our silence over racism, and our (often) concomitant verbosity over liberalism, hinder us in the task of global evangelization? G. C. Berkouwer has noted that "the church is placed in the world not as a passive observer of God's action in and with the world; rather, she is called to 'involvement,' or engagement, with the world—with the whole of human life in all its dimensions" (Berkouwer 1976:395-96). How can this engagement avoid "meddlesomeness" and become evangelistic? How can we treasure our Reformed tradition and avoid traditionalizing it? How can we preserve its riches by giving them away? Has our love of the Reformed faith made it difficult for our churches to aim for unreached peoples, because we cannot recognize the legitimacy of other evangelical churches, not Reformed, also engaged in that task? Comity over unreached peoples is difficult to achieve when you will admit only the frailties of the other body trying to do a similar task. You have to do it all yourself. Do you?

We were greatly helped in all of this by everyone who took part. Unfortunately we cannot include the case study prepared for us by Samuel Wilson of MARC/World Vision. But we can give special thanks to Dr. Ralph Winter whose papers, lengthier by far than any others in the book, reflect the wisdom and leadership he has taken in this area. It was wisdom and leadership we continued to appreciate throughout our time together. The development of this whole concept of unreached peoples, as chapter two clearly indicates, is deeply indebted to him and to the gifts the Lord has liberally showered on him.

He would be the first to admit the last word has not been spoken. And, for that reason, we have included the chapter by James Reapsome, an essay not read at the consultation. It indicates the ongoing character of the discussion. I myself found many of the questions emerging from Reapsome's survey answered by some of Winter's arguments in chapter three. But its anecdotal character catches some of the flavor of the current debate in a way that adds a dimension to Winter's more systematic arrangement. For that reason alone it seemed a wise choice to add it. It diminishes in no way from the contribution of Winter's presentations. Both augment one another.

There were many who labored behind the scenes, or better yet, between the lines. Miss Linda Porter of the Seminary staff saw to many needs before they were spoken. Miss Shannah Frame-Szto worked hard to prepare the typescript of this manuscript.

We are grateful to God for bringing us together. May we also be grateful to Him for using this book to send us away. May the vision of 48 men and women for an invisible world of unreached peoples open our eyes to see God's harvest.

Harvie M. Conn
June 23, 1983

Chapter 1
The Biblical Mandate
Robert D. Recker

The biblical story moves from the Garden of Eden to the vision of renewed humanity in the new Jerusalem of God. This story has to do with a people and peoples as they relate to the center, the sent Son of God, the true Israelite, and the glory-filled Son of Man, who victoriously reigns.

The God-created and God-placed man in the earth is exhorted by God to fill the earth, to subdue it, and to have dominion over every living thing in it. After the flood the Lord affirmed, "I will remember my covenant between me and you and all living creatures of every kind" (Gen. 9:15). God's promise to Abraham included worldwide perspectives: "I will make you into a great nation and I will bless you . . . and all the peoples on earth will be blessed through you" (Gen. 12:2-3).

Jesus exhorted the early nuclear church concerning the divinely ordained certainty that "repentance and forgiveness of sins will be preached in His name to all nations, beginning at Jerusalem" (Luke 24:47), reminding them that they were the official witnesses on His behalf: "You are witnesses of these things" (Luke 24:48).

And the seer, John, envisioned the eschatological city of God with its gates open to the whole world, welcoming the glory and honor of the nations into it, making room for the nations to walk in its light, the lamp of which will be the Lamb of God (Rev. 21:24-26; cf. Isa. 60:11).

It is this universal beginning and this universalistic vision of the end of history which form the divine parenthesis of the Scripture. And at the heart of the parenthesis is the story of our Lord Jesus Christ, a story that must be told to the nations.

The apostle Paul, in building up the great Epistle to the Romans, provides a similarly evangelical parenthesis in the words, "Through him and for his name's sake, we received grace and apostleship to call people from among all the Gentiles to the obedience that comes from faith [obedience of faith]" (Rom. 1:5). That is reaffirmed again in his concluding words, "According to the revelation of the mystery hidden for long ages past, but now revealed and made known through the prophetic writings by the command of the eternal God, so

1

that all nations might believe and obey him [obedience of faith]'' (Rom. 16:25-26).

The Epistle to the Romans reveals that Paul was gripped by the unresolved problematic of the Old Covenant, the dichotomy between Israel and the Goyim. Romans evidences Paul's attempts to deal with this mystery of God's working in salvation history. But there are many other relevant passages in his epistles. For Paul and other early New Testament Christians this was a theological problem with which they had to wrestle. His conclusion was that ''there is no difference between Jew and Gentile—the same Lord is Lord of all and richly blesses all who call on him'' (Rom. 10:12).

Israel and the Nations

What was the meaning of God's so-called ''particularistic'' dealings with Israel? Was this merely a methodological approach on the part of God over against the nations, or was this a radical choice of God for Israel and thus against the gentile world? It cannot be denied that in much of the Old Testament the gentile world is pictured as temptation and threat to Israel (Bavinck 1960:11). Yahweh is presented as living in the bosom of Israel, whereas the gentile nations were viewed as godless and without hope (Eph. 2:12). The only hope for such nations appeared to be found in a coming to Israel and thus a coming to the God who lived in the midst of Israel (Isa. 55:5; 56:3-8; 60:1-5; Ruth 1:16). In that era, to deal with the word and will of God, the seeker had to deal with Israel and thus make peace with the God of Israel. Israel was in some sense a touchstone among the nations (Gen. 12:3). She would become a byword symbolic of blessing or of cursing.

What God did in the midst of and with Israel was not done in a corner. She was living her life, as it were, in the amphitheater of the nations (Bavinck 1960:14-15). In her internal communal life she was to serve as a model to the nations, indicating what a blessed life eventuated when both God and neighbor are given their due. The law of the living God was to take incarnate form in her daily communal life. She was to show hospitality to the stranger and alien, with one law governing the life of the home-born and the stranger (Exod. 12:48-49; 20:10; Num. 9:14; 15:30; I Kings 8:41-43). The attitude of Israel to the sojourning stranger among them was to be that of love, and this mandate flowed out of the very nature of God Himself (Deut. 10:18-19; Lev. 19:34). Israel was reminded to recall its own history of wanderings (Gen. 15:13; 18:1-8, 24; Exod. 23:9). The stranger was not to be out of sight, and out of mind.

God's covenant with Abraham indicated that Israel was to fulfill a certain role with regard to the Gentiles, a role God succinctly summarized as ''being a blessing to all the families of the earth.'' At a later stage in Israel's life Zechariah was led to characterize the net historical result as more that of a curse than a blessing (Zech. 8:13). Prior to this judgment the Israelites had been reminded of God's command that they "not oppress the widow, or the fatherless, the alien or the poor" (Zech. 7:10). The book of Jonah would appear to be a critique of Israel's lack of love for her neighbors, when it is viewed in the light of the divine observation regarding Nineveh: "And should I not be concerned about that great city?" (cf. also Ezek. 36:22-23,36).

Something of this role of the people of Israel was again referred to in the making of the Sinaitic covenant. God commanded Moses to communicate to Israel the challenging words,

> Now therefore, if you will obey my voice and keep my covenant, you shall be my own possession among all peoples; for all the earth is mine, and you shall be to me a kingdom of priests and a holy nation (Exod. 19:5-6, RSV).

Here Israel is clearly set in the midst of the peoples of the earth, in the midst of an earth declared to be God's; and her role in that arena is to be an obedient community of ministering servants on behalf of God, a nation dedicated to the service of God. The entire earth is pictured as the temple wherein the Israelite priests of God serve (cf. Hab. 2:20). At a later date Peter, in writing to the "exiles of the dispersion," does a commentary on this text. He exhorts them to fulfill the role of a "holy priesthood," by declaring the wonderful deeds of God who called them out of darkness, abstaining from the passions of the flesh, and maintaining "good conduct among the pagans," that they might "see your good deeds and glorify God on the day he visits you" (I Pet. 2:5,9-12).

That this was not simply theoretical speculation is shown in Solomon's prayer at the dedication of the temple. There he pictured the foreigner as coming to the temple to entreat the Lord, having heard of the good news of this God in a far country. Solomon implored God to hear that foreigner's prayer "so that all the peoples of the earth may know your name and fear you, as do your own people Israel . . ." (I Kings 8:41-43). It is of note that the liturgical setting often appeared to evoke in Israel the consciousness of Yahweh's universal reign and of His significance for the nations (cf. Ps. 46:10; 47; 67; 95–100). The faith of Israel seemed to cry out for the universal recognition and service of this living God (Ps. 72:19; 67:2).

The prophet Isaiah envisioned a day when Israel would serve a mediating function among the nations. She would be the peacemaker among her historic enemies, and she would share her covenantal blessings with them. And thus in playing a servant role Israel would become a "blessing in the midst of the earth" (Isa. 19:23-24, RSV).

It must be recognized that on the whole the manner in which Israel was to fulfill her missionary role in the Old Testament was that of the centripetal model (Mic. 4:1-2; Isa. 2:2-3; Zech. 8:20-23; Isa. 45:14-17; 60:3). Yet there are

3

also intimations of centrifugal movement out of Israel toward the nations. Such movement is not simply in the form of outgoing rumors of what God has done in and with Israel, but rather that of a conscious, intentional proclamation of the Lord to the nations (Isa. 42:1-4, 10-13; 45:6,21-23; 49:6; 51:4-5; 52:10, 15; 54:3; 56:7; 59:19; 60:9; 61:6, 11; 66:19; Hab. 2:14).

J. H. Bavinck has rightly observed that this glorious anticipated future clusters around the appearing of the promised Messiah of God. He will be at the center of the promised renewal of Israel, and only thus will blessing come to the nations of the earth (1960:20). Though much of the centripetal movement is viewed as a spontaneous coming, the significant impact of the dramatic communal life of Israel on nations must not be minimized. She was placed in the world amphitheater as God gathered all the nations before Him in a cosmic lawsuit (Isa. 43:8-13), and Israel was called upon to be Yahweh's legal witnesses in the earth. She was to witness to the truth, to the fact that Yahweh has saved, and that there is no God and Savior besides Him: "You are my witnesses" (Isa. 43:10, 12; 44:8). The roles of the individual Servant of Yahweh and of the communal servant, Israel, are not sharply distinguished in the Servant Songs. There seems to be an interdependence built into the account. At the least we can affirm that the princely Servant is the choice instrument in the hand of Yahweh to enlighten the Gentiles. A beginning was made in this venture when Galilee of the nations saw a great light (Isa. 9:1-2; Matt. 4:12-17). Shortly thereafter in the account Jesus called His disciples to follow Him, saying, "I will make you fishers of men" (Matt. 4:19). And in the Sermon on the Mount He designated His followers as "the salt of the earth" and the "light of the world" (Matt. 5:13-14).

Thus it is not strange that Luke in the conclusion to his Gospel and at the beginning of the Book of Acts recorded that the Christ reached back for Isaianic language and affirmed that His followers were now to fulfill the old role of Israel among the nations with the saying, "You will be my witnesses both in Jerusalem, and in all Judaea and Samaria, and to the ends of the earth" (Acts 1:8). And it is worthy to note the inclusive scope of this activity; once again the entire earth is to be the amphitheater of this witness.

Both Isaiah and Luke emphasize that the outpouring of the Lord's Spirit is what qualifies His agents to witness (Isa. 44:1-5; Acts 1:8; 2:1-4; 2:32-33; see also Ezek. 36:23-27; Joel 2:19-29). The task of reclaiming the whole world in the name of Israel's Savior God will be fulfilled by the almighty power of the Spirit of this God. A new witnessing power will thereby characterize the people of God. A new boldness in aggressive, persistent outreach will mark the apostolic band (Acts 2:29; 4:13,29,31; 28:31). The new Israel of God will not be timid or shy (II Tim. 1:7). Even in the past they were characterized as a people "who through faith conquered kingdoms, administered justice, and gained what was promised, who shut up the mouths of lions, quenched the fury of the flames, and escaped the edge of the sword, whose weakness was turned to strength; and who became powerful in battle and routed foreign armies. . . . Others were tortured, and refused to be released, . . . the world was not worthy of them'' (Heb. 11:33-38). How much more should boldness characterize them in the future! The Hebrew Christians are reminded to be grateful for ''receiving a kingdom that cannot be shaken'' (Heb. 12:28), and to offer to that ruling God acceptable worship, ''with reverence and awe, for our God is a consuming fire'' (Heb. 12:28-29). The author's final blessing is a prayer to God that He might equip them ''with everything good for doing His will, and may He work in us what is pleasing to Him, through Jesus Christ . . .'' (Heb. 13:21).

But before we go on with the New Testament material we must take another quick look at the role of the nations in the Old Testament. We are first of all reminded of the unity of the human race before the face of God. ''From one man He made every nation of men, that they should inhabit the whole earth, and He determined the times set for them and the exact places where they should live. God did this so that men would seek Him and perhaps reach out for Him and find Him, though He is not far from each one of us . . .'' (Acts 17:26-27). Paul in his address in the Areopagus affirmed the unity of all mankind in that ''the God who made the world and everything in it is the Lord of heaven and earth'' (Acts 17:24). This is the note on which the biblical revelation begins. The history of all mankind takes off as it were from the very hand of God the Creator, the One who placed mankind in the earth.

Paul indicated that all peoples are ruled and provided for by this one God. He is in some sense ''near'' to them, to the end that they might seek Him and find Him. The creation account in Genesis also indicates something of this nearness of God to His creature man. People are made in His image, and they are royal agents of that God in the earth and thus responsible to Him. And much of the Genesis material underscores this truth that God calls all peoples to account. There is a solidarity among people with relation to God's dealing with them. So all people in Adam fall into sin, are judged by God, and in Adam are driven from the garden. Furthermore, the flood is an expression of God's general judgment that ''all peoples on earth had corrupted their ways'' (Gen. 6:12).

The table of nations in Genesis 10 underscores this unity of the children of men, but it also highlights the fact of their geographical dispersion. Mankind is pictured as flourishing and multiplying in their divinely provided habitat. And in the tower of Babel incident specific recognition is given of the divine word, ''Behold, they are one people, and they have all one language'' (Gen. 11:6, RSV). Verkuyl sees Babel as ''a collective effort to organize the world without God'' (1973:37); it was an expression of human self-deification, a rejection of

His wisdom and providential control. Thus God's dispersing of the peoples was an expression of His judgment upon their sinful arrogance. They were dispersed in order to fulfill their role in the earth.

Abram, the one who was called out to be the father of Israel, became the symbol of faith and faithfulness. He manifested true love for his neighbors and proved to be a blessing to the kings and the people of the plain among whom he lived. And when God Almighty again appeared to Abram, he is given the name Abraham, and assured that he would be "the father of many nations" (Gen. 17:4-6). And as a sign and seal of that covenant all the males of his household, including the foreigner, were circumcised (Gen. 17:27). They were placed in the arena of God's gracious activity.

The episode of Lot in Sodom indicated the other side of the coin. Undiscerning intimacy with wicked men will draw down God's judgment, heartache, and loss. Abraham and his seed, those who represent God in the earth, must maintain their distinctiveness in order to be a blessing to the peoples of the earth. The salt may not lose its flavor.

The identity of the people-of-God-in-the-earth required that they maintain some distance between themselves and other peoples. And yet that seemed to vary according to the historical circumstances. The sons of Jacob appeared to live in much closer proximity to the surrounding peoples than could post-exilic Israel. When we inquire from the Bible what determines the measure of distance, we are reminded of Abraham's remark to Abimelech, king of Gerar, that "there is surely no fear of God in this place" (Gen. 20:11). This would indicate that the style of our relationships is to be gauged by the level of the godlessness of the peoples about us. Lot was so guilty because he seemed to have lost his sensitivity to the depth of evil around him. His spiritual barometer completely failed him.

Paul says something similar in I Corinthians 5:9-13, where he expressly rejects the notion that the believer must withdraw from the world. Rather he rejects an intimacy with immoral people, particularly within the household of faith. The immorality of which he speaks was stealing, reviling, drinking, greed, and idolatry. The incompatibility of idolatry and the identity of the people of God was always in the forefront of the considerations of the old covenant. Nothing was to dim the splendor and witness of the exhortation that "you shall worship and serve the Lord your God alone." Nothing was to compromise the claims of the lordship of our God and Christ.

Paul speaks in the context of marriage of the "consent" of the unbelieving wife to live with the Christian husband. If we take this as a microcosm in human relations, it points us to the fact that our continued relationships with the unbelieving community around us are partly determined by their tolerance of or lack of tolerance of believers in their midst. Believers are exhorted to love and to pray even for their enemies, but at other times they must flee in order to protect their own lives. Yet as a general stance our love in Christ must overcome our fear (I John 4:18), and we are exhorted to look not only to our own interests, but to the interests of others and to the things of Jesus Christ (Phil. 2:4,21). This is to have the mind of Christ.

Biblical examples affirm that the level of unbelievers' tolerance for the people of God was an important determinant for the believers' stance. We recall the sojourn of Israel in Egypt, the relationship of Joseph to the pharaoh, the mandate given to Israel in exile to seek the good of the land, and the stance of Daniel and his associates over against the rulers of Mesopotamia. At a later time believers adjusted their stance in line with their new situation under the accord of Constantine, and later under the *pax Britannica*. Isaac had to come to terms with this stark given when the Philistines urged him, ''Move away from us; you have become too powerful for us'' (Gen. 26:16). But in God's providence the Philistines were forced to come to terms with Isaac and make covenant with him, for God was with him (Gen. 26:28-29). At a much later point in history modern missionaries came to terms with this when they were told that they were to behave as ''guests'' in the land. The sovereignty of God thus limits and curbs the autonomy of nations who seek to live apart from Him. It influences and overrules the attitudes they manifest toward the people of God. Not even nations who are zealous in their ungodliness are able to prevail with God and deny God's people room to exist and fulfill their mandate in the earth. All the earth belongs to God (Exod. 19:6).

Israel understood that the nature of their God was such that it implied a royal relationship to the entire earth. Hence the psalmist could liturgically declare and celebrate at the religious center of Israel with these words:

Sing to the Lord, all the earth,
. . . proclaim His salvation day after day.
Declare His glory among the nations,
His marvelous deeds among all peoples.
. . . Say among the nations, ''The Lord reigns.''
. . . He will judge the peoples with equity (Ps. 96).

The heavens proclaim His righteousness,
and all the peoples see His glory.
All who worship images are put to shame . . . (Ps. 97:6-7).

The Lord has made His salvation known
and revealed His righteousness to the nations.
. . . all the ends of the earth have seen the salvation of our God (Ps. 98:2-3).

It might be said that this is a proleptic celebration of an eschatological reality.

But even so it would have to be affirmed that this theological profession of faith transcended the day to day religious dichotomy that existed between Israel and the nations. As the Israelite bowed in worship before Yahweh, he was compelled to assert that the virtues of this saving God were to be recognized and acclaimed in the midst of the nations of the earth. The drama taking place between Israel and her God was of significance for the whole wide world of peoples.

So too, it was true of prophetic figures such as Isaiah, that their eschatological vision included not just a centripetal coming of many peoples to the mountain of the Lord for instruction in His ways, thus submitting to His judgments and ushering in peace among the nations (Isa. 2:2-4). It was also true that His judgments, His laws, His salvation will move outward from Yahweh to the peoples to enlighten them. The islands are pictured as waiting in hope for the active arm of Yahweh (Isa. 51:4-5). Even the centripetal movement (Isa. 49:22-23) is pictured as resulting in the knowledge and conviction of all flesh that Yahweh is Israel's Savior and Redeemer (Isa. 49:26). The worldwide visibility of God's saving acts is underscored (Isa. 52:10). Through the manifestation of Yahweh's righteous Servant, the nations will be anointed with wonder and kings will be struck dumb with conviction (Isa. 52:15).

A use is also made of the imagery of Israel entering to possess the land. Her tent prophetically is to be so enlarged that her seed takes possession of the nations and reinhabits desolate, abandoned cities (Isa. 54:2-3). Once again the theological warrant for this hopeful vision is to be found in the very nature of the Holy One of Israel, the God of the whole earth (Isa. 54:5). And this envisioned future is as certain as God's word of covenantal peace is sure. The old boundaries of the knowledge of the word of God will be transcended and nations will be annexed to Israel, because of the will and acts of Yahweh (Isa. 55:5).

But the final vision of the old covenant is a liturgical vision in which it is declared that Yahweh's house will be "called a house of prayer for all nations" (Isa. 56:7). And in a world where there is no other god, the proclamation is articulated, "Turn to me and be saved, all you ends of the earth; for I am God, and there is no other" (Isa. 45:22). As surely as God lives and speaks, the assured expectation is intoned, "Before me every knee will bow; by me every tongue will swear" (Isa. 45:23). This enlarging vision broadens out into the vision of the divine creation of the new heavens and a new earth (Isa. 65:17).

The Peoples and the Coming of the Kingdom

As one can quickly gather, the Old Testament vision of a new situation that will transcend the dichotomy between Israel and the nations was a royal vision, the vision of the victorious coming of the kingdom of God. Thus the good news that Christ brought was declared to be the gospel of the kingdom. Christ's coming to Israel was the event-announcement, certain and challenging, declaring, "Repent ye; for the kingdom of heaven is at hand" (Matt. 4:17, RSV). In the encounter with the centurion of Capernaum and his expression of faith, Christ evoked the centripetal vision of the old covenant with the expectant and prophetic words, "I say to you, that many will come from the east and the west, and will take their places at the feast with Abraham, Isaac, and Jacob in the kingdom of heaven" (Matt. 8:11). The accretions here pictured are not added to the central site and symbol of Israel, Jerusalem, but to Israel's fathers of faith and obedience. The dichotomy is therefore transcended not only on the boundaries. Rather the distant boundaries of peoplehood are collapsed right into the very fount and heartbeat of the covenantal peoplehood of Israel. They are intimately related to the historical patriarchs of Israel, and thereby to Israel's God. Even more startlingly, judgment also descends upon those who were subject to Israel's king. But in sharp contrast to gentile faith and inclusion, they will be disowned as unworthy of their privileges and excluded from the fellowship.

Jesus called to Himself the 12 apostles and sent them out. But in the early phase He confined their mission to the "lost sheep of Israel" (Matt. 10:6). Yet they too are exhorted to enunciate the messianic message, "The kingdom of heaven is at hand." And their representation is messianically qualified and authoritative in virtue of His presence. "He who receives you receives me, and he who receives me receives the one who sent me" (Matt. 10:40).

But even the salvation-history timetable of the messianic Servant of Yahweh is pushed forward by the impatient providential hand of Yahweh. So the importunate Canaanite woman in the area of Tyre and Sidon lays claim to the mercy that will spill over the historic boundaries of the house of Israel (Matt. 15:21-28). And at a later stage of His ministry the awesome prospect of judgment and displacement is held out to Israel. "The kingdom of God will be taken away from you, and given to a people who will produce its fruit" (Matt. 21:43).

As a microcosm of the people, Israel's religious leaders were confronted by their Messiah on two scores and condemned. "You shut the kingdom of heaven in men's faces. You yourselves do not enter, nor will you let those enter who are trying to" (Matt 23:13-14). In a sorrowful messianic lament for Jerusalem our Lord prophesies, "And this gospel of the kingdom will be preached in the whole world as a testimony to all nations, and then the end will come" (Matt. 24:14). This same Messiah is presented as the final judge of the nations (Matt 25:32). And the norm of that judgment will be that in their historical dealings the children of men have reacted as it were to the Messiah of God in a positive or negative fashion.

In Matthew's perspective, finally the promised King of Israel enunciates the charter of His new universal kingdom, directing His followers to claim the nations in His name and authority, making disciples and baptizing people of all the nations (Matt. 28:19). In such obedient activity the presence of the messianic Lord is assured, exercising His all-encompassing authority in and through His messengers.

This royal vision of the Messiah is already set forth in Psalm 2:8, where the nations of the earth are given to Him as His inheritance. The remote recesses of the earth are challenging bits of turf to be reclaimed, and in kingly fashion He rules with a rod. John's vision of the messianic work also fits in with this royal profile, in that "the reason the Son of God appeared was to destroy the devil's work" (I John 3:8). There is revealed in the ministry of Jesus a clash of kingdoms, and the Christ engages in an historical and powerful exposé of the false royal claims of the prince of darkness (John 12:31-32; 14:30-31; 16:8-11). Christ recognized this reality of the clash of competing kingdom claims and proceeded to drive out the demonic forces as an expression of the Spirit's presence and as an evidence of the impinging claims of God's royal rule (Matt. 12:25-28). Christ's apostolic activity was proof that the Messiah had bound up the evil strong man, and so could despoil his house (Matt. 12:29).

In line with the Old Testament use of the yoke as a symbol of submission to a king's rule (Lev. 26:13; Ezek. 30:18; 34:27; I Kings 12:4,9-14; Isa. 9:3-4; 14:25; Jer. 27:8-12; 28:2; 30:8), and in direct contrast to the oppressive nature of many of the royal yokes alluded to in the Old Testament, Christ's invitation to the weary and burdened to come to Him, to take on His yoke, and to learn from Him was and is attractive. Christ's royal yoke is recommended in that all things have been committed to this royal prince by the Father. The prince Himself is gentle and humble; His yoke or rule is easy and His burden is light. And the end of the matter is rest for the souls of those invited (Matt. 11:27-30). The stance of the king here is that of one who woos the people to own His sovereignty with the assurance that the result will be rest, and not that of oppression.

The tone of the Great Commission in Matthew 28 is more aggressive with regard to the rightful claims of this bona fide representative and vice-regent of Yahweh. Paul too, in looking over the course of salvation history, picked up the accents of Psalm 2 and underscored the promised Messiah's exercise of the rod in subduing all the nations of the earth, and in destroying all opposing forces or dominions, until all of His enemies capitulate to His rule and are put under His feet (I Cor. 15:24-28). Then the messianic Son will submit all of this to the Father in order that God may be all in all.

In all of this data there is an impetus toward a universalizing of the scope of the reign of the messianic prince who would come out of Judah. Isaiah's vision of the coming one on whose shoulder the government would rest (Isa. 9:6), and of the increase of whose government and peace there would be no end, would appear to be the outworking of the legitimate internal dynamic of the Abrahamic covenant. The gracious approach of God whereby He enters into covenant with men reveals a steadily widening horizon. The royal claims of the representative divine prince can tolerate no geographic or intensive limitations. He increasingly expresses Himself as King of kings and Lord of lords (Rev. 19:16).

It is not surprising that the apostle Paul understood and laid hold of this internal dynamic and so interpreted the promise Abraham and his offspring received as that of being "heir of the world" (Rom. 4:13). Israel thus in the person of the Christ, as the offspring of Abraham, takes possession in the name of the Lord of the whole world. As the world was viewed as the arena of the judging activity of Yahweh in His lawsuit with those rebellious to His rule, so now the world becomes the turf of the messianic prince who rides on conquering and to conquer (Rev. 6:2; 19:11-16). And the outcome of that engagement is succinctly put: "The kingdom of the world has become the kingdom of our Lord and of His Christ, and He will reign forever and ever" (Rev. 11:15).

The Book of Revelation with moving images reviews the grand sweep of salvation-history from the first coming of Christ to His second coming. It evaluates all things from the perspective of the Christ who rules in the midst of the seven candlesticks and who exercises judgment in the midst of the turbulent course of human history. It pictures the giant angel with the gospel scroll in his hand, one foot planted on the sea and the other on the land, thus symbolizing the all-encompassing scope of the claims and work of Jesus Christ (Rev. 10:1-11). And even the song of Moses, which is picked up again in the vicinity of the throne of God, includes the words, "All nations will come and worship before you" (Rev. 15:4).

The apostle John in his writings is fascinated with the truth of the universal significance of the coming of Christ. The Messiah is sent because of a love of God for that world (John 3:16), and thus can be designated as sent "to be the Savior of *the world*" (I John 4:14). No national or ethnic boundary can delimit this vision. This Messiah cannot be fenced in ethnically.

Even Peter, in calling upon believers to be prepared to give the reason for the hope they had (I Pet. 3:15), did so in the context of the royal odyssey of the Christ. The Jesus he commends "has gone into heaven and is at God's right hand—with angels, authorities and powers in submission to Him" (I Pet. 3:22). Christians are to remember this truth in the midst of a world that opposes the onward march of the gospel of Christ. And this is part of that internal activity in believing hearts, which seek to own or reverence or consecrate Christ as Lord (I Pet. 3:15). In this same context Peter plays with the old covenantal promises when he exhorts them not to return evil for evil, but rather to counter evil and insult with blessing. To this end were they called in order to inherit a blessing (I Pet. 3:9). Thus the sons and daughters of Abraham will yet prove to be a blessing in the earth.

Pauline Universalism

In Paul's pastoral Epistles the universal dimension of the gospel and of the claims of Christ come to the fore. Intercession is to be made for all men. God our Savior would "have all men to be saved, and to come to the knowledge of the truth" (I Tim. 2:4). There is only one Mediator between God and men "who gave Himself a ransom for all" (I Tim. 2:6). Here the mystery of godliness is set forth in the pilgrimage of Jesus who was "taken up in glory," "preached among the nations," and "believed on in the world" (I Tim. 3:16). Such missionary godliness must be pursued by Christ's followers, with a hope set on the living God, "who is the Savior of all men, and especially of those who believe" (I Tim. 4:10). And as Christ witnessed a good profession before Pontius Pilate, so too must his followers witness through a godliness which is blameless until the appearing of Him who is declared to be the only "Ruler, the King of kings and the Lord of lords" (I Tim. 6:15).

Paul's exhortations to Titus are founded as well on the firm foundation that "the grace of God that brings salvation has appeared to all men" (Titus 2:11). The believers are challenged to show meekness to all men, for it was God who sought us out; we did not find Him because of our good works. Rather it was God who saved us by the appearance of the kindness of God our Savior and His love for man (Titus 3:4). Thus believers are to manifest godliness and good works "so that in every way they will make the teaching about God our Savior attractive" (Titus 2:10).

James, the servant of God, was convinced that there is "only one Lawgiver and Judge, the one who is able to save and destroy" (James 4:12). Jude, in striving to deal with godless leaders, affirmed Jesus Christ to be "our only Sovereign and Lord" (v. 4), and ascribed to the "only God our Savior" all glory (v. 25). In essence these New Testament witnesses picked up the central gospel message of the prophet Isaiah and applied it to the widening horizons of their day. And that message still is foundational:

> I, even I, am the Lord,
> and apart from me there is no savior.
> I have revealed and saved and proclaimed—
> I, and not some foreign god among you.
> "You are my witnesses," declares the Lord,
> "That I am God" (Isa. 43:11-12).

> This is what the Lord says—
> Israel's King and Redeemer, the Lord Almighty:

I am the first and I am the last;
apart from me there is no God (Isa. 44:6).

I am the Lord, and there is no other;
apart from me there is no God. . . .
I will strengthen you, . . .
so that from the rising of the sun
to the place of its setting
men may know there is none besides me.
I am the Lord, and there is no other (Isa. 45:5-6).

Those tall Sabeans—
they will come over to you . . .
saying, "Surely God is with you,
and there is no other; there is no other god" (Isa. 45:14).

It can thus be seen that the driving sweep of the two Testaments precipitates into the question of the unique nature of this one God and Savior who created, redeemed, reclaims, and restores His world. And that people aligned with this God cannot but stand and cry out as His representatives to the far corners of the earth, "In the name of God, and on behalf of Christ, Be reconciled to God" (II Cor. 5:20). The living God in whom we believe deserves nothing less than the world laid at His feet, re-subjected to Him.

Thus the Christ who declares Himself to be the light of the world co-opts His followers into His passionate service of God and royally declares that they too are the light of the world and the salt of the earth. His followers within their Christ-defined identity have no choice but to be witnesses of Christ's ministry, His death, resurrection, ascension, and session at the right hand of God. They bear witness that He now calls on all peoples everywhere to repent and to believe on Him, and that one day He will return to judge the living and the dead, with all flesh appearing before Him (Acts 17:30-31; 10:36).

And furthermore the church is the temple of that Spirit (I Cor. 3:16), commanded that the congregation at Antioch "set apart for me Barnabas and Saul for the work to which I have called them" (Acts 13:2), the very same Christ-sent paracletal Spirit who "will convict the world of guilt in regard to sin and righteousness and judgment" (John 16:8).

Thus it has been demonstrated from the wealth of material in Scripture that the inner dynamic of the Scripture, in both the Old and New Testaments, presses out to the ends of the earth and lays a claim on all peoples. The final commission of our Lord and Savior Christ therefore simply and succinctly focuses the message and movement of the entire Scripture.

Though there are isolated texts in Scripture which refer to specific peoples, the most important scriptural basis for this centrifugal dynamic is its accent on the nature of the triune God Himself. It is because of the nature of this one and only living God, that He lays claim to the entire earth, and can do nothing less. This is without doubt the core gospel message of Isaiah. And again it is at the heart of the celebrative victory vision of the paslmist in the temple. Jonah had to learn that it is the nature of Yahweh to have compassion on all flesh.

Thus too, the Christ of God reveals in unmistakable fashion not only that He is the Savior of Israel of old, but that in amazing fashion He is the Savior of the world. He is the one who shows mercy to the weak, to the obscure, and to the forgotten. He is the one who insures that the glorious, impinging, weighty presence of God fills the earth. And He it is who leads nation after nation, people after people, person after person, to capitulate to the claims of the living God, whose largess is sufficient for all.

The Holy Spirit, who is sent by the Father and the Son, applies to sinners everywhere the merits of the atoning, reconciling work of Jesus Christ. And He cannot be boxed in, for the arena of the Spirit's activities is the whole world. He gives His gifts and His life to whomever He will. This Lord is not a respecter of persons (Acts 10:34; Rom. 2:11; Eph. 6:9). The Spirit's target too is nothing less than the world. And as its sovereign, He will be its chief prosecutor, convicting it of sin, of righteousness, and of judgment.

The church of Christ, which is the New Testament form of the people of God, represents this God (II Cor. 5:18-20) and is sent out by this Christ (John 20:21). As the authoritative representatives of the Christ who claims all peoples as His realm (Matt. 10:40; Ps. 2:8-9; Rev. 5:6-10), Christ equips us His messengers with the indwelling Spirit (John 20:22; 14:16-18; 16:7-16). The church thus, as aligned with this God and powerfully indwelt by the Spirit of God, is missionary to the very core of its being. Living before the face of this God it must reflect the very nature of the one who so loved the world that He gave His only Son to save it. The church is thus irrevocably set in the world, with its arms outspread after the pattern of Jesus, an intercessory prayer in its heart, and the divine gospel challenge on its lips: ''O world, why will you die; be reconciled to God.''

There is no biblical delimitation of this representative task of the church in the Bible. As this saving God's representative, who must go out to all people, she must be willing to sit down and plead even with notorious sinners. She must bring the claims of this King to all levels of life. This Lord cannot be circumscribed or provincialized; He is the Lord of all, both extensively and intensively. And thus, ''Your kingdom come'' is the watchword of this redeemed community. When the love of God has entered a community, then the mind of Jesus inevitably follows, and those so influenced ''look not only to your [their] interests, but also the interest of others'' (Phil. 2:4). Such a loving of the neighbor as self is the fulfillment of the law of this King, who sacrificially emptied Himself for the sake of others (Phil. 2:7).

No people, or pocket of people, can be ignored, overlooked, or written off. To be sure, no people is worthy of the attention and saving message of this God. But that is not the issue when we are speaking of a gospel of grace. The point is rather, that *this* God is worthy of all peoples, and that to know Him in truth is life, health, and salvation. He is the only answer to the problem of the peoples of the earth who have a bent for self-destruction. He can lead them out of their smallness, frustration, jealousy, and fratricide into the glorious unity of redeemed humanity. And in this renewed and widened circle, the richness of their own ethnic identity can flourish, come to fulfillment, and make a contribution to the richness of the entire mosaic.

Why have we as a church been so slow to fulfill this dynamic and mandate of the kingdom of Jesus Christ? It is because the church has been too preoccupied with her own life, her own internal workings, the intricacies of her liturgical life, her organizational life, her own nourishment. She has been careful to preserve her own life, apologetically defending her distinctiveness from other differing sections of the church of Christ.

The church has been inclined to forget that it is more blessed to give than to receive, that in losing her life she will find it, that in giving she will receive, and that, in the way of sharing, the manna of the gospel will not spoil but be preserved for generations to come. The church has forgotten that by an influx of new believers she herself will not be threatened, but rather invigorated.

The church has concentrated on proper christological formulations and rightly so. But she is tempted to underemphasize the challenge to stand with Christ outside of the camp, to know Christ intimately in His passion, to experience the fellowship of sharing in His sufferings, becoming like Him in His death, and feeling the power of His resurrection (Phil. 3:10). For looking into the face of our glorious Lord, we are changed into His glory (II Cor. 3:18; 4:6). Submitting to His rule, we are worked upon by that power which is able to bring everything under His control, and our lowly bodies become like His glorious body, fit instruments of the Spirit, attuned to God and His will (Phil. 3:21; Eph. 1:19-20; Rom. 12:1-2; 6:4, 13, 22; 7:4, 22; 8:11-17).

The eschatological vision of the Scripture also has something to say to the church in her pilgrimage on earth. In the redeemed city of God, and in the context of the particularistic, Israelite symbolism of the old covenant, there stands a great multitude clad in white robes before the throne of God. This numberless, acclaiming throng includes people "from every nation, tribe, people and language," standing in front of the Lamb (Rev. 7:9). The redeemed city is presented as a product of the mighty hand of God, for it comes down out of heaven, and finally resolves all of the earth's dichotomies. Babel is reversed and the leaves of the tree of life minister healing to the nations (Rev. 22:2).

We thus are called to go forward unabashedly with vigor and courage, for this God is not the God of the Jews only, He is also the God of the Gentiles. There is only one God (Rom. 3:29).

Be silent before me, you islands!
Let the peoples renew their strength (Isa. 41:1).

Sing to the Lord a new song;
sing to the Lord, all the earth (Ps. 96:1).

Chapter 2
Unreached Peoples:
The Development of the Concept
Ralph D. Winter

The Bible practically begins on the subject of the peoples of the world and the problem of their "unreachedness." Only a few pages into Genesis we are confronted by a table of the world's peoples and the fact of God's central concern somehow to reach them. Abraham was to become a nation, more specifically, a "blessed" people, and quite explicitly he and his lineage were in turn to be a blessing to all other peoples (Gen. 12:2,3; 18:18; 22:18; 26:4; 28:14,15; cf. Acts 3:25 and Gal. 3:8).

Having said only this much we are immediately catapulted into two of the most profound dimensions of the Christian faith, reflected as they are in the two words of our topic—*unreached peoples*. The concept of peoples, almost unknown to Americans, sees mankind as a set of molecules, not atoms, that is, an aggregate of "peoples," not individuals. It is not a concept that refers merely to the individuals that make up the population of our planet, nor does it have much to do with a list of the geographical territories called "countries."

The other concept within the phrase of our topic echoes the concern of God for these peoples to be somehow "reached," "redeemed," "blessed," whatever. It sets us wondering, precisely in what way were Abraham and his lineage to "be a blessing" to all the peoples of the earth? Was the effect of his reaching out to be a spiritual experience analogous to Abraham's own relationship of faith to the living God? Was this blessing to be similar to God's blessing promised to Abraham himself? For example, were the other nations also to be given land perhaps in the sense that "the meek shall inherit the earth"? Were they merely to be spiritually blessed? Or is this hypothetical? Did the Gentiles have to wait until the time of Christ in order to be brought into a living relationship with God the way Abraham was?

Concepts versus Labels

Before going on to these concepts, however, a warning is in order regarding the shifting meaning of the terms themselves. For Westerners in general, and especially American evangelicals, the relevance of the sub-concept here called "a people" is pretty much a recent rediscovery. Americans are much more likely to be heard talking about world population than about the peoples of the world. Worse still, in terms of the history of the English language, the recent phrase *United Nations* constitutes the final, irretrievable hijacking of the word nation, making it mean "country." No wonder American missionaries are more likely to speak of "winning souls" in this or that "country" than to speak within the terminology of the Matthew 28:19 phrase, where Jesus commands His followers to "go and disciple the peoples of the world."

One mission retains as a corporate objective the planting of the gospel "in every country of the world" without any reference to the more specific, biblical concept of "peoples." A recent pamphlet by another mission speaks of "unreached people" and "reaching the unreached," and in this particular case the context clearly indicates that the reference is to the winning of individuals. The word *people* has come to mean "persons." Only the grammar of phrases like *a people* or *unreached peoples* forces the word *people* to refer to a group. Unfortunately, as a result, phrases like *the Chinese people* are increasingly ambiguous grammatically. Thus Americans on hearing the phrase may more likely think of one billion Chinese individuals rather than a single, mammoth ethno-linguistic bloc consisting of thousands of peoples. By contrast, *the Chinese peoples* and a Chinese people (referring to sub-groups) represent uses of the word that sound just a bit strange to modern ears.

Similarly, then, our American senses are programed to assume that similarly ambiguous phrases like *the Gentiles,* or even *the nations,* in the Great Commission passages simply refer to masses of individuals. In English a *Gentile* means an individual, while in the Bible and in the whole non-Western world, *Gentile,* or *ethnos,* means a group.

For a quite different reason, the term *unreached* is slippery. In British English it may predominantly be used in a spatial or geographical sense, like "untouched." David Barrett, for example, speaks of unreached people as "groups without previous contact . . . [who have] not yet had the Gospel brought to them." Thus, being consistent, he defines *untouched* as "a group not yet reached . . . unevangelized," and *unevangelized* means "the state of not having had the Gospel spread or offered" (1982:847).

On the other hand, the term *unreached* among American evangelicals has for years been an adjective with theological (not spatial) flavor, and it has been applied only to individuals. That is, "reaching people for Christ" has meant "winning persons to faith in Christ." Thus when we use the phrase *unreached peoples,* we sense a tug to read "unreached *people"* (i.e., persons). If on the other hand we force ourselves to think of a group, we must realize that most evangelicals do not possess an accepted meaning for the concept of an unreached group. That is, most evangelicals do not think in terms of an unconverted group, or of group conversion as being the same phenomenon as

18

individual conversion. Thus the need for a deliberately new definition for the word *unreached*, if it is to mean more than "unexposed" or "untouched."

However, before proceeding further, I must point out that in this chapter my main purpose is not to trace the development of the meaning of the two words, *unreached* and *peoples*, or even that of the term resulting from the two linked together. My purpose will be to trace the development of what I believe to be a widespread contemporary consensus regarding a certain concept underlying these words. And I will trace the concept no matter what terms have been used along the way in the conceptual developments leading to the present. That is, I believe it is important to recognize and rejoice that there has now recently come into being fairly wide agreement about a certain concept. As a result of a gathering in 1982 (to be mentioned further below) many people now intend precisely the same concept whether they employ the terms *hidden peoples, frontier peoples, by-passed peoples, unpenetrated peoples,* or *unreached peoples.* Thus I understand my assigment to be to comment on the development of this now well-accepted concept, rather than to trace all of the history of the usage of the two specific words with which it is now identified. For example, this concept to whose meaning the phrase *unreached peoples* has recently been applied happens to be the concept to which David Barrett applies the label *hidden peoples* in the dictionary section of his master work (1982:829). Unfortunately, in another section he employs a quite different meaning for *hidden peoples* (1982:19).

The First and Second Eras

If we go back to consult mission thinking in the modern Protestant period,[1] we will note that the earliest writings by British and American mission scholars betray very little concern for the intrinsic significance of the biblically important concept we are here calling "peoples." I have found it helpful to recognize a First Era, in which William Carey and others in his train pushed clear out of the Western world to the coastlands of Asia and Africa. Carey in particular certainly confronted the vast spectrum of linguistic barriers, doing something with at least ninety different languages. But he did not effectively grapple with the significance of non-linguistic caste distinctions. Neither do the writings of Henry Venn or Rufus Anderson in this First Era deal clearly with the people entity, much less see it as the specific target of strategic biblical and missionary concern.

On the other hand, we have all read about the Indian "praying towns" resulting from John Eliot's work in the mid-1600s in Massachusetts. Too bad Eliot's countrymen later destroyed most of his work by force of arms. Furthermore, Alan Tippett, with his incomparable grasp of the Pacific, points out that as early as 1815 English missionaries in the Pacific islands had nevertheless actually precipitated what were later to be called "people movements," and that there were many such occurrences by 1850. But those movements were not quite recognized for what they were. Tippett (1971:30) quotes a British leader who, in 1847, wrote apologetically that such occurrences of rapid growth were unaccompanied by "civilizing," which is what he felt readers in England were waiting to hear and what he himself apparently regarded as the essential goal.

By 1864 the much celebrated Christian movement among the Batak people had begun. The missionary Ludwig I. Nommensen, trying to keep ahead of the advancing Islamic front in Sumatra, was unwilling to try to slow a Batak people movement down. By now facts about people dynamics became too prominent to ignore. Word began to filter back to Europe, at least to Germany. Mission leaders like the great German missiologist, Gustav Warneck, took note. But meanwhile a new emphasis was arising in England.

The Second Era is characterized by a new awareness of another kind of geographical frontier which gradually came to dominate the consciousness of the mission world. J. Hudson Taylor led the way in stressing the necessity to forge inland. He himself worked seriously in three of the many different Chinese languages. Yet I believe he too would have been surprised to encounter the contemporary concept underlying the phrase *unreached peoples*. He did at least break China down into family units as targets. He estimated the need for 1,000 evangelists to work only 1,000 days and by touching 50 families per day (!) to reach the 50 million families he guessed to populate China.

Incidentally, Gustav Warneck pronounced such calculations "unspiritual." Obviously, he could not possibly have imagined the massive wave of American and British response to this and similar appeals in the Second Era. The response came principally through the mechanism of the Student Volunteer Movement for Foreign Missions, a movement that would in fact largely ignore his and other missiological writings of the First Era.

Warneck had, however, kept his eye on things more comprehensively than Anglo-American mission leaders in regard to people dynamics on the field.[2] He was well aware of the Batak developments by virtue of his own Rhenish mission involvement. Drawing from such empirical data he, along with other German scholars, advanced concepts of the "Christianization of peoples" over which, on the continent, there had been much discussion and disagreement.

For example, Verkuyl (1978:193) quotes Warneck's classical statement, "When Jesus speaks of the need to Christianize all peoples, He means that they must be made Christian on the basis of their natural distinctiveness as a people." But Verkuyl goes on to describe Hoekendijk's (1948:93) disapproval of the basic methodology of both Keysser and Gutmann. Verkuyl summarizes, "Without exception every German missiologist writing since the Second World War has given up this naive notion of Christianizing the *volk;* in fact they resolutely avoid using the term'' (1978:193).

In any case, at least two of Warneck's students, Christian Keysser working in what is today Papua New Guinea, and Bruno Gutmann working in today's Tanzania,[3] took people dynamics very seriously. And their work and writings in the next generation (1920s and 30s) are now becoming classic. Unfortunately, the interruption and alienation of two world wars, as well as the barrier of the German language itself, have kept most of these ideas from the English-speaking world.

For these nineteenth- and early twentieth-century observers, pietism, despite all its precious and authentic spiritual blessings, had nevertheless interposed an essentially new perspective. In all honesty, it is very difficult to wed the concept of individual conversion, so significant in the pietist backgrounds of the vast majority of Protestant missionaries, and the concept of a whole tribe or ''nation'' or people being converted. Yet both did happen, and Warneck tried very hard to hold to both. Gutmann may have tended to value the Christianization of the national leadership over the conversion of any one person. Bavinck at the opposite extreme is very suspicious of the attempt to Christianize pagan social structures. According to him,

> Gutmann does not sufficiently recognize that although the tribal bonds which are still found . . . perform a restraining function in the sphere of morals, they are, nevertheless, completely connected with demonic, collective self-deification, so characteristic of heathendom. . . . The tribe must undergo a drastic change. And it is in this sense that the heathen who are converted must join the ''new fold,'' those who know an entirely different form of community from that of the tribal relationship, a form of communal life that the tribe never dreamed of (1960:119).

We must understand that these Dutch scholars (Verkuyl, Hoekendijk, and Bavinck) were acutely aware of the longstanding existence of a *volkskirche* in Germany itself. Its spirituality did not seem to be able to thwart the demonic element in the rise of Naziism, or the invasion of the Netherlands.

Meanwhile, although the *International Review of Missions* had functioned since 1912 as an agent of the cross-fertilization of concepts, not even Christian Keysser's article on his work printed there in 1924 aroused much attention in the English-speaking world (Keysser 1924).

In his foreword to the first English translation of Keysser's major work, *A People Reborn,* McGavran recognizes that ''since Hitler's day the term has come into disrepute . . . but if *volkskirche* is understood rightly as a genuine church (a congregation) of *a people,* it will be accepted as a thoroughly good term'' (Keysser 1980:x).

However, whether it was Williams, Nommensen, Keysser, or Gutmann, and whether a particular indigenous Christian movement being discussed was rapid or merely relatively fast, in all of this literature the discussion focuses mostly and rightly upon the nature of *the movement* of a people (within a people) rather than upon the nature of a *people* (group) itself. We do not have space to sketch the various earlier, mainly German, discussions of the phenomenon. But we must at least acknowledge in passing the great relevance of all this for contemporary discussions about structural social change and contextualization, as well as the ongoing concern about churches in, of, or out of peoples. We will turn to the contemporary debate later in this chapter.

Here I must pause once more and put on a different hat. Out of deference to the plain meaning of the Scriptures consulted at the outset, we must reflect on the great work in mission that the German people achieved in the nineteenth century and, to the extent the wars allowed, in the twentieth. What great blessing German Christians might have continued to spread to many nations had their own *volk* not gotten caught up in the two world wars. Those wars appear to me to be basically strident efforts to save their *volk,* to find their own sufficient *lebensraum.* What a warning this is today as equally strident variations of Americanism flit through our churches and as the United States now lavishes 99 percent of its wealth upon itself and its own self-protection! The relatively generous people of the United Presbyterian denomination, for example, give out of what they earn through their church for the blessing of peoples outside the United States not even two cents per dollar but something like two cents out of every hundred dollars. Yet this is a fairly "good record" as mainline denominations go. Is there any hope for a nation so dulled by affluence, crazed by insecurity, so impotent in reaching out with blessing to other nations? I submit that the future of America depends more upon the theme of this book and what we do about it than it does upon any kind of arms build-up or nuclear freeze.

The Third Era

Back to the story. I believe a genuinely new, Third Era began once again as another trickle of new frontier awareness appeared, this time in two places. This new awareness began to define the nature of the final frontiers. A handful of missionaries from the English-speaking world working in Guatemala—H. Dudley Peck, Paul Burgess, and W. Cameron Townsend—confronted the durability of the various Indian languages they encountered. The Pecks came from John Eliot's territory, where he had translated the Bible for Indians in the Boston area back in the mid-1600s. They and the Burgesses each concentrated specifically on one particular language (the Mam and the Quiche, respectively). Cameron Townsend worked on Cachiquel but later decided to tackle the more general problem of getting the Bible into the mother tongue of all other tribes. He guessed there were about 500 on the face of the earth(!) Due to his diplomatic and organizational efforts in the generalization of the problem, it is fair to associate him, more than any other human being, with the spiritual need of the specifically tribal peoples of the world. The mission he founded in 1934, Wycliffe Bible Translators, presently sends out twice as many missionaries as are sent out by all of the member denominations of the National Council of Churches put together. Tribal peoples are not easy to reach, and to this date embarrassingly few agencies have substantially followed his lead.

Meanwhile, however, as a result of mission work in India, non-tribal "mass movements" had sprung up within some of the lower castes. These phenomenal breakthroughs were not exactly sought for originally. They seemed to dim the hopes of the gospel's reaching higher levels of society. And, as a general phenomenon, they potentially pictured once again the meaninglessness of nominal Christianity. But the phenomenon provoked both concern and fascination.

Thus, during the same period in which the missionaries in Guatemala were confronting the "horizontal segmentation" of tribal movements, missionaries in India were confronting the "vertical segmentation" of vast non-tribal movements for which they had not planned. In 1928, the National Christian Council of India, Burma, and Ceylon brought things to a head. John R. Mott and William Paton, president and secretary respectively of the International Missionary Council, who were present at that 1928 meeting, formulated a resolution that appointed "a study of the work in mass movement areas" (Pickett 1933:11). The purpose of this study was later described in part as to help mission agencies "to think through the existing maze of conflicting opinions and experiences of the movement" (1933:12).

Out of this came *Christian Mass Movements in India,* the monumental (370-page) work appearing in 1933, and written by J. Waskom Pickett, who had been appointed to do the study. This book in turn attracted so much attention that the Mid-India Provincial Christian Council invited Pickett along with Dr. Donald A. McGavran and the Reverend G. H. Singh to look further into the phenomenon. The result of their further study inevitably confirmed and consolidated the importance of vertical segmentation, that is, the existence of another (not-tribal) type of unit which can equally be called a "people."

This further study was published in 1936 and immediately attracted international interest. John R. Mott, in 1937, wrote the introduction to the second edition, and a new concern for taking the concept of peoples seriously went worldwide. In many places the many "non-growing mission station churches" began to look more closely to see just what disparate peoples might be represented ineffectively within the same congregation.

Kenneth Scott Latourette, active in the SVM, close to Mott and Paton, and later to become the greatest of all historians of the development of the Christian movement, inevitably drew on these documents when he wrote, in 1936:

> More and more we must dream in terms of winning groups, not merely of individuals. Too often, with our Protestant, nineteenth-century individualism, we have torn men and women, one by one, out of the family or village or clan, with the result that they have been permanently deracinated and maladjusted. To be sure, in its last analysis conversion must result in a new relation between the individual and his Maker—in radiant, transformed lives. Usually the group, if won, is brought over by a few of its members who have found, singly, the truth of the gospel and have begun the new life. Experience, however, shows that it is much better if an entire natural group—a family, a village, a cast, a tribe—can come rapidly over into the faith. That gives reinforcement to the individual Christian and makes easier the Christianization of the entire life of a community (Latourette 1936:159).

However, in reviewing this literature, it must be admitted that we do not quite discern the mood of a rediscovery of the reality of peoples as the true structural fabric of humanity and the true target of Great Commission focus. Rather, we do find again and again an understandable jubilation over the discovery of how churches can begin to break out of decades-old, static, mission station, "conglomerate" congregations and begin to grow rapidly along the lines of people groups. It is, of course, not exactly a criticism to point out that this literature stresses more the growth of the church than the penetration of all peoples. However, the concept of a people is clearly there, even if we do not find a "closure" theology built upon the winning of peoples.[4]

Pickett, for example, cannot describe such movements apart from the groups within which they occur. In a crucial statement he observes:

> The distinguishing features of Christian mass movements are a group decision favorable to Christianity and the consequent preservation of the converts' social integration. Whenever a group, larger than the family, accustomed to exercise a measure of control over the social and religious life of the individuals that compose it, accepts the Christian religion (or a large proportion accept it with the encouragement of the group), the essential principle of the mass movements is manifest. The size and distribution of the group are of immense interest, but do not affect the principle. A mass movement, which we would prefer to call a group movement, may comprise either a large or a small group (Picket 1933:22).

As he says here, Pickett is not pleased with the pejorative phrase *mass movement,* which says nothing in itself about the group within which the movement takes place. Pickett himself observes, "The so-called mass in these movements consists of homogeneous groups, thoroughly accustomed to joint action" (1933:22). Yet Pickett, despite this generalized definition, never applied this brilliant insight to the high and respectable castes or to ethnic, economic, or linguistic groups in other lands. McGavran, in 1956, in preparing an amplified edition of the joint study published in 1936 (under the new title, *Church Growth and Group Conversion*), gained permission of all the authors to employ the phrase *people movement*. In his own new chapter one, he says,

> Basic to the entire point of view is the concept of a people . . . if becoming a Christian . . . means "leaving my people and joining some other people" then the growth of the church will be very slow. . . . Thus it happens that Christianity, as long as it remains outside a people, makes very slow progress, but, once inside, it flows readily throughout it (McGavran 1956:5).

But in this new chapter and in his classic, *Bridges of God* (1955), McGavran internationalized the concept, and it became a general widely discussed missiological concept, most often referred to as "the homogeneous unit principle."

Almost all discussion has focused on the empirical and practical significance of these groups in evangelism. Getting inside is the key thing. Once inside the purpose is plain: to get through to the rest of the group. This practical fact, of ease of communication within the group, is the basis of my own recent thinking. Early in 1982, I began to realize that we could define such groups as "the largest group within which the Gospel can spread as a church-planting movement without encountering barriers of acceptance of understanding." I agree with Robert Recker's very practical point:

> We must remember that no matter how transitory one would view the phenomenon of peoplehood, the gospel of Jesus Christ is addressed to and finds people where they are. It addresses flesh and blood people who are more or less communally oriented and who function more or less in communal fashion (Conn 1976:77-78).

Theological Interlude

However, no matter how practical our concern, theological problems unfortunately surface whenever we begin to talk about "group conversion." It is admittedly a complex phenomenon. In 1953, McGavran set out to explain it further under the title, *How Peoples Become Christian*. This was the original title of his classic work, *The Bridges of God*, appearing in 1955. The publisher didn't like the intended title, rightly feeling that the average Britisher or American would think the word "peoples" a misprint! This book, for which McGavran is most famous, further documents the simple fact that where great growth occurs, it does so with the peoples involved retaining their cultural

25

integrity. Some estimates suggest that three-fourths of all non-Western Christians have been won within peoples.

By now, however, it is clear that in all such discussions the deep-rooted feelings of American readers, for example, are often tied up in knots. The Dutch and Germans may conjure up fears of nominalism or even a Nazi state church. For Americans, paying attention to the differences between peoples may on the one hand seem like racism. Yet ignoring those differences will also seem like a certain kind of racism. For Americans it is thus both a practical and a theological question whether we should encourage people coming into the United States from Mexico to retain their Spanish, or encourage them to give it up. Or do we help them do what they want, whatever it is, going along with them both linguistically and ecclesiastically?[5]

There are a few verses in the Bible (e.g., Zech. 2:11; Acts 15:14; Eph. 2:15) that might allow Americans to assume that God will ultimately unite all believers into one new people consisting of one new cultural tradition. But there would seem to be far more references on the other side. Take, for example, Revelation 7:9, 11:9, 17:15, and 21:3, where in all four cases "peoples" (in the plural) describes redeemed but differentiated humanity at the very end of time. But as we note the translation of the Greek, we begin to understand how difficult a concept this is for Americans. We are not totally surprised that in only the first three passages is the consistently plural Greek word rendered by a plural English word. In the fourth case, of Revelation 21:3, most American translators (and apparently even some ancient copyists) falter, rendering in the singular "God's people" what is plural in not only the three previous contexts but what has the best manuscript evidence (see Metzger, 1971), namely "God's peoples." In other words, powerful cultural forces may affect our missiology even on the exegetical level.

History displays many subterfuges in the dealing with scriptural injunctions. Luther was just as capable of nullifying the contemporary significance of the New Testament Great Commission as New Testament Jews were able to ignore the significance of the Old Testament Great Commission. Luke 24:46 clearly implies that Jesus could have expected them to understand.

Intentions often bleed through a variety of different wordings if we will let them. If a Christian family were told to relocate in a city slum and to "be a blessing" to all the families of the neighborhood, does this wording necessarily conceal the obvious intention of evangelistic initiative?

But centuries of misunderstanding weigh us down today just as they did New Testament Jews. The subtle and supreme failure to understand is typified by the widely held assumption that Christ came to change the game plan from a passive "air wick" goodness to an active reaching out. Yet the "go" in Genesis 12:1 is no less definitive than the "go" of Matthew 28:19. In all ages we are told very simply to "go and be a blessing," all the while counting on God's willingness to be our own sufficient blessing, guaranteed by His very presence with us until the end (compare Gen. 24:15 and Matt. 28:20).

Richard De Ridder's book (De Ridder 1975) is absolutely foundational for a full appreciation of the essential meaning of the biblical story. I believe it is of significance that the earlier title of the book, *The Dispersion of the People of God* (which in effect makes no comment about the purpose of that dispersion), would in a later edition have been restated much more boldly and significantly as *Discipling the Nations*. That is, the dispersion was neither meaningless nor merely punitive. It was purposeful in the fundamental sense of Abraham's calling. And as is common in history, we see God fulfilling His purposes with or without the wholehearted obedience of His people. It is and always has been a case of very simply "Go or be sent" or "Give blessing and blessing will be given to you." But also clearly implied is Jesus' warning, "Seek to save your life and you shall lose it."

Momentum Increases

In any case, the literature of the 1933–1955 period does, in fact, lean upon a concept of peoples that is in effect defined operationally as that type of group within which a people movement can occur. We see in this literature again and again the phenomenon of "peoples" patiently described to the perturbed Western observor. But the bulk of the material is very simply and practically devoted to how people movements to Christ can be justified and promoted.

In other words, those men were much more sure about the reality and need of movements to Christ than they were ever bothered over details about the definition of a "people." Pickett described, exposited, and rejoiced about the movements occurring in India. Mott, Latourette, and McGavran surmised that these breakthroughs had general significance for the whole world. But a great deal changed when McGavran returned to the United States in 1954. His strong conviction about the general significance of people theory in missiology now gained the backing of institutional force. His 1952 manuscript, *How Peoples Become Christian*, already mentioned, was not only published (as *The Bridges of God*) in 1955 by the National Council of Churches (USA) but carried the backing of the Institute of Church Growth, which he founded in association with the Northwest Christian College in Eugene, Oregon. He then republished the 1936 book in 1956, adding a chapter, "The People Movement Point of View." Soon Fuller Seminary would discover him and assist him in boosting his concerns into larger orbit.

From this point on, the profusion of views is so great it would be unduly wearying to try to recount all that has happened. Much of the subsequent history has been described elsewhere. For example, the so-called Church Growth school of thought has produced thousands of pages within which some of these ideas are quite basic, and a great deal of interchange has resulted with virtually all sectors of the mission world.

The Lausanne Tradition

One unanticipated tailwind in the development of the people concept has been that winsome, irenic stream of energy called the Lausanne tradition. Here again we are assisted as we trace this movement since many others, including Ed Dayton, very recently, have done so (1983:23).

At this point we must zero in more narrowly on the precise concept I have described earlier as being widely accepted as the denotation of the phrase *unreached peoples*. It was McGavran's coming to Fuller that brought the writer of this chapter as well as many others (including Ed Dayton, Peter Wagner, Arthur Glasser, etc.) into dramatic and forceful contact with a man who was convinced that we are in a sunrise and not a sunset situation with regard to the preaching of the gospel to the ends of the earth. His irrepressible optimism has been contagious to all those who have had very much to do with him.

I hope a few biographical references will be helpful at this point. In spite of my ten years of field experience among a tribal people group surrounded by other groups without a church, nevertheless, it took me almost ten years clearly to fathom, formulate, or understand the contemporary meaning of the phrase *unreached peoples*. (I will call it the "Chicago 1982," or the "C-82" concept.) I am pained as I look back at my own published writings. I helped to promote the Theological Education by Extension movement. I was well aware of the fact, clear back in 1961, that such a movement would allow a multicultural denomination to foster its disparate subcultures, allowing and promoting theological education within those cultures rather than demanding a centralized or field-wide, culturally defined standard for ordination. I had, myself, worked within just such a people group, a (somewhat repressed) cultural minority in Guatemala.

But my earliest burst of insight engendered by McGavran's perspective is what I have often called "The Incredible Achievement." I wrote of it in my little book, *The Twenty-Five Unbelievable Years*, which was published in abridged form as a new chapter for Latourette's seventh volume in his *History of the Expansion of Christianity*. However, in that book, written in 1969, I merely note with appreciation the great importance of cultural minorities and cultural pluralism (pp. 16, 23, 31, and 82). I do not speak of peoples as such.

I also for my own part had discovered and written extensively about the significance of what Latourette had called a *sodality*, a structure just as churchly as that of the local congregation. But there is nothing in these writings either about people groups or unreached peoples. Another growing concern was to do something about the inadequate and fast-decaying home base of missions. But again this had no unreached people content as such.

Anyone close to McGavran would inevitably have begun to think in terms of harvest theology and even what I call "closure" theology (looking toward the end of the task). I happened to be involved in a panel discussion late in 1965, which was one of many discussions leading to the formation of MARC. The 1966 Berlin Congress on World Evangelism had an upbeat emphasis, and McGavran attended the congress (but was not utilized as a major speaker until the 1974 meeting). As MARC got started and as David Barrett's concerns for tracing indigenous movements of all kinds came into the picture in the period prior to the publication of his first major work, *Schism and Renewal in Africa* (1968), most of the discussion, as I recall, revolved around the growth of the church around the world, and its health and vitality in many remote places. The concern was to document the Christian movement. MARC produced "Country Profiles." Barrett was tracing Christian movements and soon plunged into the work which led to his truly monumental *World Christian Encyclopedia*. I recall at the time beginning to speak occasionally for an equal concern for the peoples that were not yet reached.

In late 1972, I experienced some kind of new burst of insight and wrote a little article for the tenth anniversary issue of *Evangelical Missions Quarterly* entitled "Seeing the Task Graphically." My assignment at the Fuller School of World Mission was probably the only one absolutely requiring a grasp of the overall extension of the Christian faith, my professorship being "The Historical Development of the Christian Movement." As a result it had finally broken in upon my attention, as I then explained at Lausanne in 1974, that there were massive amounts of people yet unreached in certain specific huge blocs— Chinese, Muslim, and Hindu. I saw also that the reason these massive blocs were in the main unwon was that individuals within them were "mainly beyond the ordinary evangelism of existing Christians reaching their cultural near-neighbors.   .   .   .   That is, they were at an E-2 or E-3 distance" (Douglas 1975:218-25). The vast majority of their people were walled off from Christian outreach by the protective barriers (maintained by peoples that were as yet unreached). But I didn't add that last part in parentheses, nor did I count or even guess at the number of groups. I was counting individuals. All my charts done in those days portray masses of people, not numbers of peoples.[6]

The little article, "Seeing the Task Graphically," framed as it was in terms of masses of individuals yet to be reached, was employed as the basis for the opening audiovisual at the International Congress on World Evangelization at Lausanne. In both my own plenary paper, written closer to the time of the congress, and also in my own presentation at the congress I do mention (in passing) the need to think in terms of peoples. At the congress I even introduced the concept of people blindness:

> A malady so widespread that it deserves a special name . . . let us call it people blindness, that is, blindness to the existence of separate peoples within countries . . . which prevents us from noticing the sub-groups within a country which are significant to the development of effective evangelistic strategy. . . . Until we recover from this kind of blindness we may confuse the legitimate desire for church or national unity with the illegitimate goal of uniformity (Douglas 1975:221).

I don't believe, however, that I was the one at this juncture who was pushing hardest for the significance of unreached peoples. The emergence of massive planning for the Lausanne Congress provided the occasion for a greater emphasis at MARC on the unreached peoples. Their Country Profiles had documented the existence of the churches in country after country. Now Don Hoke and Paul Little, directing the International Congress on World Evangelization (ICOWE), asked the Fuller School of World Mission, which in turn asked MARC, to do a $25,000 study preparatory to the congress on unreached peoples. Even though I was asked to write a brief, popular essay, "God Has Always Sent the Gospel to Peoples," introductory to the *Unreached Peoples Directory*, which was given out at the congress, I think I felt at the time that this fact was so obvious I even wondered why I was asked to stress it. Charlie Mellis was one who could see further ahead at that point than I could. Others did too. I had a former missionary, Ed Pentecost (now teaching at Dallas Theological Seminary), working under me on a master's thesis later published under the title *Reaching the Unreached: An Introductory Study on Developing an Overall Strategy for World Evangelization*. That book (Pentecost 1974), although now out of print, is still the best thing of its scope that I know of on the subject. Pentecost is one of the early ones to suggest the idea of defining unreachedness in terms of 20 percent of the individuals' being Christians. Working with MARC, he was the research coordinator for the unreached peoples study presented at Lausanne.

In the explanatory introduction of the *Unreached Peoples Directory* passed out at the congress, the definition of "unreached people" is not firmly established. Mentioned are both the 20-percent figure and the phrase, "[where] there is no appreciable [recognized] church body effectively communicating the message within the unit itself" (MARC 1974:26). But the directory goes on to say that "for those who prefer a single criterion, 20% is a reasonable dividing point" and that "for the purposes of this directory we consider that a people is unreached when less than 20% of the population of that group is part of the Christian community" (MARC 1974:26). Note that there is not yet a reference here to "practicing Christians."

Clear proof that the problem of a definition of unreachedness was not terribly impressed on my mind is the fact that in 1976 I was invited to address the joint meeting of the IFMA-EFMA executives on the subject of our overall progress in world missions. My talk on that occasion, ''The Grounds for a New Thrust in Missions,'' employed a new type of graphics to highlight the enormous amount of work yet to be done and the fact—very crucial in my own thinking then—that only mission agencies could best penetrate those remaining frontiers, that is, the peoples where the church was not yet established. In my mind it was very simple that all individuals who could not be brought into existing churches must then be part of other groups where there was no existing church. That was a good enough definition for me. But at that point I had not yet attempted to define or count the remaining peoples to be penetrated. I was more interested in the protection and development of that endangered species, the precious mission mechanisms (which I felt were alone able effectively to cross those frontiers) than I was in the definition of those frontiers. I recognized that some mainline denominational thinking warred against the very idea of a cross-cultural mission structure other than those which would exchange personnel with groups where there were already churches.

However, in early 1977 the 20-percent criterion suggested in the MARC Directory at the ICOWE in 1974 became with one fatal change the published definition of the Lausanne Committee's Strategy Working Group (Wagner and Dayton 1978:24): ''An unreached people is a group that is less than 20% practicing Christian.'' In my own biased recollection, the change to ''practicing Christians'' was almost instantly criticized. I had not paid much attention to the question before then. I had felt that so many groups were so obviously unreached that any precise definition was unimportant. But when the new 20-percent definition came out, I remember calling my friend Peter Wagner, who was the chairman of the Strategy Working Group, and saying, ''This is a great mistake. Almost all groups everywhere are now classified as unreached!'' But it was too late. The Strategy Working Group was an international committee, and everyone had gone home.

The emphasis on 20 percent did have the merit that it was relatively easy to quantify. I say ''relatively'' because most evangelicals thought they knew how to recognize a practicing Christian when they saw one. But they might not have been so readily able to assume that they could recognize the presence or the absence of the other criterion (mentioned back in 1974, as above): ''no appreciable church body.''

By now I was heavily involved in the development of the U.S. Center for World Mission, which was first mentioned in public at the IFMA-EFMA Mission Executives Retreat in 1976. It was a project stressing exclusively the remaining task. I spoke of the need for the establishment of a major mission center [in each country], the primary purpose of which would be to focus major attention on the Chinese, Muslim and Hindu groups. If every mission agency represented here were to lend one key person, such a center could jump into being. The idea to which I refer has been talked about now for two years, and an open discussion tomorrow noon will take it further. It involves the availability of a major former college campus in Pasadena, and would be in no way bound to any denomination, school, or mission structure. I would hope that it might beautifully complement, in the area of *the work of the world's mission agencies,* the emphasis of the Billy Graham Center on the *evangelistic outreach of the world's churches.* . . . One of the novel aspects of the center will be its avowed attempt to bring about a wedding between the professional missionary tradition and the university tradition within which more and more missionaries are being processed and formed (Winter 1977:20, 21).

In view of this presentation at the IFMA-EFMA meeting in 1976, and partly due no doubt to all the attention claimed by the actual founding of the USCWM late in 1976, I was asked to address a group of mission leaders that was to meet in December, 1977, at the Overseas Ministries Study Center in Ventnor, New Jersey. I was told, ''You have made your point about how many people there are yet to be reached. We'd like you to come and tell us how you think they can be reached.'' Others were to speak on the same subject.

The Strategy Working Group's new 20-percent ''practicing Christians'' definition came into the picture at about this moment. Thus, in my presentation to the executives at OMSC (published as a booklet in 1978 under the title, *Penetrating the Last Frontiers*), I struggled to respond to the SWG's official unreached peoples definition. I said what I have already said above about the difficulties inherent in the word *unreached.* But being reluctant to launch a counter definition for the same phrase, I proposed another concept under another label—*hidden peoples,* a phrase suggested by a member of our staff, Robert Coleman. By *hidden* he did not mean people were physically hidden, but hidden due to our people blindness. Until we identify their peoplehood, they may seem to be within reach. Thus, the concept as I defined it:

> Any linguistic, cultural or sociological group defined in terms of its primary affinity (not secondary or trivial affinities), which cannot be won by E-1 methods and drawn into an existing fellowship is a Hidden People . . . (Winter 1978:42; also in Wagner and Dayton 1978:67).

At this point I was unaware of the fact that this ''presence or absence of a church'' concept had, in fact, been mentioned (and yet at the same time left secondary), as we have seen above, in the MARC *Unreached Peoples Directory* distributed at Lausanne in 1974. Thus, if this concept is inherently more useful, I certainly can take no credit for first mentioning it.

But unfortunately, a great deal of confusion still remained. In *Unreached Peoples '79* one chapter presents the SWG 20-percent definition of the unreached peoples term (1978:24), while the next chapter (an abridgment of my "Penetrating the Last Frontiers" presentation in 1977) presents, big as life, the "presence-or-the-absence-of-a-church" definition for the hidden peoples label (Wagner and Dayton 1978:67).

By the time of the publication of *Unreached Peoples '80,* my chart in the *'79 Annual* indicating the 16,750 estimate of the number of hidden peoples was somehow misunderstood as the number of peoples in the total world population. Furthermore, the phraseology of *hidden people groups* in the same introductory essay is utilized as equivalent to the 20-percent definition of *unreached peoples.*[7]

Edinburgh 1980

Meanwhile, the preparations for the Edinburgh Conference (the 1980 World Consultation on Frontier Missions) began to boil up in late 1978. While I had very little to do with the actual organization of that conference, I was certainly willing for the convening committee (involving a wide range of mission executives) to hammer out a slightly improved definition of the concept I had already proposed for the phrase *hidden peoples:*

Hidden Peoples: Those cultural and linguistic sub-groups, urban or rural, for whom there is as yet no indigenous community of believing Christians able to evangelize their own people (Starling 1981:61).

Furthermore, the consultation itself equated this term with the phrase *frontier peoples.*

Thus, as a result of this October, 1980, meeting, the basic concept here expressed, whatever the label (*hidden* or *frontier*), went to the ends of the earth with all of the various mission agency and youth delegates who went back to their home countries. Meanwhile, the *unreached peoples* phrase, employing the new 20-percent ("practicing") definition, was now reinforced worldwide in the same year at the Pattaya Conference of the Lausanne tradition.

It is significant to note that the 171 youth leaders who attended the sister conference, the International Student Consultation on Frontier Missions, eventually sponsored three new student organizations: (1) the on-going International Student Coalition for Frontier Missions, which early published a newsletter and later introduced the *International Journal on Frontier Missions;* (2) the Theological Students for Frontier Missions, born six months later, which utilized the Edinburgh definitions unchanged; and (3) the National Student Missions Coalition, born 13 months later, which developed a slightly modified definition:

Unreached Peoples are definable units of society, with common characteristics (geographical, tribal, ethnic, linguistic, etc.) among whom there is no viable, indigenous, evangelizing church movement.

More mission agencies sent delegates to the Edinburgh 1980 Consultation than to any other meeting in history. Exactly one-third of the delegates and one-third of the agencies sending them were from the non-Western world. Also, three out of four of the major plenary papers were assigned to non-Western mission leaders. This was indeed the first large world level conference (consisting of mission executives) in which non-Western mission executives could rub shoulders as equals with their Western counterparts. Larry Keyes' diligent work in rounding up data on non-Western mission structures helped assure a larger attendance from that sector. At the very origin of the proposal for the Edinburgh conference, back in 1972, and in the formal call drafted for it in 1974, it had been unthinkable that the unreached peoples challenge should be considered on a world level without the major participation of the growing number of outstanding non-Western mission leaders. Due to the welcome presence of 171 younger leaders, it became equally unthinkable, I hope, for another world level meeting to leave them out!

Although the Edinburgh conference focused exclusively on the frontiers defined as the hidden peoples, the Pattaya conference certainly had strong emphasis on unreached peoples. By now it is unquestionable in almost all mission circles that the forward-looking vision of Christians today must be focused more and more on places where the light is darkest. One of the three simultaneous consultations planned for June, 1983, convened by the World Evangelical Fellowship, is on frontier missions.

Looking forward to the Edinburgh meeting in 1980, the Evangelical Mission Alliance in London in 1979 invited me to address them on the subject of hidden peoples. At the 1981 meeting of the IFMA a new Committee on Frontier Peoples was created. Early in 1982 I was also invited to address the Association of Evangelical Missions in Germany, at a conference whose entire theme was, interestingly enough, the English phrase *hidden peoples*. In the fall of 1982 the annual meeting of IFMA mission executives took the theme, ''Penetrating Frontiers,'' while the EFMA executives focused on the same subject under the theme, ''The Challenge of the Remaining Task.''

Meanwhile, Sam Wilson, working with Ed Dayton at MARC, had been involved in both Pattaya 80 and Edinburgh 80 and rightly insisted that the use of a 20-percent definition had always been merely a method of achieving a reasonable likelihood of the presence of an indigenous, evangelizing church. In the *1981 Unreached Peoples* annual, presenting ongoing thinking of the Strategy Working Group, the ''presence of a church'' concept was newly acknowledged (Wagner and Dayton 1981:26).

When was a people reached? Obviously, when there was a church in its midst with the desire and ability to evangelize the balance of the group.

Also, three new categories of unreached peoples were suggested, as the result of ongoing thinking in the Strategy Working Group: initially reached, 0-1 percent; minimally reached, 1-10 percent, and possibly reached 10-20 percent. The word *possibly,* I believe, especially suggests the basically predictive purpose of the percentage approach. In the same treatment a new, divergent definition for hidden peoples was suggested.[7]

Thus it was only reasonable to assume that some standardization of terminology was desirable. Late in 1981, Ed Dayton, representing the Lausanne Committee, took the initiative to invite Wade Coggins and Warren Webster to convene a meeting near the Chicago O'Hare airport, which I have already called the "C-82" meeting. A wide representation of leaders very willingly gathered, coming from IFMA, EFMA, Inter-Varsity, NAE, Southern Baptist, ACMC, Billy Graham Center, Dataserve, Gospel Recordings, SIM, NAM, MARC, USCWM, and Wycliffe. The sole purpose of the two-day meeting was to settle on a standard terminology which would foster more effective thinking and action in regard to the world's darkened peoples. A number of additional terms necessary to conceptualize the reaching of peoples were defined, such as *reported, verified, evaluated, selected, supported, engaged,* as well as *reached* and *unreached.*

For our purposes here, the key accomplishment of this meeting was the abandonment of the 20-percent concept and the adoption of a modification of the-presence-or-absence-of-the-church definition further refined for the Edinburgh 80 Consultation. What came directly out of the meeting was:

> Unreached peoples: a group among which there is no indigenous community of believing Christians able to evangelize this people group.

The result was in effect to employ the *unreached peoples* phrase from the Lausanne tradition and the *hidden peoples* concept from the Edinburgh tradition. However, in continuing to use the unreached peoples phrase, this meant the old definition would continue to circulate for a while at least.

There is no reason to assume, of course, that everyone will choose to follow the lead of the C-82 meeting in thus underscoring the presence-or-absence-of-the-church concept. There are in fact other concepts that are also valid. The 20-percent active Christian achievement is still a useful measure. David Barrett has focused attention on whether as many as 20 percent have been "evangelized" (rather than incorporated into the church). His 1982 master work defines such as unreached peoples (Barrett 1982:19). This corresponds to no definition mentioned here thus far. On the other hand, the phrase is elsewhere defined in his dictionary (1982:847) as,

Unreached peoples: ethnic, linguistic and other groups without previous contact with Christianity, who have not or not yet had the Gospel brought to them.

In regard to evangelization, Barrett has an enormously sophisticated list of all the possible ways the gospel can be "brought," which is perhaps his main concern. In his *Encyclopedia* he devotes various tables and one entire section, "Part 5," although short, to "Evangelization." Curiously, it was his earlier work, *Schism and Renewal in Africa* (1968:13), that first mentioned the significance of 20 percent of the population's being "adherents" (not merely evangelized). And this significantly affected Pentecost's thinking as he advanced the 20-percent definition for use in the *Unreached Peoples Directory* distributed by MARC at the 1974 Congress.

Concepts and Labels Reviewed

1. Barrett 1968:137. "By the time the number of Protestant or Catholic adherents in the tribe has passed 20% . . . a very considerable body of indigenous Christian opinion has come into existence."

2. Pentecost 1974:30. Unreached peoples: "We consider that a people is unreached when less than 20% of the adults are professing Christians" (Note: This definition does not require "practicing" Christians).

3. MARC 1974:26. "Unreached Peoples are those homogeneous units (geographic, ethnic, socio-economic or other) which have not received sufficient information concerning the Gospel message of Jesus Christ within their own culture and linguistic pattern to make Christianity a meaningful alternative to their present religious/value system, or which have not responded to the Gospel message, because of lack of opportunity or because of rejection of the message, to the degree that *there is no appreciable* (recognized) *church body effectively communicating the message within the unit itself."*

4. MARC 1974:26. Unreached Peoples: "For the purposes of this initial Directory, we consider that a people is unreached when less than 20% of the population of that group are part of the Christian community" (Note: does not require "practicing" Christians).

5. LCWE/SWG 1977 (See Wagner and Dayton 1978:24). Unreached Peoples: "An Unreached People is a group that is less than 20% practicing Christian" (Note: In demanding "practicing Christians" almost all groups become unreached).

6. Winter 1978:40, 42. A Hidden People: "For both spiritual and practical reasons, I would be more pleased to talk about the presence of a church allowing people to be *incorporated,* or the absence of a church leaving people *unincorporable.* . . . Any linguistic, cultural or sociological group defined in terms of its primary affinity (not secondary or trivial affinities) which cannot

be won by E-1 methods and drawn into an existing fellowship, may be called a Hidden People'' (Note: the first published definition of hidden peoples).

7. Edinburgh Convening Committee 1979. ''Hidden Peoples: Those cultural and linguistic sub-groups, urban or rural, for whom there is as yet no indigenous community of believing Christians able to evangelize their own people.''

8. Wagner and Dayton 1981:26. ''When was a people reached? Obviously, when there was a church in its midst with the desire and the ability to evangelize the balance of the group.''

9. LCWE/SWG 1980 (in Wagner and Dayton 1981:27). ''Hidden People: no known Christians within the group.

Initially Reached: less than one percent, but some Christians.

Minimally Reached: one to 10 percent Christian.

Possibly Reached: ten to 20 percent Christian.

Reached: twenty percent or more practicing Christians'' (Note: suggests a different concept for the phrase *hidden peoples*).

10. NSMC January 1982. ''Unreached Peoples are definable units of society with common characteristics (geographical, tribal, ethnic, linguistic, etc.) among whom there is no viable, indigenous, evangelizing church movement'' (Note that this definition introduces a geographical factor).

11. IFMA Frontier Peoples Committee February 24, 1982. Agreement to use the Edinburgh 1980 definition (#7 above) for all three phrases, *hidden peoples, frontier peoples,* and *unreached peoples.* (This action was taken in light of advance information regarding the mood for change on the part of the MARC group. This mood was officially expressed at the C-82 meeting, see #12.)

12. LCWE/Chicago March 16, 1982. Unreached Peoples. ''A people group (defined elsewhere) among which there is no indigenous community of believing Christians able to evangelize this people group.''

13. LCWE/SWG May 21. Same as number 12 except that the SWG voted to replace, ''able,'' by the phrase, ''with the spiritual resources.''

14. LCWE/Chicage July 9th: further revision of numbers 12 and 13 by second mail poll. Unreached Peoples. ''A people group among which there is no indigenous community of believing Christians *with adequate numbers and resources* to evangelize this people group without outside (cross-cultural) assistance'' (Note: new phrase italicized).

Sizing It Up

At this point we must try to look back and ask whether we are heading in the right direction. Underlying all these definitions (except perhaps the first, which is given only to show where the 20-percent idea may have had part of its origins) is the concern for evangelistic outreach to function in such a way that people (individuals) have a "valid opportunity" to find God in Jesus Christ. As evangelicals we tend to think this will normally take place as the response of an individual without any believing community in the picture. Yet we know better.

To exaggerate slightly McGavran's view perhaps, it is no more likely that fish will crawl out on the land to get the bait than will individuals embedded in a social matrix (especially a non-Western one) be likely to walk out to become Christians. It is rather our duty to move into their world and win people within it. We are not to be modern members of "the party of the circumcision" by demanding directly or indirectly that people ignore the social and family bonds within which they have grown up. In the New Testament, Jews did not have to become Gentiles, nor vice versa.

However, to create the realistic, culturally relevant, "valid opportunity" for people to accept Christ is not the easiest path, because it ultimately forces us to take "peoples" seriously. Reaching peoples is thus merely the process whereby the realistically valid opportunity is created. Unreached peoples are groups within which individuals really don't have that opportunity. It is not good enough to send a message or even extend an invitation people cannot accept without passing extra-biblical tests.

This need for a "valid opportunity" highlights the existence in these definitions of the word *indigenous,* and the phrase *believing community.* But it does not settle the question of the validity of people-churches. Note 5 at the end of this chapter shows some glimpses of the current debate. In passing, let it be noted that the reality and integrity of a people tends to supersede at least for a while the geographical distribution of the group. That is, a group is not unreached or hidden just because it happens to be a geographically isolated non-Christian portion of a reached people. It can be evangelized by a geographical strategy rather than requiring a new missiological breakthrough.

Also to be noted is the trend in the final definition above (no. 14), which stresses, more than any previous definition, whether outside help is needed to finish the job. In my opinion, as hinted at in number 6, the crucial question related to the work of a classical mission agency is whether there is yet a culturally relevant church. From that point of view it is the unique burden and role of a mission agency to establish an indigenous beachhead, to achieve what I would call "a missiological breakthrough," not the cessation of need for further work from elsewhere.

Thus, I believe, whether the indigenous community possesses "adequate numbers and resources" is not the crucial point, practical though it may be in another sense. The chief question would seem to be whether the missiological task has been done. In turn, that should mean, in my opinion, more than even getting the Bible in a people's own language. It should mean at least a handful of believers who had become consciously part of the world fellowship, capable of drawing upon the life and experience of Christian traditions elsewhere, and even capable of consulting the Bible in the original languages. In short, an unreached people needs very urgent, high priority missiological aid until it is quite able to draw on other Christian traditions and is substantially independent, as regards holy writ, of all traditions but those of the original languages themselves.

Indeed, it would seem to be a great strategic error for all cross-cultural aid to cease before the new church begins to lend at least some aid to the cross-cultural task of reaching all remaining unreached peoples. Perhaps every indigenous church can have, must have, a role to play in the classical missionary endeavor. Note well that this perspective is fundamentally different from preoccupation with the "three-self" type of wholly autonomous national church. History shows that autonomous, isolated, national churches become stagnated and/or heretical.

Furthermore, I consider that enough mischief has by now been done by the "disengagement syndrome," which was highlighted by Henry Venn's "euthanasia of the mission"[8] concept in the nineteenth century. I do not believe any church anywhere can ever get so mature that it has no need of continued contact and interchange with other church traditions. The "bailing out" of Hawaii in 1865 by the American Board of Commissioners for Foreign Missions certainly was only an armchair victory. Why could not the mission have foreseen the need for at least a few Christian attorneys to defend the Hawaiian believers against the aggressive land hungry mainlanders who were already arriving in force, not to mention the pressures of the not-so-holy descendants of some of the missionaries themselves?

It is certainly reasonable to question whether a mission agency as such should continue to be linked to the younger church. It would likely be better once classical mission work concludes for home church lay people, pastors and leaders to take over an on-going liaison through a regular program of interchange mediated by another kind of office. The mission then should be related, if at all, only to the corresponding mission structure within the younger church. We must face the fact that many younger churches (like many older churches) get sealed off and spend not more than *one* percent of their income on evangelizing their own people, and *nothing* in evangelizing other people who live physically intermingled with them. But to pursue this would take us beyond the scope of this chapter.

Suffice it to say, I would prefer to stress the unreachedness of a people in terms of the presence or absence of a church sufficiently indigenous and authentically grounded in the Bible, rather than in terms of its numerical strength vis a vis outside help. That is, I have all along felt in my own mind that the phrase of the Edinburgh formulation (no. 7), "able to evangelize their own people," referred back to the indigenous quality of the believing community rather than to the numerical strength of the indigenous movement. If this interpretation is acceptable; then the concepts expressed in definitions 7 and 12 should be considered basic.

We are gratified that the ultimate unity of mind and heart in all these discussions is the attempt to hasten the completion of the task. In that we must not grow weary. In due time we shall reap if we faint not. Providentially, the "we" here includes a vast, unprecedented world family of believers whose final citizenship is in heaven, whether or not that heaven preseves the magnificent diversity of the world's peoples—a diversity still irritating so often to our fellow Americans unless they too can come to see these cultural barriers as potential bridges.

Notes

1. To omit the entire post-apostolic period prior to 1600, as well as the Roman Catholic tradition since 1600, is really not fair, and in fact we do ourselves a great deal of harm to do so. But both space and the expectations of our own tradition edges us away from the many luxurious examples in this sphere on which we could well draw.

2. Unfortunately G. Warneck's greatest work, *Missionslehre,* his multivolume treatise on missiology, has never been translated into English.

3. Christian Keysser's classic work describes his fascinating experiences in Papua, New Guinea. First published in German in 1929, the English translation is entitled *A People Reborn* (Keysser 1980) and is introduced by a superb essay by Donald A. McGavran. The best treatment in English of Bruno Gutmann's work in Africa is a chapter by Donald C. Flatt in Beaver 1973. Per Hassing 1979, unaware of Flatt's article, undertakes a critical review of Gutmann's thinking and writing, endeavoring to balance out the purely favorable treatments.

4. It is not as though the leaders of the Student Volunteer Movement did not have preeminently a closure theology built into their thinking. The most famous of all missionary slogans—"the evangelization of the world in this generation"—was surely a closure theology. What I do not see in their literature specifically is the wedding of the people concept as a missionary target with a restatement of their closure goals as basically a reaching of unreached peoples. I have been slow to do so myself.

They did, however, faithfully parcel out the necessary remaining task as they saw it. Comity agreements were intended to encourage some attention to every part of the world. They (Ellis 1909:304) boldy conceived of a "Distributed Responsibility":

THE DISTRIBUTED RESPONSIBILITY

Most of the mission boards of North America have accepted a distinct responsibility for a share of the mission field. This has done much to remove the vagueness from missionary presentation. It has been figured out also by the men best informed how much money it will take to meet this responsibility. Consequently, some churches have determined the amount they should raise. The figures in the former case, so far as they are available, are given below.

Denomination	Accepted responsibility in population
Canadian societies	40,000,000
Congregationalists	75,000,000
Dutch Reformed	13,000,000
Foreigh Christian Missionary Society	15,000,000
Northern Baptists	61,000,000
Northern Methodists	150,000,000
Northern Presbyterians	100,000,000
Reformed Church in America	10,000,000
Southern Methodists	40,000,000
Southern Presbyterians	25,000,000
United Brethren	5,000,000
United Presbyterians	15,000,000

5. There is by now a large contemporary literature that argues back and forth about churches within peoples and vice versa. Space will not permit more than a few quotes.

(1) Robert Recker, in his superb essay, "What Are People Movements?" (Conn 1976:78), quotes the theologian of India, D. T. Niles, who seems to question even McGavran's idea of a "church of a people": "It is so easy to slip from a concern to build a church for the nation into a desire to build a church of the nation" (Niles 1962:256).

(2) Rev. Theodore Williams, in a letter to the editor of *India Church Growth Quarterly* (Oct.–Dec., 1982), says:

> The statement in the April–June issue of ICGQ attributed to Dr. George Samuel: "Caste can be considered as a bridge for groups of people to embrace the Christian faith without fear of social dislocation"—is very objectionable. Caste is the curse of this land. If we advocate caste in the name of Church growth, we will lose our credibility. Caste attitudes have created endless problems for the Church in south Tamil Nadu and Kerala. In my opinion, the reason for the stagnancy of the Syrian Church is its caste consciousness.
>
> Western church growth leaders and missiologists aver that caste is a harmless tool to be used in evangelisation. This may be because they do not understand our country. But those of us who are Indian must watch our words. A faith that does not break caste barriers and emphasize the oneness of people in Christ cannot be the Christian faith. Any proclamation of the Gospel which does not enable people to come into unity in Christ is lopsided proclamation.
>
> Finally, let people not think that all Indians involved in mission accept the viewpoint that caste has its advantages in evangelisation.

(3) The Lausanne Occasional Paper No. 1, The Pasadena Consultation—Homogeneous Unit, includes this quote:

> Dr. Donald McGavran's definition of a HU [homogeneous unit] is "a section of society in which all members have some characteristic in common." Used in this way the term is broad and elastic. To be more precise, the common bond may be

geographical, ethnic, linguistic, social, educational, vocational, or economic, or a combination of several of these and other factors. Whether or not members of the group can readily articulate it, the common characteristic makes them feel at home with each other and aware of their identity as "we" in distinction to "they."

We are agreed that everybody belongs to at least one such homogeneous unit. This is an observable fact which all of us recognize. Not all of us, however, consider it is the best term to use. Some of us prefer "subculture," while others of us would like to explore further the biblical concept of *ethnos* (usually translated "nation" or "people") as enjoying a "solidarity in covenant" by creation, although in rebellion against its Creator. Nevertheless, for the purposes of this statement we shall retain the more familiar expression "homogeneous unit."

(4) "We recognize the validity of the corporate dimension of conversion as part of the total process, as well as the necessity for each member of the group ultimately to share in it personally." (From *The Willowbank Report—Gospel and Culture, Lausanne Occasional Paper No. 2.*)

(5) Jim Reapsome (1983) writes:

Do we or do we not tell new converts to break down the old barriers and break out of the old castes and ghettos right away? Some say no, because that would put an unnecessary precondition or roadblock in the way of the conversion of others. Better to keep new converts in their own social and ethnic units, prejudiced as they are, for the sake of winning others. . . .

On the other side, however, we find those who say that Paul was quite blunt about the necessity of breaking down social, religious, economic and ethnic barriers. . . . Paul specified that converted slaves and masters must radically change how they feel toward and treat each other.

In short, "the new man" who now possesses a divine nature and knowledge, becomes part of a socially identifiable body that simply puts Jesus Christ and the common life in him ahead of all human, earthly, sinful, "old man" divisions and social cliques. . . .

As one weighs both sides of the debate, it appears that pragmatics tends to obscure the apostolic demand for hauling down ethnic, racial, religious, and social barriers. . . . Must we really accept the social status quo to see more people saved? I think not. . . .

It would not be too far amiss to suggest, even on the basis of pragmatics, that more people are won to Christ by converts breaking down ethnic, social, national, religious, and racial barriers than by keeping those distinctives intact. Who knows? . . .

We must resist the temptation to justify church and mission tactics on the basis of what appears to bring in the most people . . . we cannot deemphasize or make less important the experience of God's new creation in a new family that transcends the old family. By trusting in Christ, the convert enters a new social unit—bearing God's own image—and thereby explodes in a very disrupting way the old social unit.

If that gets in the way of someone else's conversion, or even drives family, friends, and neighbors away, that is the price of radical obedience.

Reapsome expresses in this lengthy quote from the *Evangelical Mission Quarterly* the sincere concern of a U.S. pastor whose role is to pick up the pieces of splintered American families and try to weld them into the new surrogate family of the local church.

Church people tend to begin with a warm vital fellowship, which is the preconceived destination of their converts. It works. But the context within which it works is more typical of America than any place else.

By contrast McQuilkin (1973:35) expresses a view more common in mission circles:

> . . . some would question the sincerity of almost any decision unless it is validated by a clean break and open opposition to one's family and society. Such is often necessary and, when necessary, is clearly a test of genuine faith. Furthermore, when present, such courage is a highly praiseworthy attitude. But we must not extend this principle and make such a position the *sine qua non* of genuine faith. We are clearly unbiblical when we demand radical individualism, which is a western rather than a biblical concept. The cohesiveness of family and people, their inter-responsibility are strong emphases of Scripture.

The most recent statement by McGavran on this subject is his article, ''The Primacy of Ethnicity'' (1983).

6. Our most recent pie chart, ''Unreached Peoples '83,'' makes a distinct shift in the direction of emphasizing the number of peoples in the different categories rather than the individuals. It is available in two sizes: 12″ x 16″ for $.75 postpaid (quantity discounts available) or in large, untearable size 19″ x 25″ for $1.50, both from the U.S. Center for World Mission, 1605 Elizabeth, Pasadena, CA 91104.

7. In the following year *Unreached Peoples 81* over-corrected things and defined the hidden peoples as groups where there is ''virtually no Christian group,'' ''virtually no Christians,'' ''no known Christians within the group, e.g., zero Christians'' (pp. 26-27). Yet on pages 140 and 141 there is a reproduction of a statistical table and a pie chart in which the original definition of hidden peoples is preserved. Thus, neither in the 1980 annual, where hidden peoples was made to mean 20 percent, nor in the 1981 annual, where it was assumed to be zero percent, was the concept present for hidden peoples the same as was set forth along ever since the original article was printed in the 1979 volume.

8. See Warren 1971:28, 172.

Chapter 3
Unreached Peoples:
What Are They and Where Are They?
Ralph D. Winter

When I was given the topic for this chapter, three subpoints were suggested to me, namely, ''the demographic picture of the unreached, current discussion regarding differences of terminology, and the progress in making churches aware of unreached peoples over the last decade or so.'' Since my earlier chapter, ''Unreached Peoples: The Development of the Concept,'' happens to cover a great deal of the discussion leading up to the present, I will try here to deal with the two basic questions of the topic: What are unreached peoples, and where are they? To cover the subpoints suggested, I'll add one more: Why are they unreached?

Unreached Peoples: What Are They?

In my earlier chapter I covered the various definitions that have been given in recent years for the term *unreached peoples*—a term now synonymous with two others—*hidden peoples* and *frontier peoples*. In March, 1982, a number of major entities involved in unreached people research arrived at a concensus to the effect that an unreached people group should be defined as *a people group within which there is no indigenous community of believing Christians able to evangelize this people group without outside (cross-cultural) assistance.*

Coming to Terms

Traditionally the task of the church has been defined in terms of extending the gospel of Christ. In our circles evangelism has so often been said to be the main business of the church of Jesus Christ that I do not believe I need to discuss the concept of unreached peoples further from a philosophical rationale, but rather from a pragmatic standpoint. We need to know which peoples are unreached, not so much to be able to separate out Christians from non-Christians or even to count how many unreached peoples there are, but primarily in order to know how the church should go about evangelizing them. The practical premise upon which all this thinking is based is simply the necessity of ''giving everyone a valid opportunity to accept Christ.'' To know what groups are unreached, then, relates to a question that is very pragmatic.

"Reach" should mean "incorporate." Some will remonstrate, however, that if we are simply trying to give everyone a valid opportunity to accept Christ, why is it necessary to emphasize the presence or absence of the church (as does our definition of an unreached people). In my thinking, and in the thinking of all those who employ this criterion, there is no such thing as "a valid opportunity to accept Christ" apart from the indigenous presence of His church. Don't misunderstand me! What I am saying is rather technical. I agree that conceivably a person can accept Christ apart from a church in his context. But normally this is not the way people become Christians, and even if they do, it is not ideal. People do not simply turn on a switch in their hearts or minds in some kind of direct relationship to God and then proceed to grow spontaneously in their new faith. Normally, they need to be incorporated into His fellowship, into His church. That is the reason why the trend has been for the various definitions of unreached peoples to take into account the presence or absence of an indigenous church.

Reaching groups is faster. Apart from the fact that it is more biblical to emphasize the salvation of peoples, not individuals only, it is also true that it is easier to give individuals a valid opportunity to accept Christ if you can get to them within their community on their own wavelength through a fellowship of believers that they can understand and by whom they will be understood. That strategy is both a better and a faster way to reach people. Some today may think it is more efficient to evangelize the world by spraying the globe with electromagnetic radiation in the form of radio or television. Such efforts are all to the good. But evangelizing at arm's length by radio is not the same as reaching people on their own personal wavelength and within their own culture. Someone once said to me, "It's possible today by satellite to project a message into every home in the world." And I answered, "What language are you going to use? Muslims alone speak 580 different languages." He paused, as he should have, because we are not speaking of mass communication when we evangelize. Jesus was not content with merely a public ministry. He poured most of His energy into one people group and became Himself a part of that group. Ultimately we are dealing with very, very specific communication to the heart, a communication that constitutes an invitation to become part of an existing fellowship of believers, within the same people group.

Reaching groups is better. Clearly, the main reason for working with unreached people (individuals) as members of people groups is that only when they, as new believers, can fit into a group of their own kind will they become firmly established in the faith. In this sense, the only valid church is one that is understandable to people because it fits them culturally in the language and custom of their people group. In the Pauline sense of the word, there is no other kind of church. The church is by definition understandable to the people involved. It isn't just an arbitrary mixture of people from different kinds of backgrounds. The Bible cries out that people deserve to be met on the level of their own language, tongue, people group. Most mission leaders today agree.

People groups are permanent. Finally, we speak in terms of a church within each people group because peoples as "nations," "tribes," and "languages" may be permanently with us. I won't take the time to elaborate on this point. Pragmatically it isn't that important. But let me say in passing that one of the factors in the picture today is a new appreciation of the fact that peoples as distinct groups are God's creative intent. We are coming to realize that all peoples are potentially of equal beauty to Him. Actually, this change of perspective is now coming to be seen as more biblical than the typical American "melting pot" psychology, in which we are to become all alike, somehow. All modern versions of the New Testament, for instance, have retranslated Mark 16:15 to say we are to preach the gospel "to all creation" rather than "to every creature," as the King James Version puts it. What is God's "creation"? Part of God's creation is what we find in Genesis 1—the heavens, the earth, the trees, animals, birds, and so forth. Another part is what we read in Genesis 10—the table of the nations, the *mishpaha,* the families, the lineages of the earth.

I am only saying that it is futile for us to ignore the people distinctions. God created them, and according to the book of Revelation, these distinctions will be with us until the very end. Our task is to see how God expects us to use these distinctives as a means of bringing mankind to Himself. And the first step in that process is to recognize which peoples now have a viable witnessing church in their culture, reaching out to those still without Christ. These are what we have called the reached people groups. On the other hand, which peoples do not have this internal witness? It would seem that once the people group is clearly distinguished, it would be relatively simple to tell if it has a viable, indigenous, witnessing church. But the facts are not quite so simple. Let me elaborate.

Pseudo-unreached groups. What are unreached peoples? There are some people groups that seem to be unreached, but really aren't, and some that seem to be reached but really aren't. First let us take up the pseudo-unreached peoples.

Let us say that among the refugees from Southeast Asia in the United States today there are 1,000 members of a certain tribal group who now live in Philadelphia. Among them there is not one Christian. Moreover, nobody in Philadelphia can speak their language. Are these people an unreached people? We cannot say yes or no until we ask a further question: "Has there been somewhere else a missiological breakthrough into this same people group?" We must recognize that the 1,000 people in Philadelphia may or may not be the entire people. Who knows, maybe in New York City there are 100,000 more

46

from the same tribe. The subgroup in New York may have strong, fast-growing churches and well-educated pastors, and the Bible may be in their language. In that event, it would be folly to treat the Philadelphia people group, 1,000 strong, as though it were an unreached people. Wouldn't it be foolish for an ordinary American to try to learn their language and translate the Bible into their tongue if someone, somewhere else, had already done this? Thus, a group of people among whom there is no church or Christians is not an unreached people if the same group elsewhere is reached. Such a people we can call a pseudo-unreached group.

Pseudo-reached groups. You can also go in the opposite direction. That is, a people may be pseudo-reached even though they have a church. Let us say, for example, that there has been a church for 1,000 years in a particular culture, but the church is invalid in a very practical sense. Its rituals and traditions not only do not lead people to Christ but actually create a barrier to finding Him. There is such a thing as a dead church; indeed, deadness and life are the essence of which we are writing. A pseudo-reached group of this sort may have some missionaries, and some Christians, but it lacks a vital church. The church present in that culture is unable to reach out and evangelize the people of the culture because the church itself needs to be evangelized. Unreachedness is thus not defined on the basis of whether there are any Christians, or whether there are any missionaries working among them. It is defined on the basis of whether or not in that culture there is a viable, culturally relevant, witnessing church movement.

People distinctives: cultural or genetic? Finally, it is not always easy to determine clearly one's own people group. There are some people who believe that in determining people groups we should consider only ethno-linguistic distinctions. I will not argue with them, but I do think that the label *ethno-linguistic* combines both genetic and cultural factors. If, therefore, we are going to combine genetic and cultural factors in our descriptions of peoples, why not admit it from the outset? Does anyone believe that genetic relationships between people are ultimately the factor we're groping for when we're trying to preach the gospel? We're trying to get through to people. And to be able somehow to get through to a group of people who are part of the same tradition, linguistically and culturally, is more significant than to get through to people who are accidentally related genetically. I heard the other day that when a group of Mennonites left South Russia, somehow one of their babies was left behind and grew up as part of a Kazakh group of people. By the time this blond, blue-eyed boy was 15 or so years old, he realized he didn't belong to these people. But that was only a genetic awareness. Culturally, linguistically, he was very much a Kazakh. For someone to urge that he should now go back to his people turns out to be an ambiguous statement. Who are his people? As far as the gospel is concerned, were he to become a Christian, he would be a superb messenger to the Kazakhs compared to his ability to witness, say, to the rest of his own genetic family. Thus, as far as I can see, the phrase *ethno-linguistic* is a useful term, but it should free us, not limit us, in our understanding of cultural realities.

How Big Is a People?

What are unreached peoples? Let us talk now in terms of the size of these groups. American traditions have so redefined the English word *people* that it only rarely means a group, and even then does not give a clue as to size.

Does English help or hinder us? For example, the English statement, ''John looked out the window and saw the 'people,' '' is ambiguous because it is not clear whether he sees an affinity group or a crowd. Does he see a family, a group of people who identify with each other? Or does he see merely a large crowd of people who are complete strangers to each other? Ordinarily in English, ''He saw the people'' means merely a lot of people or persons. Rarely does ''He saw the people'' refer to a people group. Thus the English language doesn't ordinarily suggest a group meaning for the word *people*. While the phrase *a people* requires a group meaning, it is a very rarely used phrase. Therefore, all our exegesis, all our agonizing about the word *ethne* is, I believe, strikingly accompanied, and subtly influenced, by our own cultural American English vocabulary and semantic structure. I'm not sure we're well qualified to ask whether in the New Testament when people spoke of *pante ta ethne* they were referring to a mass of individuals other than Jews who didn't obey God or whether they were thinking of a mass of peoples. We wouldn't think of a mass of peoples. Maybe they would. One thing we never find in the New Testament is the phrase *a Gentile*. That it is possible for us to say it in English betrays the possibility that we have similarly pressed the English translation of the Greek word *ethne* into the English paradigm of people = individuals.

Thus our subconscious perspective makes our exegesis exceedingly difficult. In the Bible, however, you do have different words that are used depending on the size of these groups. In Genesis 12:3 and 28:14 (the first and last of those five backbone vertebrae in the book of Genesis that have to do with the Great Commission), the word *mishpaha* is often translated improperly as the ''families of the earth.'' It would be much more accurate to say ''the kindreds of the earth.'' In any case, the word *mishpaha* is translated *ethne* in the Septuagint. Then when you move to Genesis 18:18 and 22:18 (two more cases where Abraham is reminded of his responsibility to all the peoples of the earth), the word *goyim* is used, but *ethne* is still the translation. When Isaac comes into the picture in Genesis 26:4, the same thing happens. But, as we have seen, when Jacob comes into the picture in Genesis 28:14, *mishpaha* is used again (*ethne* in the Septuagint). I cannot detect any contextual reason why there is that shifting back and forth unless, in actual fact, these are synonymous terms. And indeed they are in part. There were 60 *mishpaha* that went into the promised land (these are smaller groups).

But several of these *mishpaha* belonged to single tribes since there were only 12 tribes. One of these *mishpaha* happened to be a tribe all by itself. Thus a small *goyim* is sometimes called a *mishpaha*. Here I am drawing on an unpublished paper by Richard Showalter.

Megapeoples, macropeoples, minipeoples, and micropeoples: Even in English when you speak of the Chinese people, you refer to a billion people who represent many, many peoples in terms of missionary strategy. In groping for a terminology to define strategic units more precisely, I have tried to press into duty the following unpronounceable series of words. If, for example, we refer to the Han Chinese, we are speaking about only the "Chinese-ish" citizens of China. The tribal peoples of China would not be included in this category. But the specifically Han peoples include not only those in China, but also the Han peoples outside of China. Thus, politics and political boundaries are of lesser significance in this study. More important is what we could call peoplehood, a sense of belonging to each other. The Han Chinese, then, could be considered a *megapeople,* my largest category of definition of peoples (note that there are small megapeoples, too, such as small tribes unrelated to any other). So, let us refer to the category of all Han peoples as the Han Chinese megapeople. Likewise, we may speak of a Hindu megapeople including all those for whom the primary orientation of their lives has come from the impress of Hinduism. But the large megapeoples have significant subdivisions.

Thus, we may proceed to notice that within that massive megapeople called the Han Chinese there are *macropeoples,* smaller groups such as all those who are native speakers of Mandarin. I have heard that in China only 14 percent of the population speaks Mandarin in the home. Certainly many more understand Mandarin, since it is the official language of the country. But at home many who understand Mandarin may usually speak Fukien, or Minnan, or Hakka, or Swatow, or Cantonese. Cantonese speakers, for example, make up one of the large macropeoples within the Han Chinese megapeople.

However, even within the Cantonese macropeople there are still many mutually unintelligible dialects and thus significant barriers to the communication of the gospel. Scholars studying the Chinese seem strangely reluctant to confront the linguistic diversity of China. I don't know why. Perhaps the fact that one writing system unites them all throws us off and gives us a false impression. But to speak of all the dialects of Chinese as the same language is like speaking of all the European languages as a single language, and asking,

"Do you speak European?" or, "How many of you speak European?" Is European a language? No. There is, of course, a large family of languages called "Indo-European." Russian and English are both part of the Indo-European language family. But so what? I don't understand Russian very well, nor do most Russians understand English. Now, maybe the differences within the Chinese family of languages are not quite as great as are differences between certain of the various languages of Europe. But nevertheless they are very great. Just because many different kinds of Chinese people can read the same writing system doesn't of itself reduce those differences. The Koreans and the Japanese, whose spoken languages are utterly distinct from Chinese, also make use of the same Chinese ideographs. That doesn't make their languages the same, or even related. As English speakers, we could also learn to use the Chinese writing system to write English, if we wanted to. And we probably would if, for example, we were conquered by China! In such an event, we would probably never use a fixed symbol typewriter again since dot-matrix computer printers can easily print Chinese symbols. Why else is it Japan doesn't bother much with letter-quality printers, as they are called, with symbols that strike one at a time?

Let us grant then that the Han Chinese make up what I call a megapeople, within which are a number of macropeoples. In turn, the Cantonese macropeople, for example, comprises many minipeoples due to the existence of very different Cantonese dialects. Finally, within such minipeoples there are extended families and clans, etc., which I would call micropeoples.

The missionary target, the "unimax" level: The important thing is that somewhere along the line we have to ask ourselves, "Which of these size levels is the missionary target?" I have proposed that the easiest way to determine this is to say that it is the largest group within which the gospel can spread as a church planting movement without encountering barriers of acceptance or understanding. (This phraseology was accepted at the Lausanne sponsored meeting in March, 1982.)

In other words, the value of these distinctions is to help us evangelize. Once a group is penetrated by the gospel, to what extent can the gospel spread automatically? What size group makes for greatest efficiency? That is, what is the largest group within which the gospel can spread without bumping into linguistic or cultural barriers that are for practical reasons insuperable? We ask this because we simply want to get the gospel to everyone. If in order to get at the reality we have to work in terms of megapeoples, macropeoples, minipeoples, etc., fine! For want of a better word, I have suggested the term *unimax peoples* to refer to the maximum sized, still sufficiently unified group within which the gospel can spread without encountering barriers of understanding. I don't love this term. But for the time being I have come up with nothing better, and we do need some definition that deals with this particular unit of peoples. Otherwise, we end up with a megapeople like the Han Chinese, a people in almost anybody's language, but not an entity that is in itself an efficient missionary target in the sense we would like an unreached people to be.

Do Peoples Overlap?

Finally, we need to ask, what about individuals who seem to belong in more than one people group? It seems obvious that practically everyone in the world is part of more than one group. And in each group, whether a sports group, a vocational group, or a genetic relationship, there may be avenues of communication that are superior to all others. Nonetheless I think what we are really trying to do when we evangelize is to choose an avenue that will maximize the impact and acceptability of our message. It seems logical to me to assume that we are all trying to find that one maximally approachable group for any given individual. We can then say that for every person in the world there is only one people-oriented approach that, to the best of our knowledge, is the best way to reach that particular person. That way no one will be counted twice. Of course we might find out that our guesses were wrong and we will have to reclassify that person. Let me give you an example. When we talk about a Chinese Muslim, is he primarily Chinese and secondarily a Muslim, or vice versa? We need first to ask, "On which basis should he be evangelized?" Should he be approached as a Muslim? Or should strategies effective with Chinese be used? In a given case the person might be classified in either group but not both. Personally, I think it is better to approach most Chinese Muslims as Muslims. However, it may be that for some Chinese Muslims it should be the other way around. Whichever it is, it will not be both.

The point is that to do effective evangelism we must ordinarily approach individuals with full recognition of their peoplehood and deal with them in the group where they can best be approached. We may therefore assume that everybody in the world is in only one group, and we can then count up the groups that result without counting anyone twice. In doing things this way I have arrived, along with the advice of many people, at about 16,750 groups that can be called unreached by the definition given here.

How Many Peoples Are There?

But is the number 16,750 at all exact? When people challenge its accuracy, I invite them, just for fun, to add up the same column of people groups and see if they get a different total. The total, at least, is absolutely precise. I will admit, of course, that the subtotals being added are pure guesses! You will find that we have listed 5,000 tribal, 4,000 Muslim, 3,000 Hindu, 2,000 Han Chinese, and 1,000 Buddhist groups. These are clearly round numbers. In each case those

51

three zeros are supposed to announce to everyone that these are guesses—careful guesses, but guesses, nevertheless. At this hour of history it is too bad no one can do better than guess. This is what MARC does. This is what the different research agencies on our campus are doing. Everyone is guessing. We are all pleading for help. And every time we guess we are constantly refining our grasp of what the task really is. Thus, when it comes to the total number of unreached peoples, I think we have to realize that once we settle in our minds that everybody belongs in only one group (that one which, for that person, is the most reachable context) then we can count the groups without counting anyone twice. Some groups are already reached (about 6,550) and some (16,750) are unreached, for a rough total of 23,300.

Sombody may remonstrate, "But David Barrett says there are only 8,990 people groups, not 23,300." True, his book speaks of some 8,990 distinct ethno-linguistic peoples, and it lists specifically 432 larger clusters of peoples, most of which I would consider macro- or even mega- peoples. (Even he does not list all 8,990 by name.) However, we also need to make sure what it is he refers to when he speaks of a people.

It is clear in his table that his listing is almost identical to the number of languages he figures need translations. Now let's see where that leads us. Wycliffe Bible Translators, for example, goes into South Sudan and counts how many languages there are into which the Bible must be translated and presented in printed form, in order to reach everybody in that area. Wycliffe's answer is 50 distinct translations. What does 50 mean in this instance? Does it mean 50 groups of people? Certainly not if we are speaking of unreached peoples. In many cases quite alien groups can read the same translation.

How do I know this? Gospel Recordings also goes into South Sudan and counts the number of languages. Their personnel, however, come up with 130. Why? Because they put the gospel out in cassette form, and those cassettes represent a more embarrassingly precise language communication than does the written language. I know how this works because where I worked in Guatemala one translation of the New Testament was used for about 300,000 Quiche Indians, a good portion of the entire tribe. But when the church leaders started producing radio programs, all of a sudden they got negative feedback from all over the Quiche area with the exception of the one valley from which the radio speaker came. Quiche Indians in all the other valleys resented the twang they heard on the radio. They understood it but they didn't want to listen to it. It "hurt" their ears.

It is perfectly reasonable that if Barrett is thinking along the same lines as Wycliffe, he too will also get the smaller number. In fact, if you use the same proportion, 130/50 x 8,990, you get almost exactly 23,300, which happens to be the total number of peoples in the world Bruce Graham and I have indicated on our *Unreached Peoples 1983* chart. I'll admit that the number just happens to come out the same. I didn't derive the 23,300 total in this way, nor did Barrett vice versa. But I do think the close correspondence is reassuring. Of course if someone really wants to manufacture disagreements, look in Barrett's book under the chapter on India. There he points out that there are 26,000 different castes in India alone (the sort of thing I would call micropeoples). Yet in our *Unreached Peoples 1983* chart we list only 3,000 (unimax) peoples for India. Thus we really appear to be in disagreement there. In this case we seem more conservative whereas he had a smaller number in the other case.

If, however, you were to take his 26,000 people groups in India and multiply that figure by all the other countries in the world, in proportion to a reasonable similarity/diversity factor, you would get a world total of at least 100,000 to 200,000 peoples by that definition. Do you see what I mean? Different authors for different reasons and different organizations for different purposes are counting different things. It isn't as though nobody agrees on anything. I think there is a great deal of interesting and valuable correlation between these different studies. I find Barrett's book of immense value. Obviously, if you are counting peoples specifically for the purpose of estimating how many different printed New Testaments are necessary, you get one number. If you are trying to estimate how many different tapes are necessary, you get a larger number, closer to the unimax size, and similar to our figure of 16,750 out of the 23,300.

Unreached Peoples: Where Are They?

Now let us turn briefly to the question, Where are the 16,750 unreached peoples?

Five thousand of them are tribal peoples (not counting 1,000 already reached). They are all over the world, in every country. There are certain areas of the world like the island of New Guinea, the country of Nigeria or Peruvian Amazonia, where there are a large number of different tribal groups. The so-called "tribals" are often basically refugee populations. For example, in a space of 50 by 200 miles in West Cameroon there are 200 different languages, many of which have no similarity. It is a mountainous area, the English part of a country that is otherwise French speaking. That little neck-of-the-woods, so to speak, happens to constitute an area representing "mountains of refuge" for people of all kinds, from all over Africa. For example, there are groups there that trim their hair so that they have only one lock of hair falling down one side, in a way similar to the pictures you see in King Tut's tomb. Apparently these people hailed originally from Egypt. But there they are, in a little mountain valley of West Cameroon, too scared to go in any direction because everybody in every direction is hostile to them.

This constant fear of all other groups, this imprisoned situation, is typical of tribal peoples. This trait, even if it were a common denominator, is too tenuous to make the tribal category into a cultural bloc. The tribals of the world are a far bigger task than if they were a single megapeople.

Four thousand of the world's unreached peoples are in the Muslim sphere. Here we find a massive megapeople scattered all over the world, but nevertheless also concentrated in a number of places. As Americans we tend to think of the Middle East when we think of Muslims. Yet the Middle East is the smallest part of the Muslim world today. Only 7 percent of Muslims speak Arabic. We find larger concentrations of Muslims both east and west of Arabia, and they speak 580 major different languages. Note that although, like the tribals, many different languages are spoken, the evangelistically significant unifying factor of Islam makes the huge Muslim category a megapeople, not just a large category like the tribal group.

Three thousand are Hindu groups, mainly concentrated in India. But again, Hindus are scattered all over the world. For example, in places like Trinidad and Guyana in the Caribbean or Fiji in the South Pacific, people with Hindu orientation constitute the majority of the population.

Two thousand are part of the Chinese megapeople. Although these peoples are perhaps a bit more concentrated than any other group, they can be found in 61 different countries of the world. Since that statistic is probably two weeks old at the time of this writing, we should add another five countries.

About 1,000 are Buddhists, in a primary sense. And for vast millions of Chinese and Japanese, Buddhism is certainly a secondary factor. The heartland of Buddhism is no longer the India in which it was born but Burma, Thailand, and Cambodia, for example, where its missionary influence was more virile.

In no case above do we refer to reached peoples, only unreached. But it is not true that the Chinese peoples or tribal peoples are unreached, although the vast majority in all five categories are unreached. Furthermore, of these five large collections of related peoples—these megapeoples—four are not located in their own distinct geographical areas. Nevertheless there are certain parts of the world where each of these largest categories tends to concentrate. Highly significant to Americans is the fact that from each of these five major groups there are thousands upon thousands of individuals in the United States. Of course not all of the specific peoples within these larger megapeoples are represented in the United States, but many of them are, especially the reached peoples. One result of migration in the modern world is simply that we can no longer make any valid home/foreign distinctions. Once we see the world as 23,000 or so unimax peoples, it no longer matters where these peoples are, whether there is an ocean between us and them, whether even the peoples themselves are separated by an ocean. The question rather is whether the church is domestic within them or not. It doesn't really help us, therefore, for our mission boards to continue to be structured along geographical lines. It is like going fox hunting. If the fox jumps over the fence into a different person's yard, what do you do? We have to be able to track that fox, wherever he goes. And if there are 60,000 Gujaratis in Vancouver, Canada, well that's where they are. Peoples are where you find them. And if the Los Angeles public schools record 109 different languages spoken in the homes of their pupils, then we had better take a good look to make sure that in our evangelistic strategy we're not overlooking those which have no internal witness within their group either here or elsewhere.

The phrase *hidden peoples* was suggested originally (by Robert Coleman) because unreached peoples are normally overlooked. Even though one or two of their culture may be sitting right there in church, as a people group they are mainly outside the awareness of the church. Paul faced this situation. At the synagogues he visited he noticed that in the back rows were a few "God fearers," Greeks who represented a people which could never be first class citizens in a synagogue. And one of the most dramatic scenes in the New Testament occurred (in Acts 13) when Paul was forced to start the first Gentile synagogue. The Jews didn't mind a few Greeks on the fringes, but when crowds of Greeks responded to Paul's message, they were furious. Paul was a missionary because he could see these Greeks as a people. To others they were visible only as individuals. Taking seriously their peoplehood created the explosion of the Pauline missionary effort and brought into the New Testament perhaps its most radical concept, a reflection and clarification of the meaning of Genesis 12:1-3 and Isaiah 49:6. He quoted the latter verse in Acts 13:47, the former in Galatians 3:8.

Finding the peoples, then, is not easy. Take, for example, the Kazakhs. According to David Barrett's ethno-linguistic classification, the Kazakhs speak one language and comprise only one of his 8,990 ethno-linguistic groups. Perhaps one printed translation might suffice. But, let's be realistic. The Kazakhs number more than 10 million. It is likely that they are, in fact, a macropeople comprising many minipeoples of the unimax definition. To be content to observe merely that they speak one language and are one people is wishful thinking. Even geographically they are scattered. Today they are found in northwest China, and in southeast and south Russia. Large numbers live in Afghanistan and Iran. There are a million Kazakhs in Turkey, refugees who walked back and forth across the Russian-Afghan or Iranian border, going in and out of the U.S.S.R., finally ending up in Turkey. Today, because of the European Economic Community, we find 10,000 Kazakhs in Munich. So, if you want to reach the Kazakhs (perhaps more than one variety of them), go to Munich, Germany. Do you see what I mean? Geography is not as important as peoples. Once that is clear, the question of *where* they are is a very exciting one.

It is very significant what can happen in Munich, Germany, once we focus on peoples instead of countries.

Unreached Peoples: Why?

Finally, what about the why? This is the question that energizes me the most. The other questions of what and where I would call simply technical questions. But *why* this subject is important is the mandate of the gospel itself. But it is more than that. Let me recapitulate a bit.

I think we are living in the third and final era of mission history. Speaking of only the Protestant tradition, the first era missionaries went out to the coastlands of the world, and after a number of years the work became somewhat stagnated. People seriously did not believe it was useful or safe to go inland. Finally a few missionaries broke through the resistance and opened new inland fields. As a result a whole new wave of awareness engulfed the Protestant world. All the mission agencies had assumed it was impossible to go inland until Hudson Taylor and his followers actually did it. Then, gradually, after about 25 years of respectful watching and waiting, the older mission boards in England and America rapidly retooled, motivated to a great extent by the impact of Moody and the rising demands of the Student Volunteer Movement. And a new rush of recruits went out into these new inland frontiers, epitomized by the 1910 Edinburgh Conference, which made as its focal point the unreached areas of the world.

However, because they weren't invited to that conference, thousands of missionaries and dozens of mission boards were outraged. The most offended were working in Latin America. The conference leaders, those young student volunteers, now grown up, hadn't looked carefully enough at Latin America. They didn't realize the separate challenge of aboriginal peoples in Latin America or take seriously enough the fact that many of the Europeans in Latin America are only superficially Christianized. But the frontier zealots at Edinburgh didn't want to be bothered with Latin America. They were thinking geographically, not with people-vision. They wanted to go to the predominantly non-Christian areas of the world. However, their hearts were right. Their motive and their zeal in 1910 were clearly for the frontiers. A frontier mood epitomized that second wave. As a result the inland areas of the world, especially in Africa and Asia, were their main thrust.

Nevertheless, at the very end of this second, student volunteer, era, some of the younger missionaries once more began to tinker around and broke through to still another reality, which in the earlier stages was too small to be bothered with. In my earlier chapter I have mentioned the whole sequence: Eliot, Nommensen, Keysser, Gutmann, then Pickett and, preeminently for the English-speaking world, McGavran and Townsend. Cameron Townsend, as a colporteur for the American Bible Society in Guatemala, noticed that the Indians were considered almost wallflowers, part of the environment. Everyone assumed that eventually they would learn Spanish and become "real" Guatemalans. But somehow it didn't work out that way. In the United States, for example, every year for the last 38 years a higher and higher percentage of the Navajos have not spoken English. Likewise among the U.S. blacks the so-called "black power" tradition of self-determination has blown sky high our easygoing American assumptions of integration. We now must face the fact that these small groups are not fading away that easily and we must confront the fact of their reality.

Townsend symbolizes attention to "horizontally segmented" small groups in Guatemala and later, as head of the Wycliffe Bible Translators, to tribal groups in general. Townsend, recently deceased, was a wonderful man with a wonderful career and a wonderful impact. More than any other person on the face of the earth he has been responsible for the evangelization of the world's tribes. His fields are less easily contested or ignored than McGavran's, although McGavran's more generalized concern includes far more peoples—tribal plus all the rest, whether horizontally or vertically segmented.

Today, Townsend's organization sends out twice as many missionaries as all the member denominations of the National Council of Churches combined. Such a fact calls into question the sense of mission and the alertness of those National Council denominations such as my own. But, I believe that the older boards will eventually retool massively as they did almost a century ago at the beginning of the second era.

In a two-week period recently our campus was visited by denominational leaders of the Methodist, United Presbyterian, American Baptist, and the Reformed Church in America denominations. Among all of them there is a tremendous new awareness, in particular within the residual mission-minded minorities of those groups. I don't believe we need to worry that the mission agencies of the world, especially those of the United States, will continue to overlook the final unreached people frontiers. It is a wonderful, wonderful achievement that a new awareness is here. No one agency can be credited with this accomplishment, not the USCWM or MARC or any other (although the Lausanne tradition can certainly take a great deal of credit). I believe this new interest is the work of the Spirit of God. This is the thing that makes you tingle, the overwhelming sensation that we are watching God work, bringing the theme of our book, unreached peoples, to the fore among us. The mission agencies, I think, are a clean sweep in this area.

However, the question is, How can the mission agencies operate without an increasing awareness among the people, the people in the pews? Once again, I think the people concept helps a great deal. For years people in the pews in my denomination have been told that the job is over: "We've turned it over to the nationals; we're going home." But the so-called "nationals" turned out to be, for instance in Pakistan, part of a very tiny sub-community of former Hindus in that country. They have no significant ethnic or cultural connection to the vast bulk of Pakistanis, even though their language is more or less the same. But if my church were to assume that the Presbyterians in Pakistan were able to effectively evangelize the rest of the country, it would be about as absurd (and I use the word advisedly) as to suppose that if Navajos were the only Christians in the United States, seven Navajo-speaking congregations—one in Chicago, one in Seattle, one in Portland, and so forth—could be expected to win the rest of the country by themselves. I'm not stretching the truth. Those Navajo Indian congregations could try their best and could accomplish a great deal. But it is absolute folly to assume that the job is done because among certain peoples we have gotten in and made our missiological breakthrough. How foolish to assume we can now wash our hands and go home without even communicating a sense of external mission to our mission field churches.

The people back home can't easily understand this complexity. We can project the countries of the world on the screen, and they will recognize them. What we need to do now is to project on that screen the *peoples* of the world. On the map of Africa we would have to show that 800 of the people groups are split into two or perhaps three pieces by a political boundary. Take, for example, the Massai. Half of them are in Kenya, half in Tanzania, although at any given point you're not sure which side of the border they are on because they do migrate back and forth. Those in London in their drawing rooms sketching the political boundaries on their maps missed completely the significance of the peoples thus affected. Somehow those politicians saw Africa as a geography to be divided rather than as a mosaic of already long-existing people groups.

But as missionaries we are concerned for the peoples, and we must not be dazzled by the boundaries of countries any more than God is. People back home can be brought to understand this fact. One book that helps is *The Refugees Among Us,* produced by MARC. Another way for people in the pew to understand this people view is to get them to read *Perspectives on the World Christian Movement,* which has an accompanying 175-page *Study Guide.* Together these two books constitute a four-unit college course, for which a number of schools will give credit. Geneva College, for example, is offering credit to a group of about 55 students at Carnegie-Mellon who are taking that course (and nothing else) from Geneva College. They study right on their own campus, and Geneva College simply handles the academic arrangements and the audiovisuals that week after week are sent in to go with the 20 lessons. An Inter-Varsity staff member on campus at Carnegie-Mellon actually coordinates the course. In Pasadena we have now set up a one-week intensive program to train these coordinators. Right now there are perhaps five or six hundred students going through that course. But we hope that within the next two years at any given moment there will be 10,000 students studying that book. It can be done. It doesn't take any money. It doesn't take any more people than are now involved in the educational enterprise. It simply takes management.

Then I want to recommend a little booklet to which I referred earlier. It is part of the Frontier Fellowship movement and, I assure you, is not just an invention in California. Its basic idea of praying daily for the unreached peoples of the world came from Burma. That is why every copy each month has a little picture of a village in Burma and refers to the Burma plan. It was from a tribal Christian from Burma that we got the idea of a daily devotional discipline that will carry vision, excitement, and inspiration into the life of the average person.

Let me leave you with one last thought. Is there any way that you can more rapidly and more profoundly influence the vision and the purpose of an individual than to get into his hands something he will read every day? I'll answer my own question. All the other things we've ever done—even these courses I've mentioned, which are really hefty—carry people into an experience. But time wears that experience away. We've tried everything from Hidden People Sundays to day-long seminars and courses and all kinds of things. We often collaborate in truly wonderful annual mission conferences. But we have concluded that all the other activities we have ever launched are by comparison hit-and-run activities if vision is what you want to implant deeply into the lives and hearts of people. "Nothing that does not occur daily will ever dominate a life."

If it were possible for people to realize how nearly within our grasp it is to evangelize the unreached peoples of the world, it would be a revolution of new hope for people all across this country. The reason our mission boards are not receiving the candidates and the funds they need is that people in the pew have lost hope. If 30,000 missionaries are going to retire in the next 10 years and, as somebody has guessed, only 5,000 are going to replace them, then the present level of giving and going needs to be multiplied many times over. Research is necessary on those statistics as well if we are to turn this situation around and be the blessing to all the families of the earth that God expects us to be simply because He has so greatly blessed us. But we need to communicate hope to people. We need to tell them that 16,750 people groups is not that many after all. I don't care if it's 10,000 or 20,000 or what the number is, but it's a finite number. And whatever the number you come up with, just divide it into the number of dedicated evangelicals on the face of the earth today (258 million). You'll get at least 10,000 Bible believing, committed believers who are ready, if awakened, to reach out to each one of these people groups—10,000 per group.

Let me ask you, is that an unrealistic goal for the year 2000? Every week there are 1,000 new churches in Africa and Asia alone. But all these churches are new churches where there are already churches. All we need is to found 1,000 per year within these untouched groups and we'll be through with this initial job of penetrating the remaining frontiers by the year 2000. I'm not going to tamper with your eschatology, but at least we ought to try to do this. That's my eschatology. We at least ought to try to do what is plain in Scripture, what we are expected to do in terms of the blessings we have received. I don't believe there is any hope for this country if we cannot get beyond the syndrome of only accepting and trying to preserve and protect our blessings with MX missiles and horses and chariots and not realize that our only real safety is to give the blessings God has given to us to those for whom He intended them.

Chapter 4

Definitions and Identities:
Samples from the Ongoing Discussion

James W. Reapsome

In this chapter we shall discuss answers to two questions about the world's unreached peoples: first, Who are they? and second, Where are they? The answers are based on a survey of leading missionary thinkers, representing institutions of higher education, specialized research agencies, and missions agencies themselves. What follows are answers submitted to *Evangelical Missions Quarterly*, Wheaton, Illinois, as part of a survey to find the status of current thinking. First, then, Who are the unreached people groups?

Definitions

Samuel Wilson, director, Missions Advanced Research and Communications Center, Monrovia, California: "'Unreached people group: A people group among which there is no indigenous community of believing Christians with adequate numbers and resources to evangelize this people group without outside (cross-cultural) assistance.'' This definition is also the one accepted by the Strategy Working Group of the Lausanne Committee for World Evangelization, Edward R. Dayton, chairman; by the U.S. Center for World Mission, Ralph Winter, director; and by Patrick Johnstone, international research secretary, Worldwide Evangelization Crusade, England, author of *Operation World*. However, Winter adds, "I would prefer to stress the unreachedness of people in terms of the presence or absence of a church sufficiently indigenous and authentically grounded in the Bible, rather than in terms of its numerical strength vis-a-vis outside help.''

Warren W. Webster, general director, Conservative Baptist Foreign Mission Society, Wheaton, Illinois:

> An ethnic, linguistic, or other people group within which there is no viable indigenous, evangelizing community of believers. Where there is such a Christian community that group can be said to be at least initially penetrated or minimally reached with the gospel whether or not their numbers and resources are adequate to evangelize the rest of their people without outside—cross-cultural—assistance. The remainder of the task of reaching

61

those people is a matter of progressive evangelization, whether totally from within the group or assisted by outside resources.

Richard D. Sollis, chairman, research planning department, New Tribes Mission, Sanford, Florida:

(1) A tribe with no believers and no missionary work—the classic un-reached group; (2) A tribe with few, if any, believers and no evangelical missionary work being done; (3) A tribe with few, if any believers and where the only evangelical work being done is by missionaries or others with limited objectives which do not include active evangelism and church planting, e.g., some missionary linguists/translators; (4) A tribe where there is an existing church, but where the existing church is "incapsulated" and not demonstrating its potential for reaching the rest of the tribe.

Wilbert R. Shenk, vice president, Overseas Ministries, Mennonite Board of Missions, Elkhart, Indiana:

A people group may be considered unreached by Christian witness when it has had no meaningful and sustained contact with Christians so that the Christian Scriptures are not available to it and a Christian fellowship has not emerged in its midst.

Frank E. Robbins, executive vice president, Wycliffe Bible Translators International, Inc., Dallas, Texas:

Our concern is with what we call Bibleless groups. Each of them is a separate people group, but some single linguistic group may constitute more than one people group. Similarly, many of the Bibleless groups are also unreached people groups, but some of them have been long mis-sionized and have churches. They are just crippled churches for the lack of the Scriptures and the language that speaks to their hearts. Thus, the question we ask is how many groups do not have the Scriptures and in the language that speaks best to them.

Allan Starling, field coordinator, Gospel Recordings, U.S.A., Los Angeles, California: "We are talking about groups of people who are isolated from hearing the gospel message by a cultural, political, geographic or language barrier."

George W. Peters, Fresno, California, professor emeritus, Dallas Theological Seminary, Dallas, Texas: "It is utterly impossible to be exact and correct in stating precisely figures and to speak of so and so many 'hidden people groups' in the world. 'People groups' is a practical but subjective, arbitrary concept."

Lloyd Kwast, chairman, Department of Missions, Talbot Theological Seminary, La Mirada, California:

A group in which less than 20 percent are practicing Christians. By "practicing" is meant that if some criteria of measurement were set up, such as church attendance, one would discover that these people are working out their Christianity in a regular and faithful way.

John F. Robinson, executive director, Missionary Internship, Farmington, Michigan:

To define people groups only in sociological terms gives little help in the task of enumeration beyond the framework of the particular sociological group in question. When one begins to try to enumerate more broadly, the tremendous problem of overlapping classifications makes it very difficult to talk meaningfully about progress. People can be both reached and unreached at the same time, depending upon which sociological category they are placed in.

Terry C. Hulbert, dean, Columbia Graduate School of Bible and Missions, Columbia, South Carolina:

A people group in which there are no believers, or in which the believers are so few or ineffective, that there is no reasonable potential of the group being evangelized indigenously. Strictly speaking, they may have been "reached" in terms of some members having heard the gospel and believing. More accurately the group is "not being reached" or "not having the potential of being reached" under present circumstances.

J. Philip Hogan, executive director, Division of Foreign Missions, the General Council of the Assemblies of God, Springfield, Missouri:

The whole hidden peoples and unreached peoples puzzle and the research that has followed it is far more for North American and Western consumption than it is for the churches and the leaders in the third or developing world. For instance, our work in Nigeria is very strong, fast-growing, and well-led. They have 300,000 members, are totally indigenous, and are sending out their own missionaries by the score. The names we place on some of these groups and the information we publish strikes them as being just another attempt by we [sic] Americans to use our computers and pour out information. They know all about their groups that live in their territory long before we ever publish anything about them.

David Hesselgrave, Trinity Evangelical Divinity School, Deerfield, Illinois: "A people group which, within the compass of any generation, has not had a culturally meaningful hearing of the biblical gospel and has not had knowledge of, or access to, a Christian source of that message."

Cal Guy, Northborough, Massachusetts, retired distinguished professor, Southwestern Seminary, Ft. Worth, Texas:

I'm trying to raise a caution signal about planting forces in places that have numbers of unreached people before we have some research in the genuine potential for response to the gospel. We need not only to know if they are unreached, but also if they are reachable. To that end I have long suggested that I would spend 10 percent of any mission board's total income on research, and then expect to double or better the fruit of the investment of the other 90 percent.

Wesley L. Duewel, special assistant to the president for evangelism and intercession, OMS International, Greenwood, Indiana:

> I have had grave misgivings and hesitations from the very beginning of the "unreached peoples" and "peoples groups" emphasis. Anything which urges reaching the unreached thrills me. But the methods used by the protagonists have greatly disturbed me. Strategic warfare for Christ and against Satan is best guided by those God is using in leadership in the battle out on the front lines, not by people thousands of miles away trying to decide on the basis of theory and incomplete information what should be done. To me, the important questions are: How many unreached are you reaching? How much church planting are you really involved in? What percentage of your people are personally involved in evangelism or church planting? And how can we pinpoint prayer in the special areas where the Spirit is working or where Satan is fighting?

J. Ronald Blue, department chairman, World Missions, Dallas Theological Seminary, Dallas, Texas: "A group that has no viable, continuing witness within that unit of society. In other words, unless someone is sent to penetrate that group of people with the gospel, they will remain in spiritual darkness."

Wilson W. Chow, acting vice president and dean, China Graduate School of Theology, Kowloon, Hong Kong:

> The concept of unreached people groups has developed from a First World perspective and is undergirded by a strategy of sending missionaries from the First World countries. Since it is still in the initial stages in the West, it is inconceivably difficult for Asian and other Third World countries to work through such an advanced area of missions. Our national churches and theological institutions are still endeavoring to accomplish basic missionary enterprise among our own people. Nevertheless, the unreached people groups concept has made us aware of the existing cultures within our own societies.

Harvie Conn, Westminster Theological Seminary, Philadelphia, Pennsylvania:

> The terms, "people groups" and "unreached people groups" are not ontological struggles. They are functional attempts at blocking out the job that still needs doing. The "ontologists" are heavily oriented to technol-

ogy and its requirements. They must have a definition that computes, or one that they can demographically engineer. The value of a definitional struggle is that it serves as a pedagogical tool for stirring up interest in reaching the lost. As a technical instrument, it can become so loose that it creates as many problems as it solves.

As can be seen from the above, there is not much significant difference in the actual definitions of who the unreached people groups are. Rather, the differences are more related to the basic premise of narrow social definitions of people groups. Obviously, some thinkers are more comfortable with this idea than are others. Nevertheless, there does seem to be general agreement that, for purposes of expanding the outreach of the gospel, it is useful to strive for some basic concepts that help to define the scope of the task remaining to be done.

Identities

Where are the unreached people groups? Just prior to the International Congress on World Evangelization at Lausanne, Switzerland in 1974, the Missions Advanced Research and Communications Center (MARC), Pasadena, California, began to produce *Status of Christianity Profiles* on a number of countries. By the time of the congress, MARC had produced 53 *Status of Christianity Profiles* on countries and major states of the world, and an *Unreached Peoples Directory* listing 424 specific unreached people groups. Speaking at the congress, Ralph Winter said there were over 2 billion people isolated from the gospel by cultural, social, religious, and other barriers. Following the ICWE, the Lausanne Committee for World Evangelization was organized to coordinate and communicate the task of world evangelization. To that end, similar conferences were held in Kenya, Nigeria, Papua New Guinea, Ghana, Malaysia, and Singapore, as well as the Chinese Congress on World Evangelization, a pan-African conference, and an all-India conference.

The effort to locate unreached people groups was also a major reason for Ralph Winter's founding of the U.S. Center for World Mission in 1977. He popularized the concept of "hidden peoples." This he expanded to the concept of "frontier missions." In 1980, the Lausanne Committee for World Evangelization convened the Consultation on World Evangelization at Pattaya, Thailand. The research of MARC and the Strategy Working Group of the Lausanne Committee for World Evangelism was published in a book by Edward Dayton and David Fraser, *Planning Strategies for World Evangelization,* and in a condensed, simplified booklet, *That Everyone May Hear.* The first edition of *That Everyone May Hear* was published in preparation for the consultation in Pattaya, at which 18 mini-consultations discussed evangelistic strategies for specific people groups.

The most widely available lists of unreached people groups are those published by the David C. Cook Company, Elgin, Illinois. These annual directories were begun in 1979 and were also published in 1980, 1981, and 1982. The 1983 edition, entitled, *Reaching the Unreached: A Status Report,* was published by MARC. The forthcoming *Mission Handbook* of North American cross-cultural agencies, also published by MARC, will list the number of people groups each agency is attempting to reach. Meanwhile, MARC has sent out a survey to be published in *Unreached Peoples '84,* which will stress the status of the cross-cultural attempts, both local and foreign, and share the results.

In his *World Christian Encyclopedia* (Oxford University Press, 1982) David Barrett lists the peoples of the world according to five races, 13 geographical races, seven colors, 71 ethno-linguistic families, 7,010 distinct languages, 432 major peoples, and 8,990 constituent peoples, sub-peoples, and additional ethnic groups. In addition to statistical analysis, this work includes an index of peoples and languages.

Barrett concludes that there are "some 2,100 distinct ethnolinguistic groups or cultures who are still in varying degrees unevangelized, which on our definition means with populations of whom less than 60 percent have been evangelized. . . . On our definition, the only people groups who can correctly be called unreached are the one thousand or so whose populations are each less than 20 percent evangelized." He further narrows this figure to 636 people groups that have "no numerically significant evangelizing church" and are located "in countries with only a miniscule Christian presence." These groups may be found in the encyclopedia's various tables.

The most widely disseminated reference point for the location of unreached people groups is, "Unreached Peoples of the World, 1983," a chart published by the U.S. Center for World Mission. It lumps the unreached peoples into nine major groupings: tribal, Muslim, Hindu, Han Chinese, Buddhists, other African, other Asian, other Western, and U.S.A./Canada. According to this estimate, there are 23,300 peoples in the world and of this number 16,750 may be considered unreached. The U.S. Center does not have a list of these people groups. The numbers are estimates only.

Wycliffe Bible Translators and Gospel Recordings have lists of the unreached people groups that fit the specific definitions of their specialized ministries.

What becomes apparent from the survey done by *Evangelical Missions Quarterly* is that the U.S. Center's figure of 16,750 unreached people groups has become widely quoted and accepted, not because it is a precise listing, but rather because it symbolizes a statistical concept that many find useful. The EMQ survey produced the following answers in regard to the statistics for unreached people groups.

Samuel Wilson:

It is possible to count the number of linguistic groups that exist, provided one is able to distinguish languages (mutually unintelligible dialects) from minor dialect differences. The same can be said of major groupings by some other dimension: e.g., geography, religion, etc. This has the purpose of giving some indication of the status of evangelization in total or global terms. We are interested in planning strategies for evangelization. While we see the motivational merit to some finite number that could be used to motivate the church to her task, the fact is that we believe the job is only "doable" as small groups are defined which are tractable to the definition and carrying out of a Spirit-led plan to plant the church. The exact number, therefore, holds small interest for us. Barrett means *only* ethnolinguistic groupings, and Winter has never offered anything but an *estimate* of the numbers or groups that might exist.

Warren W. Webster:

Enough of us are thinking along similar lines, that there is hope for the emergence of a mutually acceptable terminology and approach, if we can somehow surmount the sociological concepts that have been rather heavily incorporated into many of our present definitions and strategies. The use of sociological definitions of people groups tends to cloud and confuse the picture when employed on a global scale. Within a single ethnic nation or culture, the sociological people groups may be helpful in pointing out segments of society that have been missed in the evangelizing process.

We know that, with a few exceptions, the church has taken root in nearly every independent nation on the face of the earth. We also believe that modern nation-states are not the same as the biblical "nations" our Lord has committed us to disciple. So our strategies must also include the 9,000 to 10,000 ethnolinguistic groups of which we arc aware. We must locate and describe those in which the church is not yet represented by a viable, indigenous, evangelizing community of believers.

Charles R. Taber, Emmanuel School of Religion, Johnson City, Tennessee:

In any modern society each person meets and interacts with many others, many strangers, many quite different from self, and tends to have stripped down, role-to-role "simplex" relationships with any one other. The social structure is "complex" in that there are many specialized and compart-mentalized institutions, each serving only one or two needs. The individual belongs to many groups, each serving one need or interest, and the membership of the groups overlaps very little. One belongs to some ethnicity, to some social class, to some occupation, to some employer, etc. Consensus in any one and commitment to any one can be very narrow and even provisional.

Allan Starling:

We do not have a directory of unreached peoples, but our directory shows all the languages in which we have recordings, some 4,200 to date. Both Wycliffe and Gospel Recordings are dealing with language groups, while the U.S. Center for World Mission, MARC, and others are referencing people groups. Sometimes a people group may speak more than one language; sometimes a language may be spoken by more than one people group. With regard to an apparent contradiction between information put out by Wycliffe and Gospel Recordings, we feel there could be as many as 10,000 languages and dialects that need recordings, whereas Wycliffe talks in terms of between 5,000 and 6,000 needing translations. The reason is because Wycliffe is dealing with the written word, whereas Gospel Recordings is dealing with the spoken word. There are many cases where two or more groups may be able to read the same translation. However, when it comes to listening to oral recordings of the gospel message, there may be enough difference in their pronunciation or dialects to make it hard for them to understand each other. Or one group may be prejudiced enough against another group to make recording unacceptable to them. Gospel Recordings, therefore, makes finer distinctions between the language groups than does Wycliffe.

Richard D. Sollis:

In most cases, the unreached people groups are identified and surveyed by our missionaries already working within the given country. Our field leaders are expected to identify and survey new groups sufficiently in advance to keep the field expanding as opportunities and resources permit. If the existence of a given group is known, it is not generally too difficult to discover in what geographical area they are located. However, there are still many "undiscovered" people groups which have not come to the attention of mission and church groups. In the case of tribal groups, this is usually due to geographical remoteness and/or location in a country or area closed to mission work. In general, knowledgeable sources within a given country would likely know, or could find out, where a given group is located. It would, however, be of help to have an indication of geographical location. It would seem as if there should be some form of cross referencing where references to a given people group could be found in the index by looking up (or accessing) either the group name or the general geographical location, or perhaps the group language.

With reference to data currently being entered in unreached peoples data bases, it is not difficult to find inaccuracies. However, my personal observation is that the problem is not so much one of incorrectness as it is one of incompleteness. Two major types of data which would be very helpful are: (1) more detailed information as to the quantity and quality of current evangelical gospel penetration of the people group, and (2) detailed, regularly updated information on each country explaining if, and specifically how, new missionaries or mission boards can gain entrance to the given country to the unreached people groups. Until a data base developed by the evangelicals in each country is rather extensively developed, I question whether a truly adequate, comprehensive, and accurate international data base can be developed.

To a greater or lesser extent, detailed unreached people data bases are feasible and would be of help, but to what extent are they wise? Missionary endeavor—particularly pioneer efforts aimed at unreached peoples—is encountering ever-increasing hostility from national and international groups and organizations dedicated to stopping evangelical missionary effort. To what extent should evangelical church and missionary organizations place into a data base information relative to their presence and objectives? To believe that such a data base could exist without permitting access to cults, Marxist organizations, unscrupulous journalists, and other enemies of the gospel and evangelical missionary endeavor is to be totally unrealistic. How to aid our friends but not abet our enemies is a question at least worth asking.

Wilbert R. Shenk:

By making people groups the strategic key it seems to me to seriously distort the actual situation. This approach biases our thinking and action toward rural, primal peoples, whereas the dominant phenomenon of this generation is urbanization worldwide. While not all of the major language-ethnic groups are urbanized, urbanization has touched nearly all of them.

Frank E. Robbins:

In our 1978 *Ethnologue* (a new one scheduled to come out this year) 634 groups are listed with definite needs for Bible translation, and 2,645 groups are listed as possible needs (the definiteness of which has not yet been determined).

D. John Richard, general secretary, Evangelical Fellowship of India, New Dehli, India:

As per Ralph Winter, the world contains 16,750 cultural groups and sub-groups. But that is a debatable issue. It is quite possible that a single person may belong to two or three groups, unless we narrow down the definition to more detailed specifics, such as, the Tamil coolie laborers serving in building construction works in Delhi. We have Tamil coolie laborers serving in road construction works, too. So, these latter will have to be classified under a separate group, so as to prevent a person belonging to more than one unreached group. If such a narrowing down is not done, then the number of people groups will swell up. There also are other Tamils

69

working as domestic helpers and perhaps even as factory hands in a city like Delhi.

In actual practice, generally speaking, in our outreach efforts, three main considerations are taken into account. These are the spoken language, the educational level and the economic status. The latter two are ordinarily closely linked together, though this is not always the case. There are Tamils in high places in Delhi, too. In terms of the definition of the Strategy Working Group, India is yet an unreached nation comprised of thousands of unreached groups. But we know India can never be billed as an unreached nation. Not only are there diverse kinds of missionary and evangelistic activities going on; not only are there a number of house groups quietly springing up; there is also a gathering animosity towards Christ and his gospel. It is the latter that certifies that we are on the right track, that a hornet's nest is being disturbed. All our planning for strategies for evangelizing the unreached groups in India will be unproductive, if the twin strategies of prayer and love are not given the due place they deserve.

George W. Peters:

The figures expressing the unreached people groups are practical, but arbitrary and not scientific groupings. It must be admitted that no scientific lines exist. Therefore, arbitrariness, convenience, and practical reasons (at times, perhaps, propaganda motives) enter and determine us to set up our own standards to delineate people into groupings. It is utterly impossible to be exact and correct in stating precise figures and to speak of so many "hidden people groups" in the world. As evangelicals who profess to proclaim the truth, we ought to be more cautious and conscientious and at least state clearly an exact definition of the meaning of terms. Otherwise, it becomes only disguised propaganda. To build a philosophy and strategy of missions on it may be at specific times and under specific circumstances practical sociology, but we should not make theological claims for it.

John F. Robinson:

Simply defining a people group, an unreached people group, and a reached people group is inadequate, because it gives no way of relating those terms to the other kinds of categories in which statistics are discussed. If a taxonomy of useful categories were listed, and a single global statistic for each category were given, then people could have some idea of how the people group terminology relates to the other categories that are so commonly used to talk about world need and mission progress.

Patrick Johnstone:

Unfortunately, what has become a good rallying cry has left people enthused, but with no clear vision as to where to go and to whom to go to get the job done. This would appear to me to be because of: (1) a definition of ''people group'' that is sociological; (2) failure to relate people groups to geographical locations and political nations. The pendulum has swung too far away from the very real political nations that often are seeking to blur or eradicate the very divisions that we are making, though this may be wrong, too; (3) poor statistics that discredit the whole thrust of the challenge.

This has some rather unsatisfactory results: (1) The open-ended proliferation of people groups into as many subgroups as a researcher can find. Thus we have the jeepney drivers in Manila, the high-rise flat dwellers in Singapore, Chinese businessmen in Hong Kong, etc. (2) The artificial compartmentalization of peoples into such groups, without relating them to the very real and very complex world in which we live, i.e., the fact that there are no churches among jeepney drivers does not mean that they are necessarily unreached, for there are many churches in most of the areas in which they live, and quite a number would, in fact, have connections with such. (3) Any given person may belong to up to ten different sociological groupings, but we need a definition of people group that will count each person only once. (4) The MARC unreached people annuals have been useful to focus our attention on the need to think in terms of biblical peoples, but fall short on motivating people to do anything, because of confusing and incomplete data. The total of all people groups in a country is hardly ever 100 percent, and no clear mention is made of Christians living among them, or Christian missions already seeking to reach them. (5) Ralph Winter's figure of 16,750 hidden peoples is based on the sociological breakdown, but he clearly is distancing himself from the definition on which these figures are based. Using David Barrett's narrower ethnolinguistic definition, there could be 9,000 to 10,000 people groups in the world. But if we use the ''people within a nation'' concept, the number will be much higher, depending on cutoff size used. Would ten Zimbabwean Venda people in the United States constitute a people group?

Edward R. Dayton, vice president, mission and evangelism, World Vision International, Monrovia, California:

How many unreached people groups are there? If you approach the question from the viewpoint of evangelism, the fact that one needs a unique strategy to reach each people group, then a rough estimate would be something over 100,000, perhaps as high as 500,000. If you asked the question on the basis of wanting the sum of all the people groups of unreached people groups to equal the sum of all the non-Christians in the world (approximately 2 billion), then you must stick with ethnolinguistic groups, and the estimate of 16,750 is as good as any. What is being missed in this discussion is the reason for defining the world this way. The reason is one of evangelistic strategy. It is the recognition that there is no one strategy that can be used to reach every group.

Wilson W. Chow:

Although on paper the various geographical movements, directions and locations have been analyzed and discovered, it is very difficult in actuality to locate specific people groups that are unreached. It is difficult enough locating people groups. For example, the illegal immigrants of mainland China now living in Hong Kong are classified as a people group, but their actual location is difficult to trace, since they are so scattered among Hong Kong society. This is understandable, due to their illegal presence in the colony, unlike the Vietnamese who can easily be located, since they are detained in refugee camps established by the government. The various sources of information are not entirely adequate or accurate, for the following reasons: (1) societies are constantly changing, therefore, it is difficult to publish up-to-date material that parallels the changes; (2) all methodology, including computer data, is dependent on and operates from the West; (3) the data is acceptable in theory, on the basis of strategy, but the real situation reflects a far more intricate and complex field of observation. The factors are not as visible as the data presents.

Harvie M.Conn:

The very definition makes it extremely difficult to understand the figure of 16,750 groups. If you have a definition of "peoplehood," which sees the groups as more than simply ethnic (including linguistic, social, behavioral), each person in the world could belong to from 40 to infinity groups. Talk about uncontrollable statistics! On the statistical side, I find that information regarding the three major groupings of peoples—Hindus, Muslim, Chinese, to be as useful for my purposes as anything. I'm distressed that so little attention goes to the cities and the urban character of so many peoples. Tribal, animistic groupings get a lot more attention.

Bob Waymire, director of research and planning, Overseas Crusades, and task force chairman, Global Mapping Project, Santa Clara, California:

With the help of some amazing technology, there is a way to visualize all the vital information needed for developing strategies to reach the unreached peoples. A new organization, Dataserve, Inc. has formed to help mission agencies meet the technological challenge. One purpose is the mapping of all the people groups and frontiers of the world, depicting their location and identity and status. Another purpose is to reflect the location/distribution, identity, status and dynamic analysis of the forces for evangelism and the church planting. Our first step is to have a map produced that has superimposed on it information reflecting the precise locations of people groups. The next step will be to locate and show the status of all known ethnolinguistic groups. Having computerized mapping capability will certainly enhance the efforts of those who are working to reflect the location and status of the world's peoples.

In these responses, one notes a certain feeling of unease about quantifying the task of world evangelization that remains to be done according to rather narrow social definitions and arbitrary boundaries of what constitutes a reached or unreached people group. A certain amount of confusion is bound to ensue when different proponents use different terminology and different figures. However, the more basic concern that emerges is that of the validity of a Western technological approach to world evangelization. Some scholars, of course, have reservations about the validity of social groupings as the base for evangelistic strategy. However, what remains to be seen in the future is whether or not the current high priority being given to research, the compilation of computer files, and computerized mapping will accomplish more effective evangelism and church planting.

Right now, it is clear that considerable interest has been generated by the Strategy Working Group of the Lausanne Committee on World Evangelization, by the Missions Advanced Research and Communications Center, and by the U.S. Center for World Mission. However, as the respondents to the study done for *Evangelical Missions Quarterly* indicate, on the level of missionary education and missionary strategy by specific agencies, there are serious questions that need to be faced about the wisdom and practical value of the unreached people groups approach to world evangelism.

Chapter 5
Some Strategy Questions
Roger S. Greenway

The December 27, 1982, issue of *Time* Magazine gave unprecedented coverage to the Christian missionary enterprise. When America's leading news magazine carries on its cover the picture of one of God's servants, Bible in hand, preaching the gospel to New Guinean tribesmen, you have to take note of what it says. *Time's* seven-page article was fairly accurate and complete. Writer Richard N. Ostling and his staff of reporters did credible work piecing together examples of mission work, Catholic and Protestant, from Asia, Africa, and Latin America, and explaining some of the issues facing modern missionaries. It was obvious that they had talked with missiologists as well as practitioners. Tucked away among the comments was the following observation, which relates directly to our subject:

> The most important change in Protestant missionary strategy in the past ten years has been to identify and seek to contact some 16,000 tribes and social groups around the world that have been beyond the reach of the Gospel.

The purpose of this chapter is to examine this "change in Protestant missionary strategy" from the viewpoint of the questions it has provoked in the last decade. From the start, the slogan, "Reaching the Unreached," signaled renewal in missionary thinking. After more than a decade of declining interest in, and support of, evangelistic activity on the part of many churches and mission boards a new spark was lit. Given the state of theology in North America, the enthusiasm with which the idea has been embraced in some sectors of the church is quite amazing. The concept, at least, has gained broad acceptance without any serious challenge. The exposure it has received at major international conferences has established it firmly as the most significant new concept in missionary strategy today. Whatever is said in this chapter by way of questions and challenges is not in the least meant to detract from the writer's appreciation for the renewed focus on unreached peoples in evangelism.

Question 1. Are Western churches ready and willing to increase the ranks of cross-cultural missionaries to the levels required to reach the unreached?

The studies produced as a result of the new perspective indicate that three billion people still need to be reached, most of them by way of cross-cultural evangelism. This represents a colossal assignment, and given the growth of global populations, especially in non-Christian areas, the task increases every minute. Are churches ready to hear this message and act on it? Are they conditioned for fresh pioneering?

Early in the discussions about unreached peoples it became clear that in many Christian circles there was not that readiness. Since the mid-1950s, some denominational leaders had hammered incessantly on the theme of the "end of the missionary era." Missionaries, they told church members, had successfully "worked themselves out of a job," and whatever evangelistic work still remained to be done could be taken care of adequately and better by Third World churches. This was hailed as good news. In view of rising costs, growing restrictions against missionaries, and hostility against white Americans in some places, it seemed that the natural thing to do was to turn over evangelistic work to the Third World churches. Assurances were heard that national Christians would pursue the task zealously.

Not only were the ranks thinned in some cases; missionaries on the field were shifted away from evangelism and assigned to institutions and service work. They were viewed primarily as doctors, nurses, teachers, and administrators, rather than evangelists and church planters. Churches back home were educated to expect this from the people they supported overseas. Evangelism, they were told, was being done by national Christians, and missionaries served behind the lines in positions that developed and strengthened the ministries of the churches.

The very existence of the national churches, in itself a great cause of rejoicing, came to have a negative influence on the missionary enterprise wherever it was interpreted in such a way that it distracted and deflected attention from the original purpose of mission, namely, the reaching of the unreached with the gospel of salvation.

About a decade ago, a new note was sounded. Unreached peoples were "discovered." Suddenly, a generation of Christians that had mainly heard one single line, that "old fashioned" evangelism was no longer expected of missionaries, but that missionaries were sent out to assist the established churches in their programs, now heard that thousands of people groups were unevangelized and would probably remain in that condition unless evangelistic missionaries were sent out to reach them.

Most Sunday school children are bright enough to catch the contradiction and raise some questions. For that reason, as promotors of the unreached peoples concept are very much aware, any strategy to reach the unreached will have to begin at home with a patient return to pioneer missionary perspectives in the supporting churches.

> *Question 2. Where do the national churches of the Third World fit into this new perspective, and how do missionaries of the new kind relate to those who are assisting overseas churches in programs other than evangelism?*

A number of interesting questions have surfaced in unreached peoples literature regarding the attitude of national churches toward new evangelistic work by expatriates within the borders of their countries. Some national churches, partly out of reaction to the days when mission boards went ahead and made decisions without consulting the national leaders at all, now insist that all evangelism in their countries be controlled by them. How, we must ask, do they feel about the new strategy being promoted in Western churches? Will they take graciously to the reordering of mission budgets so as to provide funds for pioneer work beyond the range of existing churches? And, as the churches of the Third World increasingly enter the missionary enterprise and send out their own workers, will they participate in this strategy, committing their own financial resources and personnel to reaching the unevangelized?

Several observations have to be made. First, I am confident that the call for a return to basic evangelism will, in the long run, find a favorable response among Third World Christians. Many of them have been waiting for this for a long time. They have watched the expatriates force their own agendas on the developing churches, but they longed to see once again missionaries who were exuberant about the gospel's power to save sinners and eager to reach out to the lost. Seldom has a proven soul-winner, a missionary who demonstrated evangelistic gifts and church-planting zeal, gotten in serious trouble with national church leaders and been asked to go home. Because the Third World churches have generally remained more sensitive to the primacy of evangelism than their Western counterparts, I believe they will respond favorably to the shift to pioneer work. The sooner the new perception is translated from the scholars' books and conference papers to actual practice on the field, the better it will be. Many of our brothers and sisters have been waiting for the day.

Second, it needs to be affirmed that inter-church assistance as it is now carried on continues to be needed and should be maintained in many of its forms. It would be irresponsible, and severely damaging to church development, if all missionaries were abruptly pulled away from what they are doing and sent to work as evangelists in tribal areas.

But the return to the original, biblical idea of a missionary must and will take place. When it happens, it will kindle fresh enthusiasm for evangelism in the national churches as well. It is a fact that when the foreign missionaries stopped evangelizing and settled down to housekeeping duties, a large share of the national leadership lost interest in evangelism too.

This brings up another issue we must not pass by. It is the exciting new growth of mission involvement on the part of non-Western churches. On the one hand this is the best bit of news the missionary enterprise has heard for a long time. But on the other hand, if it is mishandled and used as an excuse for less evangelism on the part of Western Christians, it will detract and deflect from obedience to the Great Commission in the same way that the idea of the coming-of-age of the national churches did a few decades ago.

Along with the change of Western Protestant missionary strategy in the direction of classic evangelistic efforts toward the unsaved and unreached, this other change is occurring. How they will relate to each other may be the number-one question for missions in the next decade. In an article that appeared in the *Evangelical Missions Quarterly,* in October, 1982, Lawrence E. Keyes reported on the changes he saw in mission involvement. Comparing his recent study with earlier surveys (1972 and 1976), he observed that ". . . non-Western mission agencies are growing even faster than their North American counterparts." The recruitment of non-Western missionaries is five times as fast as reported North American recruitment. The total number of Third World missionaries working cross-culturally is now over 15,000, and they come from at least 57 different countries. This appears to represent a new and mighty wave of missionary advance.

But there are problems, one of them being the financing of Third World missionaries. Many of them must take care of their own needs in the new land. A second problem, which Keyes noted, is candidate training. Training programs and administrative structures are growing, but the Third World churches still lack the mission infra-structures that Western churches established over the years.

In what directions will missions from the Third World go? Will they work mainly among people of their own race and language dispersed in other countries, the approach that has characterized most of the initial effort? Or will they target the unreached peoples in the cities and jungles around the world?

This leads me to the next observation. In planning and implementing the new initiatives in missions the participation of evangelism-minded leaders from the Third World should be sought at every stage. Charles R. Taber's strong words on the subject were spoken more than a decade ago at one of the early consultations on frontier missions. You can hear them echo occasionally in speeches and books. But to this very day their message remains largely unheeded:

> I said in my introduction that I would not primarily present concrete techniques. One reason is that this would be premature in the absence of

Third World leaders in significant numbers. Surely it is time to stop thinking and acting as if conferences in the United States or Europe, attended largely by Westerners, can provide a blueprint for world evangelization, when most of the unreached peoples are in the Third World. It should be a matter of principle that the wisdom and experience of Christian thinkers from the Third World be called upon to play a fundamental and even a determinative role in primary planning as well as in final execution. I would hesitate to hold another conference such as this one without a majority of Third World leaders, for fear of doing more harm than good by perpetuating old paternalistic patterns (Beaver 1973:120).

Taber went on to point out that in addition to being a basic principle, the inclusion of Third World missions leaders at all stages of planning and implementation is also a very pragmatic issue. For unless the vision of reaching the unreached is shared by Christian leaders on a global scale, with support and cooperation from all sides, it is doubtful that the new thrust we are talking about will get far off the ground.

If we continue as we are now doing much longer, it may be too late. What has happened in North American cities serves as a warning. There was a time some decades ago when minority church leaders were looking for opportunities to discuss urban evangelization with white churchmen. But they were ignored. And now the white Christians who want to serve God in the city must come with hat in hand, their intentions distrusted until they have proved themselves. Third World leaders are about at that point now. Thanks to Ralph Winter, Edinburgh 1980 was an exception. But let there be a few more mission conferences, and a few more major strategy decisions with only token recognition of the role of Third World leaders, and the opportunity for genuine partnership and interdependence between Western and Third World churches will be gone.

Question 3. How can missionaries participating in the work of reaching the unreached be protected from repeating the mistakes made in earlier periods?

In many cases, though not all by far, the unreached peoples are tribes and social groups that are susceptible to cultural imperialism, just as their counterparts were a century ago. Granted, mission studies have moved a long way in the past decades. Today it is recognized more clearly that the gospel ought not be identified with any nation or culture but must be given authentic, indigenous cultural expression.

But there are no guarantees that the old mistakes will not be repeated by modern missionaries. Many of the same forces that produced yesterday's errors are still around. How few denominational mission boards, for example, working overseas or among ethnic minorities in North America, really dare to trust the Holy Spirit to develop a new church in His own way, under the direction of the Bible and in the hands of brothers and sisters themselves, without the governing hand of mission authorities upon them?

It seems to me that the specialized evangelism called for by the concept of reaching the unreached demands the kind of missionaries, and mission executives along with them, who possess great sensitivity to the issues involved in the proper contextualization of the gospel and development of the church. This should be a prime requirement of all who would enter upon primary evangelism.

Anthropologists, politicians, and ideologists who carry their own agendas for social change continue to attack missionaries for daring to interfere with tribal people. They aim their attacks against national evangelists as well as expatriate missionaries. They would prohibit all outsiders from interfering with the life of tribal peoples and traditional religions. They would reject with passion everything that we are discussing about the evangelization of indigenous peoples.

The document known as "The Declaration of Barbados" was produced in 1971 by a group of anthropologists participating in a Symposium on Inter-Ethnic Conflict in South America. It was sponsored in part by the Churches Commission on International Affairs of the World Council of Churches, though the symposium's final statement did not necessarily represent the WCC's position. One section of the Declaration dealt with the question of the guilt attributable to Christian missions for the tragic condition of Indian society in Latin America. Say what we will about the prejudices and anti-religious bias of the Declaration's framers, it tells us how our work is viewed by some outside observers. It cautions us to avoid whatever mistakes may be discerned in past missionary endeavor, whether Catholic or Protestant. And it underscores the importance of preparing missionaries who are sensitive to cultural and anthropological issues. For the record, here is the section dealing with missions and tribal peoples:

> Evangelization, the work of the religious missions in Latin America, also reflects and complements the reigning colonial situation with the values of which it is imbued. The missionary presence has always implied the imposition of criteria and patterns of thought and behavior alien to the colonized Indian societies. A religious pretext has too often justified the economic and human exploitation of the aboriginal population.
>
> The inherent ethnocentric aspect of the evangelization process is also a component of the colonialist ideology and is based on the following characteristics:
>
> 1) its essentially discriminatory nature implicit in the hostile relationship to Indian culture conceived as pagan and heretical;

2) its vicarial aspect, implying the reification of the Indian and his conse-
quent submission in exchange for future supernatural compensations;

3) its spurious quality given the common situation of missionaries seeking
only some form of personal salvation, material or spiritual;

4) the fact that the missions have become a great land and labour enterprise, in conjunction with the dominant imperial interests.

As a result of this analysis we conclude that the suspension of all missionary activity is the most appropriate policy on behalf of both Indian
society as well as the moral integrity of the churches involved (Beaver
1973:369-95).

*Question 4. Dare we plunge into the work of reaching the unreached
until the issues raised by contextualization have been probed more fully
and their implications understood by field missionaries?*

There are in the world several thousand ethnic groups with their separate
languages and dialects, and no two of them have identical cultural configura-
tions. Many of them are among the unreached we want to evangelize. I suggest
that before we go much further we face the question whether the Christian
missionary enterprise in general and the board or agency we represent in
particular are prepared to take seriously the issues involved in the contextualization of the Christian faith and the church in other cultures. If we plunge ahead
willy-nilly, we will soon face serious problems, as well as earn the criticism of
secular anthropologists and the like.

I submit that when we honor the unique character of a race, tribe, or people,
in the bush or in the city, we honor God in whose image they were made and the
shadows of whose glory they still bear. On the other hand, we dishonor God
whenever we misuse or exploit the culture of those same people, even in the
interests (as we may interpret it) of their religious conversion. The problem as I
see it in evangelism is how to preserve and promote the particular genius of a
people while at the same time conveying the full gospel, which attacks the evil
in any culture and eventually will transform it.

There are a host of theological as well as practical issues involved. They were
raised by Roland Allen earlier in the century when he challenged mission
workers to trust the Holy Spirit to shape and develop the younger churches
without the imposing hand of the foreign missionary. A half century later, and
possibly standing on the edge of a great new missionary era, do we dare be the
kind of evangelists who communicate the faith simply and clearly and then set
the new Christians free to be led by the Holy Spirit along the lines of their own
peculiar culture? Tensions and challenges galore await us, to be sure. Imagine
what it will mean when the number of culturally unique churches is multiplied
tenfold and increasingly each becomes an active member of the world wide

fellowship of believers! When that happens, and I believe it will, new dimensions will be added to our understanding of the church catholic.

Let us remember that it is one thing to talk the language of cultural catholicity, and quite another thing to practice it. At one point in his ministry, the apostle Peter stood tall in his perception of cultural catholicity (Acts 11). But at another time and under different circumstances, he lost it and Paul had to call him down publicly (Gal. 2). Through the years, missionaries of the Christian faith have encountered new peoples and cultures time and time again. Sometimes they stood tall, and at other times they failed. Mission history records tensions, anguish, sometimes schism, and sometimes renewal over the question of faith and culture. As new chapters unfold, perhaps more rapidly now than in the past, missionaries and local church leaders in every land will struggle with the issues of contextualization. How far are we willing to go in the expression of the principle that no culture is unredeemable, but that through all the myriad human cultures the truth in Christ can become incarnate, contemporary, relevant, life-enhancing, and truly catholic? It seems to me that we have to wrestle with these issues more before implementing further the unreached peoples concept.

Question 5. The evangelism of unreached peoples requires cross-cultural missionaries with special gifts and training. Are boards, churches, and schools prepared to recognize this and willing to spend money and effort to equip properly the missionaries sent out?

We are talking about E-3 evangelism, work among people of a very different language and culture from that of the missionary, and in places where there is still no viable church capable of carrying on alone. With the exception of such organizations as Regions Beyond Missionary Union and Wycliffe Bible Translators, most missions are not specializing in this kind of work. Some are not involved in it at all. Nor have the new efforts emanating from Third World churches, to my knowledge, placed any stress on mission work where Christ is not yet named.

The training and orientation programs of Western and non-Western workers must be enriched by studies dealing with the relation of culture and Christianity. The principles and methods of cross-cultural mission work are an essential part of all pre-field training.

The bicultural workers needed for expanded E-3 missions must be people who, like the apostle Paul, could participate with ease and effectiveness in more than one culture. He bridged the Graeco-Roman and the Hebrew worlds. Better than most Christians in his day, Paul could achieve a high measure of cultural transcendence. He himself represented, and by his work promoted, the cultural pluriformity of Christianity. Most of Paul's battles were with people who professed to be followers of Jesus, yet who maintained that the Jewish culture alone provided the right setting for the development of the new faith. Paul fought that position. And in Acts 15 we see that the first great theological crisis in the church had to do with the relation of faith and culture. How many more battles have been fought through the years over similar issues! And some of them were lost due to the ethnocentrism of dedicated Christian workers who could not cross the cultural bridges.

It is not always necessary to travel thousands of miles to meet a major cultural gap that must be crossed. In North America, a single neighborhood, such as the one in which my wife and I live in Philadelphia, can have ten to twenty different ethno-linguistic communities within it. Some of these do not have gospel-preaching churches of any size, and each probably requires a special strategy of evangelism tailor-made to meet its needs.

Nationals of any country become cultural foreigners the moment they leave their own environment and enter a territory where unfamiliar tongues and customs prevail. A country like Mexico has well over a hundred separate cultural groups. Each is distinct, with its own language or dialect, customs, values, beliefs, and world view. For a Mexican Christian from the capital to go and reside in Oaxaca, learn an Indian language, and work to plant a church requires as much adjustment, training, specialized skills, and determination as it would for an expatriate missionary.

George Samuel, an Indian church leader who has taken it upon himself to obtain cross-cultural training for evangelism, describes the challenge in his country as follows:

> In view of the social situation in India, we need to propose a discipleship that is realistic in the light of the various ethnic units. We must take care not to insist that they must follow any of the patterns of the existing congregations. New disciples can form congregations of Bible-obeying Christians while remaining in cultural harmony with their own people. Since a very large number of sociological groups remain undiscipled, we must think in terms of helping each of them to become Bible-believing, Bible-obeying and Christ-honoring Christians in their own cultures. Instead of following a foreign culture, whether Western or non-Western, they should develop social structures which are more in harmony with God's will according to the Scripture (Wagner and Dayton 1978:93).

Samuel knows that if India's villages, towns, and cities are to be evangelized, it will have to be done in the main by Indian Christians themselves. India's cultural divisions are horrendous, its people divided by language, caste, and class barriers. Communal feelings and class distinctions separate people rigidly, and the courage it takes to cross over those barriers for the sake of the gospel, only the love of Christ can engender. It is more costly for an Indian to do it than for an expatriate. Yet that is the price Indian Christians will have to pay if their country's masses are to be engrafted into Christ's body on earth.

And beyond the personal sacrifices there are the skills, perceptions, and deep understanding of the gospel required in order for Samuel's dream for India to be realized in every culture. With the principle that Christianity not only can, but should, take on the "flesh" of one new people after another, none of us has a problem. But how to do it requires much prayer, specialized study, cross-cultural training, and patient experimentation. This means that creative new programs must be developed by Western and Third World agencies to prepare the workers for unreached peoples evangelism.

Question 6. How can the new emphasis on unreached peoples be kept from becoming just another fad, which will eventually fade away and be replaced with some more clever idea to raise interest and funds for missions?

Ted Ward, professor of Curriculum Research at Michigan State University, said in an address at Dallas Theological Seminary:

I thank God for the current vigorous campaign to redirect mission outreach activities toward "unreached peoples." At the same time, I fervently pray that this enthusiasm will not become just one more clever movement. The story of missions in the second half of this century includes too many cases where smart managers and visionary promoters figured out really neat schemes to show God how to get on with the job of reaching the world (Ward 1982:106-7).

The survival and amazing growth of the church in China, Ward points out, should teach us all some sobering lessons. God has resources other than North American Christians, and ways of carrying out His purpose of which we would never think. The best strategy is still that which confesses humbly that the job is too big for us, the problems far too complex, and we can only turn ourselves over to God to be used, to help Him if He cares for our services.

Great slogans come and go, in missions as in every other field. The un-reached peoples emphasis has produced some good ones, they sound biblical and right to our ears, and their language appears everywhere in current missionary literature. But do we mean it? Are we sure that this will not be a temporary fad? Convictions about this must be evidenced all through the ranks by realigned budgets, aggressive recruitment for primary evangelism, new cross-cultural training programs, and an emphasis on church planting. Without this, I am convinced that it will prove to be a fad.

Then there is the theological issue which makes me feel uneasy. I find it hard to explain the new interest in basic evangelism in some circles when I examine the theology that comes from the pulpits and seminaries. Granted that the Holy

Spirit may be doing a new thing among them, but if that is the case it must translate into other changes before evangelism can be rooted in good soil. The new thrust in missions is going to be costly in many ways, and it requires sound theological underpinnings in the churches and schools. Either theology undergirds it or theology will be its downfall. If for some the unreached peoples movement is really not more than a bandwagon they have jumped on, they may just as easily jump off when the momentum slows down.

There is still another matter, and I address it particularly to conservative evangelicals, traditionally the most mission-minded group. If God chooses some other way, as He has been doing in China, that is radically different from everything the missions strategists write books about and our promotional literature conveys to the churches, can we accept His "no" and lay our plans aside? Mission history records many occasions when God did just that, and mission enthusiasts were cast into despair. If the Muslim world remains resistant, and unreached remain unreached for another generation, can our faith take it? Can we rest our best efforts and the state of the world in God's hands, and apply personally the doctrine that He is sovereign?

When the issue of submission to God's sovereign and surprising will is settled, we can lean back and discover joy in world missions. Missions must never become our business, our professional career, our task, our main "job." Because then the joy goes away and our words sound hollow.

Even worse is the attitude that views evangelism as a heavy burden, a horrendous task God lays on us and watches how we perform. I see in the unreached peoples emphasis, if wrongly handled, the potential for misplaced guilt. If God is somehow portrayed as the Scorekeeper who expects His people to win the missions game, a lot of painful guilt trips lie ahead.

I hope the wrongs of both neglect and misplaced guilt can be avoided, and that churches and mission agencies will pursue the task of reaching the unreached with diligence and joy. Let the joy of missions grow as we work, remembering all along that ours is the God of the unexpected. We may see Him perform China-like wonders in India, in the Muslim world, and among the urban masses before He winds up His plan for mankind.

Chapter 6
Backgrounds for a New Thrust
Paul G. Schrotenboer

When God's people are faced with the challenge of a great thrust forward in mission, they may plunge in without taking time to reflect on where they are and why they have not taken this forward thrust before. In order not to do that, we would pause to consider first the past mission efforts of evangelical churches in the Calvinist tradition and then their present status. Therefore, with a view to the global cooperative effort of Reformed churches to reach the unreached peoples of the world, we shall now look to our heritage and to our present circumstances.

Features of Reformed Missions: from Voetius to Verkuyl[1]

We shall not attempt a history of Reformed missions or try to survey Reformed missiology. Either one would require a separate treatise, which others are more qualified than I to write. It will be of greater benefit to set forth the salient features of mission work done in our Reformed tradition. We shall focus largely on the missionary work of evangelical Reformed churches.

We have established churches in our own image. Evangelical Reformed churches have set as their goal to establish Reformed churches. The theology held by the missionaries has been Calvinism, and the churches that they have established have been persuaded to adopt the Reformed creeds. The church government they have adopted, at least when the influence of the missionary prevailed, was Presbyterian. Often the church architecture and liturgy, including the music, bear the stamp of the Reformed Western church.[2] Third World church leaders tend to imitate the missionary. When it is possible, they eagerly study at the missionary's alma mater.

We do not mention this image-making mission by way of denigration. If done rightly, it is both commendable and in some respects necessary. We have sought to establish Reformed churches holding to the Reformed faith because we have been convinced that this is the gospel pure and sound. To have done otherwise would have caused one to be less than faithful.

The question does arise, however, whether the occasion of establishing a new church in a new cultural environment in a new age is not the appropriate time to reexamine our Reformed heritage and test it in the new situation. Continuing self-examination is an essential part of that heritage.

There has been no uniformity of missionary method. The Reformed mission has not been characterized by any one method. At times the mission work was done as evangelism where no gospel witness had as yet been made. At other times the mission has worked where others were already active. Sometimes the aim has been to form national leaders from the start; at other times the goal has been to establish churches and then, at a later stage, to inquire about training local pastors. The highly successful Nevius method, which stressed indigenousness, was followed in Korea, but in Indonesia a method that kept the national church dependent for decades upon the sending church was followed. In Nigeria and China the Western church assumed officially the work started by individual members on a free-lance basis. Some churches have followed a strict evangelism-only approach, and others have followed a comprehensive approach that includes building and maintaining schools and hospitals, farming, and, more recently, social uplifting. One and the same church has followed one method in one field and another method elsewhere.

Generally speaking, the Reformed mission has been the mission of the church as institution, not of the parachurch agency, nor of the independent faith mission. Here too, however, there has been no full uniformity.

Also, generally speaking, the Reformed mission has collaborated with the colonial government. Only with the changing political situation in the last few decades did a change in mission policy occur. Today we universally decry the effects of the colonial era.

One would be hard pressed to state what is the distinctive Reformed method of mission. The variety among Reformed mission agencies and churches has been as great, perhaps, as in any other tradition.

There is no consensus on ecumenical relations. In terms of relation to other churches and mission agencies the spectrum among the Reformed churches is wide. It ranges from Reformed Presbyterian churches, which seek to establish small and separate churches holding to their distinctive principles of psalmody and worship, such as in Japan, to those churches which cooperate in establishing or strengthening existing national churches, such as in India and Zaire. Here also such churches have no distinctive denominational tradition in terms of Western features. Some churches follow one method here and quite a different method there.

There has been a great variety in training national leaders. Let us take the Christian Reformed Church in North America as an example. This church's theological education on the mission field, both with and for the national churches, ranges from establishing separate seminaries manned exclusively by expatriates (as in Mexico, the Philippines, and Puerto Rico) to cooperating in a major theological center (such as the Instituto Superior Evangelico de Estudios Teologicos in Buenos Aires). At times it has also taken the form of cooperation with other evangelicals as in the Theological College of Northern Nigeria (TCNN). It has also used the method of Theological Education by Extension (TEE).

Perhaps the only conclusion that may be reached from this variety in theological education (which can be duplicated in other churches) is that we have no specific policy, apart from the insistence that our missionaries must teach from the Reformed perspective.

True to our tradition, we have emphasized an educated ministry. As recently as in 1976 the RES Cape Town Mission Conference centered on the training of national leaders.

It should be added that in spite of our emphasis on training, we have not been very successful in training Third World leaders of outstanding ability. Perhaps this is due largely to the fact that we have so strongly insisted on doctrinal uniformity that we allow for relatively little initiative or deviation on the part of the leaders. Churches of other traditions who have been less insistent on doctrinal orthodoxy have been more successful in developing imaginative leaders who speak forcefully to their specific ethno-social context. From them many international leaders have arisen. The paucity of such leaders will have an impact on the cooperation that is needed to reach the unreached.

There is not a uniformly held world view among our churches, nor have we instilled it in Third World churches. A world view is more than a system of doctrine. It is as well a pre-doctrinal commitment that accepts, besides a body of truth, also a system of values. It will embrace a particular theology for the church but will also hold to a social philosophy that takes all life zones into its horizon.

With regard to a world view or cosmoscope there is a large difference between the context of the churches in the West and that of the churches established in the Third World. The Western context is characterized in the main by a bifurcated world view; one area, the public domain, is secular, the other area, the church, is sacred. There is one realm for Nature and another for Grace. Church (that is religion) and state must be kept separate. In the church faith must lead, but the rest of society should be run by reason in all men of good will, or at least by people who share the secular values in the ever growing area of Nature, while the church continues to speak in the area of Grace. This holds as well for Roman Catholicism as for mainstream Protestantism. Today it is common among evangelicals also to speak of the spiritual and material as two components or realms of human experience, whereas in fact the opposite of spiritual is carnal and the only counterpart to Nature is God. Moreover the opposite to Grace is wrath.

The Western context is also largely post-Christian. Actually Western society is a mixture of two dominant conflicting motifs, namely Enlightenment rationalism and the Christian gospel. The former proclaims the autonomy of man; the latter confesses the lordship of Christ. A modern offspring of the Enlightenment is the widely accepted idea of human autonomy in ethics. And one of the consequences of the gospel's claim that Christ is Lord of all is the current emphasis on holistic mission. Of these two major motifs of our society (human autonomy and the gospel), the former continues to advance in the public domain while the latter (in spite of the Moral Majority, the electronic church, and evangelical influence) continues to recede.

The biblical world view is a fundamental religious perspective that recognizes the lordship of Christ for the whole of life. It sees the entire creation as the theater of God's glory, and recognizes man's place and task in God's world as God's vice regent to rescue mankind and restore the creation.

This biblical world view, however, has not been legal tender among Reformed churches and their missionaries. I strongly suspect that a survey would reveal that a majority of missionaries sent overseas by Reformed churches hold that religion is for church, home, and a part of school. They have often been pietistic. Or, if they acknowledge the universal lordship of Christ, it has not become a directing force in their lives or, therefore, in the converts they win for the faith.

The context of the Third World churches, to speak in general terms, is that of a more holistic, sacral life view, one in which the traditional religion made its impact felt in every facet of human experience, both public and private, both civil and personal. And when the converts accept the Christian faith, they often exchange the holistic world view of the previous traditional religion for the claim that religion is for the church, but only in a tenuous and indirect way for other societal activities. The goal of mission is to establish the church, but not to renew society.

Reformed Mission Churches?

In the light of these salient features of Reformed mission work we should ask: To what extent, and in what sense, can we say that the churches established by the Reformed mission are theologically and confessionally Reformed? We ask this question because their tradition, which is a decisive factor in their makeup, is vastly different from that of the church in the West. Their Christian experience extends back one generation, or two at the most. Their recent ancestors held to a form of paganism. It would therefore be strange indeed that when they claim to be Reformed they mean the same thing as the missionary does when he or she makes the claim. This means that the historical epoch called the sixteenth-century Reformation can never directly be a living part of their own ethnic and religious heritage. At best it becomes a part of their heritage in an indirect or borrowed sense. They see the Reformation for what it is because the church of the missionary sees it as extremely important. Moreover, since the tie between the missionary and the national body is strong, the national leaders accept what the missionaries teach.

The shortness of the Christian heritage of the new churches means also that the lingering effects of the traditional religion from which they were converted are still forceful. It means that, because of the existence of the pre-Christian influence in their own village and nation, the influence of their past can easily lead to a kind of syncretism. This means, in Indonesia, for example, of prime importance is the stress upon the unique saving power of Jesus Christ, the "only name," not predestination as opposed to human free will.

Moreover, the daily experience of churches in the Third World is vastly different from that of churches in the West. Therefore, in view both of their history and of their current social context, it is not immediately apparent what it means that the churches planted by the Reformed mission are Reformed.

Several years ago I spent a number of days in Pakistan, where I visited churches comprised of sweepers of Karachi and farmers in the Punjab. One place where we met was a building without a roof; another was a structure of simplest design and almost devoid of furnishings. There were no musical instruments and no teaching aids. The gospel was communicated solely by word of mouth. When we arrived in the course of the weekday, the people came from their homes nearby, and we soon had a fine audience. There were two straight back chairs, one for the pastor and one for the visitor. The rest of the people stood or sat on the bare floor.

Soon after returning home I attended a meeting of the adult education committee of my home church. The local churches were well furnished with facilities for worship and educational materials for all ages. Our committee was considering what additional materials it could produce for adults. Not for all adults, but for the age group of 25 to 39. Not for all people in that age bracket, but for those who were married. Not for all married couples, but for those whose marriage was not ideal and was not yet hopeless. For that relatively small sector much time, talent, and money were spent to produce materials.

The contrast: one church almost without facilities or materials, the other amply supplied with both, worshiping in comfortable pews, seeking to fill a gap for one relatively small group which could stand more attention. The question: To what extent can the communal thought patterns of the two churches be considered similar?

Nevertheless, in spite of these differences, there are a number of characteristics of Third World churches that warrant their being called Reformed. First, they are the products of Reformed churches with all that this entails: loyalty,

89

love, a feeling of belonging to that part of the church that is denominated Reformed, including accepting (at least some of) the distinctive teachings.

Secondly, their loyalty to the Word of God puts them squarely in the arena of true Reformational activity. For in basic import the sixteenth-century Reformation was a return to the Word of God. Here, in spite of the difference, there is true identity.

Thirdly, the churches established by the Reformed mission tend to put greater stress on their relation to the church universal. Of all branches of the Protestant Reformation, the Calvinist branch has emphasized most strongly the unity of the worldwide people of God. This is surely true of John Calvin, who declared in his often quoted comment that he was willing to cross ten seas to restore the unity of the church.

The Third World churches, in part because of their tradition and their condition of dependence, both upon the Western church and upon fellow Third World churches, sense a greater need for fellowship and cooperation with other churches. The doctrinal differences with other Protestants often do not seem to be as important as the unity they feel as a small minority in a pagan society. It is understandable that they have fewer inhibitions in joining national councils than their parent churches in the West.

Of all Western Reformed churches, the evangelical branch is the least ecumenical. One reason may be that they keep to themselves for the sake of self-preservation: the smaller the church, the higher the self-built enclosing wall. Another reason may be that they so closely identify their teaching with the gospel that any deviation from the former is seen to be a departure from the latter. In this respect the Third World churches have not always followed the lead of the Western institutions but have reached out a hand for fellowship and cooperation with other churches.

The Current Situation

We turn now from our Calvinist tradition to our current situation. For it is necessary, before we propose guidelines for interdependence, to reflect upon our identity, the pressing issues of our age, the new mission, and the new missionary. Else we shall lack the relevance and concreteness that a strategy for mission requires. We do not pretend to be complete.

Our Identity

As we reflect upon our mission, we should keep constantly in mind four important facts as to who we are: (1) we are Americans; (2) we are affluent and technically advanced; (3) we feel increasingly more insecure; and (4) we continue to cherish our treasured heritage.

We are Americans.[3]   Americans are at one and the same time outgoing and self-centered. They are friendly travelers to all parts of the world. Their outgoing character is evident not only in their tourist activities but also in their mission work. No other area of the world has sent out so many emissaries of the gospel.

But they are also self-centered. They expect other people to learn their language and to accept, or at least appreciate, their democratic institutions. They are, generally speaking, convinced that the United States is the last bastion in the world that can save mankind from Russian communism. Jorge Lara-Braud, himself a Mexican, may well be right when he calls our strong anti-communism a negative ideology.

We are rich. Americans are rich in material possessions but also in other resources. Some other countries may have for the time being a higher average wage, but none surpasses us in wealth, climate, and the variety of resources.

Along with our affluence goes our technical advancement. This is perhaps most obvious today in the area of information and communication, from the satellite to the cassette player, from the broadcasting media to the written page. We are supersaturated with TV programs. Even if we wanted to, we could not read through the heavy daily newspaper. One cannot read even all that is being written on missions.[4]

The financial support for the traditional kind of missionary family from the United States is currently estimated at between forty and fifty thousand dollars per annum, including project expense. In contrast, Third World missionaries require about a tenth or even a fifteenth of that amount.

We feel insecure. Another characteristic of Americans is that although we are strong politically and economically, our sense of insecurity is growing. We, the most powerful nation in the world, lost our pride in Vietnam; we are the richest nation of them all, but our economic policies do not work. According to the national pulse, the only means to bolster our feeling of security is to increase our national defense. This may well be our nation's greatest idol, for in it we have put our trust. This desire for national security has in recent years greatly overshadowed our concern to promote human rights overseas and has caused a severe cutback in welfare programs at home and in development aid abroad.

One can only be ambivalent, therefore, about our national identity, for it works both for us and against us. As Jorge Lara-Braud says (1983:3), it fills us with unease and with hope. We must identify with the nation, and take distance from it. And it is as Americans that we must proclaim the eternal gospel to the regions beyond.

We treasure our heritage. People of the Reformed tradition draw often on the words of Jesus, "No one can come to me unless the Father has enabled him" (John 6:65). The sovereign grace of God has been a source of sustaining strength to our forebears and to us. It underscores the fact that mission is fundamentally *missio Dei*. We pray for fruit, but know that God asks us only to be faithful. And since He is faithful, we know that the fruit will come.

Ours is a heritage of communal confession, which we continue to embrace with conviction. It has in it elements both of stability (conserving what is good of the past) and of dynamic change (reforming according to the Word of God what is in need of revision).

It is instructive to note that in Jesus' parable of the talent the word used to explain what the servants did with the talents is *parédōken,* the word means "tradition" (Matt. 25:14). What we have received must be passed on, not in the precise form or in the exact amount of the talent that was buried, but as the heritage that undergoes enrichment in our handling. To be traditional in the true sense means to be progressive. It means to be faithful to the heritage, eager for the increase, assured of the Lord's word of commendation.

We need not feel ashamed that we are Reformed (so long as the designation does not become a perfect passive participle), nor should we shy away from establishing Reformed churches, provided they are instilled not only with that love for the heritage of the Word but also with the drive to continue the unfinished Reformation. By the same token, we should not hesitate to reassess our position, provided we do not toss aside the pearl of great price.

Issues That Agitate

Along with the features of our national life and church heritage as co-determinants of the current situation, we should consider the issues that are most in discussion today. Here we can note a distinct change from the pre-war years.

In all branches of Christendom, Roman Catholic or Protestant, whether ecumenical or evangelical, there has come a significant shift in emphasis from doctrinal distinctives to ethical or lifestyle issues. The old debates, such as between infralapsarianism and supralapsarianism, are generally seen to be esoteric and sterile. The debate between the advocates of predestination and free will has receded to the background. The mode of baptism is not seen so often any more as of decisive importance. The time of Christ's return relative to the millennium does not have the same force in separating churches and Christians as was previously the case.

Other issues, lifestyle issues, now occupy the minds of churchmen and fill the agendas of ecclesiastical gatherings, whether ecumenical or evangelical. Even the orthodox churches have begun to give more attention to these issues. We mention five that are much in discussion; all of them concern the church's mission. All of them should be held in view in devising strategies to reach the unreached.

Mission and culture: Of all issues in missiology, few if any are discussed as much as mission and culture.

There is a reciprocal relation between the gospel and culture: (1) Culture forms the voice that brings, and shapes the ear that hears, the gospel. (2) The gospel passes judgment upon all cultures, both of those who speak and of those who hear. There should therefore be a continuity and a discontinuity between the pre-Christian culture and the culture influenced by the gospel. However, this must not be looked at as a quantitative partitioning, nor as a static division (part Christian and part non-Christian). Rather there should be a dynamic transformation of culture by the gospel, both of the church that sends and of the church that is planted.[5]

Another consequence of this reciprocal relation is that, since the gospel both makes use of and passes judgment on human culture, the tension between them will remain. We tend to minimize this tension in our own culture (as when a civil religion develops) and tend to maximize this tension in the culture we traverse in bringing the gospel (as when we condemn relatively harmless aspects, such as chewing betel nut, as incompatible with a Christian life style).

It is important for us to recognize that even in areas where the gospel influence has been strong, such as in the West, other conflicting forces have often been stronger, for example, the eighteenth-century Enlightenment and twentieth-century secularism. There is no civilization that is a perfect environment for the gospel.

The current stress on the cultural context, both of the biblical revelation and of today's gospel proclamation, is not without its pitfalls. Instead of the gospel's becoming the transforming power of culture, the culture deeply alters the gospel. Or, if this is not openly done, the cultural context speaks so loudly and so often, the gospel text can hardly be heard.

Another danger, coming from the opposite direction, is that we overlook the influence that culture has had upon our Western churches and assume, at least tacitly, that our culturally conditioned understanding and presentation of the gospel is culturally unstained and should be adopted globally by those we convert. The transformation of culture should be our aim.

The question may be asked, why, in a conference on reaching unreached peoples, the issue of the cultural context must once again be mentioned. The answer is that in planning strategies one must pay attention to the culture, for we are in most instances dealing with cross-cultural cooperation. It would appear that many of the pitfalls in cooperation are due to a lack of due recognition of the dynamics of the multi-cultural situation.

Poverty: Poverty in large parts of the world is said by Senator Mark Hatfield to be one of the two greatest unsettling factors in human society today. It is also crucial in our work of mission.

It is estimated that four-fifths of the world's population is poor. Not poor in the sense that they are all seriously undernourished (that figure is estimated at about 500-700 million), but poor in the sense that the average GNP for seventy percent of the world population is $1,000 or less. Waldron Scott has said that we in North America are like an island of affluence in a sea of poverty.

This image of a rich island in a sea of poverty is of course an oversimplification. Parts of Europe run a close second to the United States. Also, some OPEC countries have average incomes higher than ours. And there are rich people in the poor nations whose standard of living does not fall much below ours. Yet, given these qualifications, the fact remains that a vast majority of humanity is poor, and that is especially true of those as yet unreached by the gospel.

The nuclear arms race: Senator Hatfield has also mentioned that the race to build up nuclear arms is the other greatest unsettling factor in today's world. Idols have a way of biting the people who worship them! These two factors, poverty and the arms race, tend to exacerbate each other. The money spent on arms (29 percent of the U.S. national budget) draws vast sums away from the war on poverty. And the spread of poverty adds to the sense of insecurity for which a greater arms arsenal must be built.

We recall that Jesus said, "Blessed are the peace makers, for they shall be called the children of God" (Matt. 5:9). War in the West has in the past greatly damaged the credibility of Western missionaries in the Third World.[6] Imagine the problem European missionaries in Africa had to explain the First World War between Germany and the allied nations to the tribes that they had told to live in peace. The fact that the gospel still finds entrance in spite of war attests to the reconciling power of the gospel.

The issue of nuclear armament and peace today greatly agitates Reformed churches. The Reformierte Bund of West Germany in 1982 went on record to declare that the position taken toward weapons of mass destruction is tantamount to the confession or the denial of the gospel. More recently the General Reformed Convent of East Germany declared its agreement with the statement of the West German churches.

In terms of nuclear war, the just war theory has become obsolete. Fought with conventional weapons, a war may be just (as was World War II, which freed Europe from Nazi domination). The World Council of Churches may advocate the just revolution but not if it is fought with nuclear arms. The prospects of mass destruction are horrendous and would make it impossible for humankind to carry out the purpose for which God has put them in the world, including, obviously, reaching unreached people. It is this great new fact of nuclear war that causes increasing tension among churches, especially in North America and in Europe, not to mention that between churches in the West with those in the Third World.

Racism: Among evangelical Reformed churches, few factors have been as

94

divisive as racism. This is the case in at least four of the Christian world communions: the World Council of Churches (WCC), the Lutheran World Federation (LWF), the World Alliance of Reformed Churches (WARC), and the Reformed Ecumenical Synod (RES). The Dutch Reformed Mission Church in South Africa, a member church in the RES, has followed the lead of the WARC in "Ottawa '82" and made the issue of apartheid a matter of *status confessionis:* To advocate apartheid is contrary to the gospel. Apartheid is driving a wedge between Reformed churches.

It should not be overlooked that the Dutch Reformed Church of South Africa (NGK), which still refuses to disaffiliate itself from the South African racial policy it helped to design, has during the past century engaged in mission work that is unparalleled anywhere in Africa or in the world. The 13 churches established by the DRC in Africa have attained a total membership of over 2 million. Does this perhaps mean that God's condemnation of apartheid is not as absolute as ours?

At the present time the position of the DRC is being challenged by the churches it has planted both in South Africa and in the surrounding countries. In 1982, five churches in Central Africa planted by the Dutch Reformed Church wrote a stirring letter to the DRC to express their deep concern over the church's support of the South African racial policy because of its serious effect upon the future of the church. Obviously, racism is a decisive negative factor in determining how churches can interdependently cooperate in proclaiming the gospel.

Confessional convergences: No presentation of the present situation would be complete without the recognition of a remarkable theological convergence among the ecumenicals, the evangelicals, and the Roman Catholics. This includes more than the debate on evangelism (note the convergence in Baptism, Eucharist and Ministry (BEM) of the 1982 Commission on Faith and Order of the WCC) but does indeed also deal with mission. We list three events: the statement of the Roman Catholic Bishops (Nov. 21, 1964),[7] the Consultation on the Relationship of Evangelism and Social Responsibility (June 1982),[8] and the Ecumenical Affirmation of the WCC (July 1982).[9] These convergences would seem to indicate that the possibilities for joint action in mission are greater than they have been in the past.

The New Definition of Mission and the New Missionary

We face today in some Reformed churches as well as in the churches at large a new definition of mission. Traditionally mission meant to evangelize and plant churches. The cultural, social, and economic services of the mission were considered auxiliary to the real task of converting people. At present mission is sometimes described by younger missiologists in quite different terms.

The new definition sometimes goes like this: "Mission is to give shape and form to the Gospel of God's judgment and promises by creditably speaking, living and acting in concrete conflicts between the Kingdom of God and human life"[10] (Filius, 1982:9). This task includes calling by name the social ills that beset society and taking up arms against them.

The new view of mission questions giving priority to evangelism. It is asked, Should mission agencies not increasingly devote their resources to inter-church aid rather than to reaching the unreached peoples? One answer with considerable currency is that we should indeed aid the churches in the Third World but leave it to them to reach the unreached in their area. The consequence of this view is that less attention is given by churches in the West to the evangelism of those who have not been faced with the gospel claims.

There is not only a new view of mission that has gained credence but behind it a new image of God. If the traditional view of God was that He is the sovereign cause of the universe, the new image is that God sympathizes with His suffering creatures. He is not the Great Origin, but the God of the future. Our thoughts about God center therefore not so much on the beginning as on the end. We have to do with a God who can be found in history, and ours must therefore be a theology of hope. We must now discern "where God is active in history," namely, in the struggle for justice and freedom. In other words, we should look for God primarily in human experience. These views are propounded by avant-garde Roman Catholic as well as by liberation theologians. They also enjoy currency among ecumenical strategists.

Along with the new view of mission and the new image of God has come a new missionary. Unlike his predecessor, today's missionary, since he knows that political conditions may soon force him to leave, seeks to make himself unnecessary. One's aim is to form a truly independent and indigenous church. One's task today is much broader than in former times.

Time Magazine (Dec. 27, 1982) describes the new missionaries as follows: "In contrast to their predecessors, the new missionaries agree that as much as possible, the preaching of the Gospel should be shorn of Western cultural trappings and adapted to the civilization of the people to whom it is offered. Instead of Christianizing Africa, so the policy runs, missionaries should help to Africanize Christianity."

The new view of mission, even if we do not accept it in the form it was presented above, the new image of God, although we do not hold to it, and the new missionary, even if he does not quite fit our mold, force us to look for ways in which patterns of interdependence between the churches of the West and of the Third World can be developed. To that we turn in another chapter.

At this point we should strive to get clearly in mind just what it is for which we strive. We do this by way of a definition that may serve as the goal for our mission and churches. Our aim is a mature missionary church, grounded in the eternal gospel, with a zeal to propagate the gospel, to make disciples of all nations, and to establish churches capable of training their own pastors and evangelists, eager and competent to win the lost, undertaking an indigenous program (as agent, catalyst, or midwife), to initiate a Christian presence and task force in the whole of society and to transform the national culture by the light of the gospel.

Notes

1. Gisbertus Voetius (1589–1676) was a Dutch theologian who wrote on missions. Johannes Verkuyl, retired professor of missiology at the Free University of Amsterdam, upon retirement in 1978 published a pamphlet, *De Onvoltooide Taak der Wereldzending* (1978a).

2. In Amoy City, China, the first Protestant church structure ever erected in China was described thus by a missionary of the Reformed Church in America: "Built high on a promenade, the large colonial-style structure with its massive white pillars and cupola-capped roof was an astounding sight in contrast to the small conglomeration of ancient houses surrounding it."

3. Jorge Lara-Braud has written a perceptive article on "The Role of North Americans in the Future of the Missionary Enterprise" (1983). As he sees it, of all countries, the United States has the strongest church life and is most in the grip of secularism.

4. *Missionalia,* a publication of the South African Missiological Society, has appeared three times a year for the last ten years. In those ten volumes, it has included 6,356 abstracts of books and journal articles pertaining to its discipline.

5. Compare this with the Roman Catholic position: "Anything whatever that is inextricably bound up with superstition and error, is at all times weighed sympathetically and, if possible, retained intact and unmarred" (*Summi pontificatus,* par. 92).

6. "One overmastering cause [for no stable and enduring churches in distant lands in the Medieval Age was] . . . the tragic unsettlement of the times, and the recurrent calamities caused by one invasion of the barbarians after another" (Neill 1964:133).

7. "The present historical situation is leading humanity into a new stage. As the salt of the earth and the light of the world (cf. Mt. 5:13-14), the Church is summoned with special urgency to save and renew every creature. In this way all things can be restored in Christ, and in Him mankind can compose one family and one people. Hence this holy Synod gives thanks to God for the splendid accomplishments already achieved through the noble energy of the whole Church. At the same time she wishes to sketch the principles of missionary activity and to marshal the forces of all the faithful. Her intention is that God's people, undertaking the narrow way of the cross, may spread everywhere the kingdom of Christ, the Lord and Overseer of the ages (cf. Sir. 36:19), and may prepare the way for His coming" (Abbott 1966:584-85).

Note also: "The Church, consequently, equipped with the gifts of her Founder and faithfully guarding His precepts of charity, humility, and self-sacrifice, receives the mission to proclaim and to establish among all peoples the kingdom of Christ and of God.

She becomes on earth the initial budding forth of that kingdom. While she slowly grows, the Church strains toward the consummation of the kingdom and, with all her strength, hopes and desires to be united in glory with her King" (Abbott 1966:18).

8. "Evangelism is the proclamation of this Kingdom in the fullness of its blessings and promise, which are also called 'salvation.' Moreover, Jesus did more than preach the Kingdom; he demonstrated its reality with 'signs of the Kingdom,' public evidence that the Kingdom he was talking about had come. We believed that signs should validate our evangelism, too, and we have spent time discussing what they should be.

"Since the 'reason the Son of God appeared was to destroy the devil's work' (I John 3:8), he inevitably came into collision with the prince of darkness. The signs of the Kingdom were evidences that the devil was retreating before the advance of the King. As Jesus put it, once the strong man has been overpowered by the Stronger One, his possessions can be taken from him (Mt. 12:29; Lk. 11:22)" (*Lausanne Occasional Papers No. 21* 1982:30-31).

9. "At the very heart of the Church's vocation in the world is the proclamation of the kingdom of God inaugurated in Jesus the Lord, crucified and risen. Through its internal life of eucharistic worship, thanksgiving, intercessory prayer, through planning for mission and evangelism, through a daily lifestyle of solidarity with the poor, through advocacy even to confrontation with the powers that oppress human beings, the churches are trying to fulfill this evangelistic vocation.

" 'We preach Christ crucified, a stumbling block to Jews and folly to Gentiles' (I Cor. 1:23). The Good News handed on to the Church is that God's grace was in Jesus Christ, who 'though he was rich, yet for your sake he became poor, so that by his poverty you might become rich' (II Cor. 8:9)" ("Mission and Evangelism—An Ecumenical Affirmation" 1982:430).

10. This definition by the Netherlands Reformed Church is not greatly different from descriptions of mission by other churches. For instance, J. G. Davies has said that the task of mission is one of "entering into partnership with God in history to renew society" (Conn 1976: 93,94). And, from the *Drafts for Sections* prepared unofficially for the Uppsala 1968 gathering of the World Council of Churches: "Today the fundamental question is . . . that of true man and the dominant concern of the missionary congregations must therefore be to point the humanity of Christ as the goal of Mission" (*Drafts for Sections Uppsala* 1968:34).

Chapter 7

Guidelines for
Interdependence

Paul G. Schrotenboer

When Jesus, shortly before His crucifixion in Jerusalem, was faced with the possibility of a new ministry among the Greeks (John 12:20ff.), He rejected this tempting new strategy by declaring that the servant of God must renounce Himself. He must become a seed that has to die, else He would not bear much fruit.

It is clear from this incident that Jesus had a definite strategy in mind for His work of mission. He had a comprehensive plan that would promote the glory of God and would draw people of all nations (not just Jews and Greeks) to Himself. His vision was for multi-ethnic growth to the glory of God. According to His plan, His death would accomplish more than His life. Only when He would be lifted up would He draw all men to Himself. He made His plan at a time when the whole of mankind, with the exception of His small band of disciples, was unreached.

Jesus made it clear on that occasion that the disciples would have to choose the same path He had chosen. A voice sounded from heaven at the time assuring Jesus that His desire to glorify God would be fulfilled. That voice of the Father, said Jesus, came not for His sake (for He had firmly made the choice), but for the disciples (for they must still resolve). Jesus also made it clear that if the disciples would follow Him and be willing to lose their lives, God would honor them as well. The path that leads to true church growth (bearing much fruit) and to the glory of God is radical self-denial.

There are two reasons for mentioning this incident at the outset. The first is that according to Reformed missiology the glory of God has been seen as the final goal of missions. Gisbertus Voetius (1589–1676) saw the goals of mission as the conversion of the heathen, the establishment of churches, and the glorification and manifestation of divine grace. The question is, however, whether we Reformed people are willing to follow the path that leads to that goal.

This brings me to the second comment, namely, that Jesus accentuated the fundamental life disposition demanded of His disciples. Life renunciation is not a subordinate part of the strategies we design; it is the *sina qua non* of our success. Specifically we would set out the guidelines that are needed if Reformed churches are to cooperate interdependently in confronting the unreached masses of humanity with the gospel.

Before we propose guidelines on how churches can together reach the unreached, we should be clear in our minds that cooperative efforts in mission are desirable. It is not a foregone conclusion that we all do agree to this, for our tradition has often followed the policy of non-cooperation. We have often done the work of mission in isolation, or as much as possible by ourselves. Some of us have considered it to be highly doubtful that churches of the Reformed persuasion should cooperate with non-Reformed evangelical churches. Even comity arrangements among evangelical Protestants were sometimes looked upon with misgiving. It was also considered doubtful whether missions and Third World churches of various parentage should cooperate with others in theological education.

The Theological College of Northern Nigeria (TCNN) is a case in point. For years the question was debated in the Synod of the North American church, among the missionaries on the field, and within the Nigerian churches, whether it was not somewhat disloyal to the faith to train young men and women for the ministry of the church in cooperation with those who were evangelical but did not hold the distinctive Reformed truths. When all was said and done, it was the national churches who decided. Some chose for a union seminary, and others established their own theological school.

This dispute of some two decades ago has been superseded largely by the broader consideration of the cooperation of churches worldwide, in the international family of Reformed churches, in the work of the Lausanne Committee for World Evangelization, and the World Evangelical Fellowship. It concerns relations to the World Council of Churches, in fact to all branches of the world church.

Our approach to the issue of cooperation is based on the consideration that, according to both the Scriptures and the Reformed Confessions, our fundamental identity is that we are not our own but belong, body and soul, for life and for death to Jesus Christ (Rom. 14:8; Heidelberg Catechism, Answer 1). If this is our fundamental identity, then the affiliation we have with the Reformed churches or family of churches cannot constitute more than a subordinate, relative, and partial identity. We are first and foremost united to Christ and to all who acknowledge Him as Savior and Lord. Our identity with Him is radical, absolute, and comprehensive.

From our identity our task derives. In other words, Christ calls upon us to live out what we are. We are a unity (with all its diversity) of co-workers with Christ. Our strategies must therefore take account of the entire people of God.

Partnership in mission cannot be avoided without at some point denying the gospel.

This does not mean that cooperation among Reformed churches themselves is not necessary. It not only is necessary but should also take top priority.[1] But it does mean that no strategies for interdependence can ignore cooperation with all the churches. To do less is in effect to deny our fundamental identity and the basic oneness of the people of God.

It is instructive at this point to note what the Heidelberg Catechism says we understand by the communion of the saints:

> First that believers one and all, as members of this community, share in Christ and in all his treasures and gifts. Second, that each member should consider it his duty to use his gifts readily and cheerfully for the service and enrichment of the other members (Answer 55).

In other words, who we are as members of one worldwide body determines what our task is toward that body, and for and with that body. That body, moreover, is global in scope.

This is a confessional, not a pragmatic, argument. It has been in vogue to lament the divisions of the church and to decry "the scandal of our division," because a divided church is a hindrance to the proclamation of the gospel and the planting of churches. We do not want to detract from this argument. Jorge Lara-Braud put it this way: "Disunity in places where people struggle for freedom is tantamount to complicity with the oppressors."

Yet the fact cannot be denied that there is a greater scandal than that of our divisions. It is the loss of the conviction that God's Word is truth and the decline of zeal that has resulted in the discontinuation of many programs for evangelism. It is an anomaly that this loss of conviction has been most prevalent in united churches. Over the last two decades an ever increasing percentage of missions have been conducted by independent mission agencies and non-ecumenical churches. All the while the mission forces of the Western ecumenical churches, including a number in the Reformed tradition, have been diminishing at an alarming rate.[2]

We do not deny that unity must serve mission. Nor do we want to detract from those who, in accordance with the prayer of our Lord, seek to make unity visible, "so that the world may believe" (John 17:21). But the fact that unity has in many instances not resulted in greater mission but has rather been followed by a loss in mission effort at home as well as abroad should alert us to the fact that any strategy, however good it may be in intention, is bound to fail if it is not driven by the right spirit. Unity in itself does not produce mission.

We should note further that some of the fastest church growth among Reformed churches has been in South Korea, where church divisions run rampant. The current projection is that South Korea will be 50 percent Christian at the turn of the century. Obviously the Lord God causes the church to grow even where there is division, and so division in itself does not destroy mission. Actually, when God makes the church to prosper, it is in what are always imperfect situations.

We should be alerted here to the danger of monocausality, to the thesis that the only significant hindrance to the gospel mission is the division of the churches. In actual fact it is only one of many hindrances. We shall have to hold in view all the multi-causal hindrances to mission, not to single out one to the exclusion of our downgrading of the rest.

Let us now form some tentative guidelines on how we should work in meaningful interdependence for the advance of the gospel.

Confessional Commitment and Ecumenical Obedience

Since we must seek to comprehend the love of God "with all the saints" (Eph. 3:18), we must strive for cooperation with the whole church of God.

Again this is not a pragmatic but a confessional argument. It is part and parcel of our being Reformed and reforming churches. Once we have accepted the idea of the *ecclesia semper reformanda,* and recognize that this concerns both our life and our teaching, we must be ready to relativize all our formulations of the truth. They are only human constructs that are contextually conditioned. Although we are loath to admit it, we have sometimes given Protestant, Western polemical slants to the truth. Revealed truth and the Reformed faith may never be strictly identified.

None of us would affirm that our formulations of the truth are wholly perfect. But we come close to saying that when we ignore what others are saying. The felt need for consultation grows as one comes to see that we know only in part and others can make a contribution.

This does not mean that we should strive for a cooperative effort where there are fundamental differences, or that we should relativize the truth. But the cooperation should be as complete as possible without harmful compromise. In the discussions with others our task is to contribute to, hopefully to enrich but, in any case, to learn from the other—all on the basis of our cherished and yet relative heritage.

Actually some of the emphases of the Calvinist tradition have found acceptance both in Nairobi (WCC Fifth Assembly 1975) and in Lilongwe (Association of Evangelicals of Africa and Madagascar Assembly 1981). Such themes were reflected as the importance of the local church as locus of action and the kingdom of God as the most comprehensive thought frame for understanding the biblical message.

The objections we have had against cooperation, and perhaps even consultation with churches and missions of other traditions, are made less relevant today by the fact that, as we have noted, the doctrinal differences have lost some of their relevance. By the same token, inasmuch as the ethical issues that now press to the fore in the discussion are often those on which we have no official or traditional position, there is an openness that can lead to a new consensus or at least a convergence.

I question whether there is a Reformed missiology in the sense that we may speak of a Reformed theology. What are the "five points" of Reformed missiology? It would appear that our theology is Reformed, but our missiology is nondescript, except that it must be biblically correct, stress the sovereignty of God, and be church-centered. For the rest of the issues that demand answers we must proceed along other lines than our fathers have followed, rubbing shoulders and bouncing off ideas with those who, like us, are struggling for the first time with today's pressing issues. Most evangelicals are not Reformed. Moreover, we will likely find that we are closer in our mission policies and practices to certain non-Reformed evangelicals than we are to certain fellow Reformed churches. This again points to a truly new and open situation. It is a situation in which we must heed the call to partnership in mission. And before partnership there must be consultation.

The consultation I refer to should include not only meetings with evangelicals but also with the WCC. We should enter the ecumenical forum alert to both the possibilities and the dangers of participation.

No evaluation of the WCC and its stand on evangelism can neglect the Ecumenical Affirmation of 1982 ("Mission and Evangelism—Ecumenical Affirmation"1982:427-51). Its strong emphasis on Word proclamation makes earlier negative evaluations of the WCC's Commission on World Mission and Evangelism such as by Harvey Hoekstra (1979) and Arthur Johnston (1978) out of date.

Waldron Scott has rightly said that at Melbourne (1980) the WCC had much to say about how to carry out our mission where the church is, and was virtually silent about witness where the church is not (Anderson 1982:43). This means that we should not look there first of all for guidance on how to reach out to the unreached.

For cooperation in our mission to the unreached, we should rather look first to the evangelical groups—the Lausanne Committee for World Evangelization, the World Evangelical Fellowship, the international mission agencies, and many parachurch organizations, such as Wycliffe Bible Translators, the World Home Bible League, World Vision International.

But when with the help of these evangelical groups we tell the unreached of the Only Name, we cannot forget the emphasis the WCC has given to aspects of the gospel we all have tended to overlook. We should surely mention in this connection the stress upon social responsibility. Evangelicals learned it from the Bible after the ecumenicals had (one-sidedly) repeated it often enough. Fortunately now we can all say it together.

Cooperation in Mission

Bringing the whole gospel by the whole people of God to the whole world for personal and societal transformation cannot be done by any one segment of the church. What is needed is an interdependence on three fronts.

The first concerns cooperation among the so-called ''sending'' churches. The second deals with cooperation between the ''sending'' church through its mission and the ''national'' church. The third has to do with consultation and cooperation among ''national'' churches.

We have shied away from cooperation with other sending churches mainly for doctrinal reasons. We have at times been reluctant to cooperate as partners with the planted church for lack of faith in their judgment. For both reasons we have not encouraged these mission churches to cooperate with other churches in their cultures. In taking this posture (which has not been constant and, fortunately, is changing) we have allowed our subordinate identity to obscure our fundamental identity.

The current danger is that we fail to accept the guideline because of fear of negative effects on how it will be applied. The best approach would be to adopt the guideline of cooperation and then apply it with wisdom and care.

Reforming the Reformed Faith

To be Reformed in mission today does not surely mean to cast away the truths of the Reformation. But it does mean to engage in the ongoing task of reforming the Reformed faith, as well as the Reformed churches. We list three examples that affect directly our work of mission.

1. The stress upon election as personally being selected by God to enjoy the blessings of salvation by grace should be replaced by an emphasis on election of God's people, one and all, to salvation and service. This great doctrine, called the *cor ecclesiae,* was largely self-directed, limited to salvation, neglectful of service. It was also given an individual rather than a communal thrust.

2. The idea of total depravity should be extended to cover, besides the pervasive influence of sin upon our personal lives, the general negative effects of sin upon the entirety of society, including the political and economic systems that have developed in the ''Christian'' West and that some still consider to be sacrosanct.

3. A third example is the doctrine of the sovereignty of God. Good in itself as a doctrine (for God is indeed sovereign!), it fails to do justice to the idea that, better than any other, encapsulates the total message of Scripture, namely, that

of the kingdom of God. Because of the coming of the kingdom in the days of Jesus of Nazareth, when He by His dying and rising again established the rule of God over the living and the dead (Rom. 14:9), we can never be satisfied with only a doctrine that God is sovereign. We must bring our world view and our lifestyle into conformity to this normative idea. Our world view must recognize the lordship of Christ on every terrain of human experience and engage in communal discipleship in every life zone. Then the idea of the kingdom of God becomes a life program, not just a tenet of faith, or a mere theological proposition.

It is in the teaching of the kingdom of God (God's comprehensive rule over the creation) that a link may be forged between the teaching of the expatriate and the political task of the Third World church. We are all aware of the demise of the colonial era. The day is past when the missionary can bask in the defense of the colonial government. Today's missionary knows he or she can be deported within 24 hours if pronouncements are made that are critical of those in power or are judged political (such as birth control!). The temptation is to avoid saying anything about politics.

This is a temptation, for since social justice is such a significant component of the gospel, one cannot be silent about it with impunity. Granted, expatriates cannot enter into party politics, especially in one-party states; but they should make their political task plain to those they teach, a task they share with all Christians, irrespective of their citizenship. Else they have in effect withdrawn from the lordship of Christ that area where most of the important everyday decisions for human society are made.

The Challenge of the Poor

This challenge has been mentioned so often, it scarcely seems necessary to repeat it once more. Yet since there is as yet only a half-hearted response to this challenge, we must stay with it until there is a surge of activity by God's people.

Our affluence is both an asset and a barrier. It is an asset that we can employ modern technology (transportation and communication) to reach the unreached. Think of the Wycliffe organization's reducing unwritten languages to writing.

Riches become a barrier for they make a gulf.[3] William H. Hannah has made the wry comment that American church persons are surprised to learn they have little credibility with the poor, the oppressed, and the exploited. This would not be so serious were it not for the fact that the vast majority of the unreached in the world belong to the poor.

It should also be made clear that if we are to reach the poor unreached, then we shall have to come to terms with our own affluent lifestyle. In a world of abundance, of enough to meet the needs of more than four billion inhabitants, we shall have to learn to share the resources, to care for the creation, on behalf of succeeding generations as well as ourselves, and to pare, to cut down on the waste and over-consumption. The issue of riches and poverty is bound to increase, as resources diminish, as the gap between rich and poor widens, and as the means of communication reach even greater masses of people.

That we speak of the truly poor also sets the form of our message. In the West the approach is often: Accept Jesus Christ and that will give you joy, peace, health, and prosperity (Bosch 1981:7). These are not quite what the poor and destitute have on the top of their list of priorities. For them the concern is, How do I stay alive? To such people Jesus Christ must be presented as Savior and Lord meeting them in their concrete situation, offering them hope for this life, as well as for the life to come.

Aid from the Emerging Churches

Perhaps a good way to consider the aid that emerging churches can give in reaching the unreached is to look at the names given to different kinds of churches. The various terms used to express the relationship of churches to mission (sending church/mission church; mother/daughter; older/younger; Western/Third World) all have a large measure of validity and all fail to express adequately a true state of interdependence. All express a dimension of reality; none describes it fully or states the ideal.

Some of these terms gained currency in a colonial, imperial era, an era of Western domination and Third World dependence. They have thus taken on connotations of that era and that relationship. The era of economic imperialism, we remind ourselves, is not yet over.

By the same token, the rejection of these terms to express the interchurch relationships stems from the current criticism of colonialism, paternalism, and the relation of dominance/dependence. The rejection of these terms runs the same danger of one-sidedness as their use, for it fails to recognize the partial validity they express. It would appear that the various terms may still be used, provided it is recognized that they express only a partial reality and each one represents at best a stage on the way to a state of full interdependence, for which there is no universally accepted term.

If one tries to peer into the future of a church-mission-church-mission process, then it may be expected that the church started by the mission today will itself engage in mission with the purpose of establishing a church among the unreached tomorrow and will then encounter conditions relative to the newly planted church somewhat similar to those we face today. The inescapable conclusion would seem to be that we should at no time anticipate a state of full interdependence among equal churches in the mission enterprise. For there will always be emerging, less experienced churches with less adequately trained leaders. The guidelines we devise for interdependence should therefore take these continuing inequalities into account. This will become apparent as we mention the large people groups we hope to reach with the gospel.

The largest groups of the unreached are the Muslims, the Hindus, and the Chinese. Taken together, they comprise 60 percent of the human race. These are the ones most difficult for us to reach. Some are out of reach because of the opposition of their atheistic governments. Others firmly hold to their own religion and would gladly convert us. With others our political loyalties are a high barrier and we are the problem. This means that the church on the scene may be the only effective way to reach these unreached masses.

It is therefore imperative to enter into cooperation with the churches in the Third World, for they often don't face the barriers under which we labor. They hold the key to open the door that is closed to us. They and we shall have to become partners of obedience in the service of the gospel, we with the economic and technological resources, they with the lingual expertise and cultural access to the unreached. And we should do our planning together.

Holism in Mission

Much attention is being given to the holistic approach in mission. In a former age the debate was between comprehensive mission and strict evangelism. Often the comprehensive approach was connected with the social gospel, or even a religious relativism that saw all religions as ways to God. This was firmly rejected by evangelical Reformed churches. But much has changed since then.

In Uppsala (1968) the key word was humanization, but there was little concern for the spiritually lost. In Lausanne (1974) the emphasis was on evangelism, with a recognition of the gospel's social demands. Since then there has been to a degree a rapprochement between the WCC and the Lausanne Committee.

Holism in mission means to begin with evangelism and social responsibility. The Consultation on the Relationship of Evangelism and Social Responsibility (CRESR) meeting of June, 1982, sponsored jointly by the Lausanne Committee for World Evangelization and the World Evangelical Fellowship, expresses well how a growing segment of evangelicals look at the relation of evangelism and social responsibility. After affirming that evangelism has a logical priority over social responsibility, the report succinctly mentions three ways in which the two are related: "Social activity not only follows evangelism as its consequence and aim, and precedes it as its bridge, but also accompanies it as its partner. They are like the two blades of a pair of scissors or the two wings of a bird" (Lausanne Occasional Papers 1982:23).

Holism in mission, however, means more than evangelism and social responsibility. It means, in addition, advocacy of the poor and politically oppressed. It also means earth-keeping as an essential part of our stewardship of the creation. And for the mission of evangelism it means to teach all these as consequences of the gospel of the kingdom of God. It need not mean any lessening of the call to personal commitment.

If we as Reformed churches are to take seriously the cherished doctrine of the sovereignty of God over the whole of life, and if this is to occupy a constitutive part in our proclamation to the unreached, then our message must include bearing witness to the regnant global injustices today. We must respond to the economic dominance of the North over the South, the dominance of national self-interest over justice among nations in foreign policy, including nations with constituencies that are largely, or at least nominally, Christian.

Holism in mission is far more than making the gospel credible. The gospel will always remain a *skandalon*. But a holistic approach that tells of the love of God, embodies the compassion of Christ, and meets the demands of social justice will remove at least some unnecessary obstacles. Our mission should be executed in such a way that the only objection people can have to becoming a Christian is that of the demand of the gospel itself: self-denial and obedient faith.

Of greatest promise is the integration in one mission program of word-deed ministry that works hand in hand to proclaim the good news. We call for a program that shows in concrete deeds of social uplift the compassion of the Lord, and trains converts to become agents of justice. In this no part of the church can go it alone. Not the churches of the West, nor those of the Reformed tradition, nor those of the Third World. Among all of them we should seek for a network of interdependence.

We would not belabor the point of a holistic gospel except for the fact that in our desire to reach the unreached we may settle for less than the holistic gospel of the kingdom with which we reach them and thus not proclaim the whole counsel of God (Acts 20:27). Of course the whole gospel can be, and should be, presented in nuclear form right from the beginning. And it is that whole gospel, not just some part of it, that we should constantly keep in mind.

Mission and Office

In seeking for a state of true interdependence in mission more attention should be given to the biblical idea of office and to the related teaching on the gifts God has distributed to His people (Rom. 12; I Cor. 12; Eph. 4; I Pet. 3:10).

Office, the Bible teaches, is for service to God, for ministry to fellow human beings and the stewardship over the creation. The office-holder is a servant of God and His representative. The office-bearer speaks on behalf of God, and God works through that officer. God gives the authority and gifts needed to enable, to accomplish the tasks. And when one is persecuted for the name of

Christ, the Lord Himself identifies with the persecuted servant in the most intimate way (Matt. 25:19-30). Office means both *administration* and *service* or "ministration." The *servant* of God is also a servant-*ruler*. It is endowment with authority.

The missionaries are office-holders who are sent by God to speak on His behalf, beseeching the world to be reconciled to God (II Cor. 5:20). They bring the Word, and God opens the heart (Acts 16:14). The work therefore is the *missio Dei*. We should therefore not consider mission (the being sent) apart from the assignment, gifts, and authority God gives to those He sends.

It may further be observed that the idea of office is applicable to the communities of believers as well as to individuals in the church. Some communities are called to do this, others to do that. The same holds for the gifts God has bestowed. Some come to every believer (I Cor. 12:1), others fall on certain persons. Some gifts are given to this church, and other gifts are given to another church. These offices and gifts should be recognized and freely used for the building of the saints to equip them for work in His service (Eph. 4:12). The church should become a working body to carry out God's mission in the world.

But two things must be borne in mind. First, the gifts and offices are for the whole people of God, not an elite part, and least of all for the office-holder.

Second, the biblical idea of office forces us to think beyond the pale of the institutional church. The body of Christ, with all its muscles, bones, and nervous network, is called to observe all that Christ has commanded. What is needed are communal Christian presences in every life area, normed by the Word of the kingdom, fitted to the time and place, driven by zeal to do justice, love mercy, and walk humbly with God. It is with the whole gospel, with its offer of pardon for sin as well as the demands for justice, that we must reach the unreached. For all this, and more, God sends us out into the world.

Conclusion

We mentioned earlier that Reformed churches have founded mission churches in their own image. This should continue, provided that we give due recognition to the need that Reformed churches be reforming churches. This holds for the church that sends as well as for the church that is planted. The alternative would be to stay with the status quo and take a nonchalant attitude, which will not win many people to Christ.

As we search out those unreached groups far away, or address those which, like refugee peoples, have become the unreached next door, we may be sure that they will imitate us, whether we want them to do so or not. We should therefore ask ourselves, Are we worthy to be the image they will imitate? And the answer to this question lies in the response to another one. Do we as church and mission truly reflect the image of Christ? We may urge that they imitate us only if we follow Christ. Then the fact that we planted them (gave them their subordinate identity) will fade as their fundamental identity is brought into bold relief as people of God. Our concern is then no less than that of the apostle Paul, who said to the Christians in Galatia, "My dear children, for whom I am again in the pains of childbirth until Christ is formed in you" (Gal. 4:19).

A second question is this: Can we, as churches from different cultures, together, become mature so that, "speaking the truth in love we will in all things grow up into him who is the Head, even Christ" (Eph. 4:13)? The intent of the apostle would seem to be that we all become mature together. No one church can go it alone, not even the affluent, tradition rich, theologically self-conscious churches of the West.

We stand squarely in the line of our Reformed tradition when we make use of all the means at our disposal to build the church and seek the kingdom of God. We therefore do not hesitate to spend much time in planning strategies of interdependence for the work and to do it together, "contending as one man for the faith of the gospel" (Phil. 1:27).

The apostle in the same passage instructs us to stand firm in one spirit as we conduct ourselves in a manner worthy of the gospel of Christ. That spirit, without which all our efforts will fail, was expressed by Jesus Himself when He informed His disciples that whosoever would be great among them must be their servant, "Just as the Son of Man did not come to be served, but to serve, and to give his life a ransom for many" (Matt. 20:28).

I was reminded of this when a few years ago I walked through the cemetery at Nkhoma, Malawi, and read the names of the missionaries—men, women and children—who died on the field, a surprisingly large number. The church they planted is today one of the largest Reformed churches in Central Africa. The seed that died bore fruit a hundredfold.

From the guidelines we have proposed, one aspect stands out, namely, co-operation. For our strategies of interdependence cooperation must begin in the planning stage. Therefore we plead that our readers,

> recognizing the inadequacy of missiologists, mission secretaries, or even churches of the West, to undertake alone the vast challenge of reaching the unreached, take the necessary initial steps to arrange for a consultation-workshop of Reformed and evangelical churches from the West and Third World to implement jointly the objective of effective interdependence in reaching the unreached.

Notes

1. The Reformed Ecumenical Synod has arranged Mission Conferences in Baarn 1968, Sydney 1972, Cape Town 1976, and Nimes 1980 in order to facilitate such cooperation.

2. The number of missionaries of the United Presbyterian Church in the USA, for example, has dropped from 1400 to 300. The churches affiliated with the World Council of Churches perform only 10 percent of the total work of missions.

3. Waldron Scott asks us to see the image the "rich" missionary projects in the light of the first of the Four Spiritual Laws ("God loves you and has a wonderful plan for your life"). To the poor this means that God has a wonderful plan for the life of the rich (Anderson 1982:47).

Chapter 8
Avoiding Past Mistakes
Paul B. Long

One of the keys to successful navigation is the recognition of drift from the selected course and the early administration of minor adjustments to deal with constantly changing environments. If deviations can be noted and corrected as they appear, one can remain on course and can avoid unnecessary dangers and drastic corrections. Just as preflight planning is necessary, so are inflight corrections essential for successful arrival at desired destinations.

Our mission objective is to evangelize, in our generation, people who are not now professing Christians and to help them become productive members of existing or new worshiping communities. An unreached people has been defined recently as "a people group among which there is no indigenous community of believing Christians with adequate numbers and resources to evangelize this people group without outside (cross-cultural) assistance" (Evangelical Foreign Missions Association, 1982).

A consensus working definition of what constitutes a mistake is more difficult to identify. "Beauty is in the eyes of the beholder," it is said, and it is not always possible to convince others of the beauty we appreciate. "Two men looked through prison bars. One saw mud, the other stars." What constitutes a mistake in mission strategy? I will define mistake as anything that causes unnecessary deviations from the selected course to our chosen destination. That destination is making disciples among all the people groups of our generation and helping them to establish living, growing churches to continue the Christian mission.

Persisting Problems

Calling

One of the most difficult problems facing most mission sending agencies today is that of finding qualified people who are clearly called and spiritually equipped to initiate new Christian work among unreached people groups. It is a serious problem confronting many candidates for mission service. It becomes a very serious problem for new missionaries when they begin to understand the necessary sacrifice and the degree of commitment this ministry entails. When the novelty of the unknown is replaced by the reality, the dangers, the hardships, the loneliness of Christian living among non-Christians, most missionaries reexamine their understanding of God's call for their lives.

The answer seems to lie within the "old guard," who have proved to be effective planters of churches among unreached people groups. But here again problems persist. The former pioneers have become deeply involved in perfecting the churches they have planted. Leaders must be trained, organization demands their attention, quality control depends upon their wisdom and their presence. So new churches among neighboring unreached people groups must remain a priority rather than a practice.

An obvious solution to the problem of finding people called by God to continue His pioneer evangelistic mission lies with the new Christians leading the new churches. But these leaders are essential for the development of the young churches they lead. Later, of course, they can move into new country, but not now. The young church's need is too urgent. Others must wait.

The remaining solution seems to be to employ poorly trained evangelists with a poor salary and with poor equipment to move into new, unevangelized people groups to do work they are frequently not called by God to do. They become sent, paid workers without missionary models and are frequently severely criticized for lack of productivity.

In my judgment the greatest need in missions today is for God-called and Spirit-equipped people to move into new, unreached people groups to teach and model the gospel. Such people do present themselves for mission service, are well trained for their mission, and are frequently tied to existing works fulfilling the vision of others rather than the call of God for them.

This serious missionary problem is reflected in the churches we plant. Mission mobility is replaced by non-growth stability. Unreached neighbors remain unreached.

Commitment

Jesus said, "Unless a grain of wheat falls into the earth and dies, it remains alone; but if it dies, it bears much fruit" (John 12:24). The expansion of His church among the peoples of this world is marked by the blood of His martyrs. Christ Himself modeled the ministry for those who would become His disciples.

Yet one does not find any great propensity toward martyrdom in the usual cadres of our mission force today. The words of the Jesuit missionary, Isaac Jogues, when captured by the Iroquois in 1642, seem strange to us, do they not? He was captured, escaped, but returned to share the fate of his colleagues, saying,

Could I indeed abandon them without giving them the help which the Church of my God has entrusted to me? Flight seemed horrible to me. If it must be, I said in my heart, that my body suffer the fire of earth, in order to deliver these poor souls from the flames of hell, it is but a transient death, in order to procure for them an eternal life (Marshall 1977:77).

After more than a year of captivity and torture, Father Jogues escaped. After serving as France's ambassador to the Iroquois Nation, he requested reassignment to mission work among the Indians. He wrote a friend before his return to work among them:

My heart tells me that if I have the happiness of being employed in this mission, I will go and not return; but I shall be happy if the Lord will complete the sacrifice where He has begun it, and make the little blood I have shed in that land, the earnest of what I would give (Weigle 1928:28).

Stories of suffering abound from the days of the cultural revolution in China during the 1960s. Young people volunteered to join the ranks of the persecuted people of God to share the shame and hardships. What kind of modern missionaries will be necessary to work beside these Christians when God opens the doors for foreigners to participate in the evangelization of unreached peoples in China? Most certainly it will demand a commitment and a willingness to suffer for Christ and His mission. A recent prayer letter from the Zhegang Province in China recounts present-day beating and torturing of Christians in that area, saying:

Thanks be to the Lord, through these fiery trials the faith of many brothers and sisters becomes stronger than ever. They now have a much clearer sense of destination. . . . May God cause us to be more faithful in propagating the Gospel so that we may welcome His glorious return without shame (*Partners* 1983:12).

This past summer I visited Christian brothers east of Austria in a Communist controlled country. The price for being caught evangelizing fellow countrymen is the loss of employment for both husband and wife, the loss of influence, possible jail and possible loss of children to be reared by foster parents more acceptable to the state. Knowing the risks involved in my friend's Christian activities, I questioned, ''What if you are caught?'' ''If I am caught?'' he said. ''I know that I must some day be caught. But I am willing to pay whatever the price may be to serve the Lord I love.'' What kind of missionary commitment would it take to serve beside such a person?

Cultural Baggage and Communication

Ethnocentrism prompts cross-cultural communicators to interpret and evaluate behavior and objects of a host culture by reference to the standards of his or her own culture rather than those of the culture to which they belong. It remains commonplace in most mission structures. We cannot, and perhaps should not, travel without our cultural baggage. But we should not measure others by our own yardstick, which never fails to present us in the better light. We owe the people we seek to win as brothers and sisters all of the best we have to share. We also need to do our best to share with them Christ, who is the transformer of peoples and their cultures. If they fail to become His disciples, any alteration of their culture through our influence is of relative and passing value. The legitimate agents of changes within cultures must be members of that group rather than the cross-cultural communicators. And they must lead in the changes as they are led by the Lord working in their lives and groupings. We Western missionaries have not always practiced this principle, and we may become annoyed when we see our mistakes repeated and compounded by the new waves of missionaries from the so-called Third World churches. The same mistakes need not be repeated if they are corrected by minor adjustments to keep the mission on course. Failure to adjust will result in either drastic changes later or loss of direction and failure to reach the goal.

Part of our Western cultural baggage includes a general scientific, logical framework of our world view which is, in my judgment, naive in regard to the occult world of spirits. We have been conditioned by both culture and training not to believe in the spirit world and its interaction in the worlds of humanity. A superior smile, gentle ridicule, or angry condemnation of things we do not understand or refuse to believe have too often closed the door to communication with those whose lives are shaped, directed, and, at times, enslaved by spirits. We have been better teachers than learners in the world of the occult, and we are poorly prepared to confront its activities in our own culture, friendship circles, and families.

Prevailing Patterns

Major patterns in cross-cultural church planting in the past have demonstrated great capacities for success and for failure. For example, the rapid extension of Christianity during the periods of colonial expansion indicates great advantages for the church and the new religion approved by the ruling powers. Fewer missionaries are killed, fewer missions are destroyed, and great masses of people are influenced rapidly. However, the sword and the scepter in service of the cross exact a price for protection. In spite of frequent, widespread acceptance of the approved religion, state religion produces shallow commitment and deep resentments. When the patronizing power is replaced, the church has great difficulty disassociating itself from former oppressors in the minds of the masses. Roman Catholicism under the Belgian rule in the Congo is a modern example, as is Mexico under former leaders. Nominal conversion to

Christianity has produced large numbers of Christo-pagans throughout Latin America. Post-colonial Africa has forced the once favored churches to drastically alter their former methods of mission.

Another effective pattern for planting churches in new people groups is the mission station method. A small Christian community is established within the people group, usually ministering to a felt need of the people served. From the original service response by the mission, a full-orbed, whole-person ministry usually develops with religious, educational, medical, and technical programs established. Development of central programs takes precedence over evangelism in the larger area. Large budgetary allocations are necessary to meet the growing needs of the station services, and more missionaries are assigned to these works. The relatively few people served by the growing institutions become further and further removed from their non-Christian families and friends, and an insulated, encapsulated Christian community consigns itself to slow growth and limited influence. Unreached people within the larger group remain unreached. A good method of planting new churches among unreached peoples becomes a bad method for continued evangelistic outreach to the fringes of the group. Unfortunately, older missions committed to the station pattern for mission ministry seem to find it very difficult to adjust to the changes needed, and frequently they continue good works to the neglect of unreached neighbors and effective mission outreach.

Institutional patterns of mission have proved very effective in opening new works among some unreached peoples. Schools have been established on all levels to meet needs of the peoples served. Many have been converted through the daily contacts with Christian professors and have been trained to follow the examples of their missionary models. In the 1950s almost all the education in Africa south of the Sahara was in the hands of religious organizations, and most of the people being won to Christ came from the student population. I administered a regional school system in Zaire (then the Congo) during that period with more than 5,000 students representing five major tribes. During those days it was a rare occasion when adults who had not studied in a Christian school made professions of faith and joined the church. Almost all of our new church members came from the student population, even when the old tribal leaders requested our schools, paid for the necessary constructions, helped support the teachers, and sent their young people to the schools. In the early days of the institutional mission patterns, rapid progress was often noted, widespread acceptance was frequently experienced, and great anticipation prevailed.

Later, however, this beneficial pattern of educational mission lost much of its evangelistic vision. Nominal Christianity became the norm and continued evangelistic outreach to non-Christians was replaced by a dedicated educational ministry providing higher education for the children of existing church members. Thus a useful method of penetrating a new unreached people with the gospel became a service program without evangelical returns. Our experience in Zaire with education as a method for continued mission mobility has proved to be a general pattern in our mission work in Brazil and elsewhere.

Medical institutions have also been used by God to advance His kingdom in new, unreached people groups. Great, long term mission institutions have developed and have been faithfully maintained and manned at tremendous cost, rendering outstanding human service. However, the contributions of these institutions to reaching unreached peoples for Christ need to be carefully and courageously monitored if they are to remain truly mission institutions.

Other special-needs patterns of mission have been, and continue to be, developed and deployed in unreached people groups with great effectiveness and lasting results. However, each of these mission services needs to be constantly monitored to keep them on course as truly mission programs, and priorities of the Great Commission must not be forgotten. Christian literature, Christian radio, and specialized ministries to meet the needs of selected groups all have great potential for effective witness. All are presently being used by God in His mission, yet all need to be regularly evaluated when fine tuning can still keep them on course and productive. Otherwise we allow them to drift into only good services for a selected few and there is a loss of true mission direction and mobility.

All of these major patterns in cross-cultural, pioneer mission have been and can be productive in winning people to Christian faith and in establishing new churches among hitherto unreached peoples. All of them also have a built-in potential for drifting off course and diverting resources from the primary goal of making disciples of Jesus Christ among the people of the world. What can be done to help keep our mission efforts on course?

Possible Solutions

We have identified the basic problem of reaching unreached peoples as spiritual. Scripture affirms the battle between the lordship of Christ in the lives of individuals and enslavement by Satan as a conflict between supernatural powers with eternal consequences for all people. Jesus promised the necessary spiritual resources for His followers to engage in this battle when He said:

> All authority in heaven and on earth has been given to me. Therefore go and make disciples of all nations, baptizing them in the name of the Father and of the Son and of the Holy Spirit, and teaching them to obey everything I have commanded you. And surely I will be with you always, to the very end of the age (Matt. 28:18-20).

"Going," "baptizing," and "teaching," we are to "make disciples" (the controlling verb) among all peoples.

To accomplish the spiritual mission incumbent upon the followers of Christ, Scripture affirms that all Christians are endowed with spiritual gifts for service within the church and for fulfillment of its mission. Some Christians are called to mission service (Wagner 1979:105). Paul and Barnabas are examples. When the Christians in Antioch were gathered for worship, the Holy Spirit said:

> "Set apart for me Barnabas and Saul for the work to which I have called them." So after they had fasted and prayed, they placed their hands on them and sent them off (Acts 13:2-3).

The two of them were "sent on their way by the Holy Spirit" (Acts 13:4a). Strategies for the fulfillment of their mission depended upon the direction of the Holy Spirit and the manifestations of His power. The basic conflict is spiritual, and the people involved become instruments of the Holy Spirit as He works in and through their lives.

This kind of Spirit-equipped, Spirit-directed, Spirit-empowered communicator of the gospel is desperately needed today for continued obedience to the demands of the Great Commission. The church needs to pray for this kind of representative to send out to today's unreached peoples. Furthermore, the established missions need to help these specialists reach the unreached rather than hold them back to carry on other good works.

The cost of commitment today to evangelism and church planting among unreached peoples is one's life. Either it must be laid down as a martyr or continually surrendered for sacrificial service as an instrument of God's Holy Spirit. The day of martyrs is not past. There have been more martyrs in our century than any preceding century in the history of the Christian church. Complete surrender to the will of God is still a prerequisite to great usefulness in His mission.

New waves of cross-cultural missionaries are now rising to obey the call of God for mission service. Many of them are not from North America or Western Europe. They come from many cultures and political and economic backgrounds. Some are the products of our earlier mission works and share many of our convictions concerning mission goals and stategies. Yet they come with the authentic stamp of their own cultures and those cultures' accompanying strengths and potential dangers. How can we best fulfill our mission? I believe great new strength can come for mission outreach into new areas of unreached peoples through the partnership of Christians from diverse backgrounds uniting for evangelical outreach. Each group can add strengths to the mission and help to balance the weaknesses of the others. North Americans and Western Europeans can learn much from Third World brothers and sisters in mission service concerning the occult and the religious traditions from which they have come.

Concerning strategies for pioneer missions we have discussed, I would suggest that all of the older patterns that have been productive in the past have value and potential for today's missions. Their shortcomings lie in the ever-present danger of losing sight of the goal and the purpose of God's mission. The goals must remain faithful to the purpose of God revealed in Scripture to disciple the peoples of this world through faithful witness by His people and the transforming power of His Spirit. With a fixed, clear purpose ever before us, flexibility in methods becomes as necessary as a pilot's inflight corrections to keep his ship on course. Failure to adjust to changing needs results in loss of direction and failure to arrive at the desired goals.

Dr. Donald McGavran, in his book, *Understanding Church Growth*, encourages us to "evangelize to the fringes" all the people in the group we are serving (McGavran 1980:410). Furthermore, we should not only share with them our vision of reaching unreached peoples, and train them to carry on as effectively as possible the mission among their own neighboring people groups. We must model for them the evangelistic missionary in action. In this last and necessary step, I fear we have failed too frequently. And the results of our ministries reflected in the lives of the people we have served condemn us. Therefore I suggest that we give serious consideration to increased partnership in missions to the unreached with those who can strengthen our weaknesses and profit by our strengths.

Chapter 9
New Means of Reaching the Unreached
J. Dudley Woodberry

Ecclesiastes 1:9 says, "There is nothing new under the sun." This is borne out when we look at means for reaching the unreached. Virtually all current means except those involving high technology have appeared or been used before. However, there are some contemporary movements and phenomena that can be considered forces for evangelism. In addition, there are some methods of evangelism whose time has come, which are being dusted off and refurbished. In the providence of God "the fullness of time" for them has come. The present study will be divided into these two parts.

Contemporary Movements and Phenomena

Tentmaking Ministries

As the name implies, tentmaking is not a new means of evangelism but has its roots in the apostle Paul. It continued with, for example, the Nestorian merchants in China during the Tang dynasty (seventh to ninth centuries) and with more modern missionaries like William Carey. However, the hiring of thousands of expatriates with petrodollars by formerly closed countries like Saudi Arabia makes this a means of witness whose time has come as never before. J. Christy Wilson, Jr., has written a foundational study of the topic in his book, *Today's Tentmakers* (1981).

There are two types of tentmakers—one whose witness is primary and whose job is secondary and the other whose job is the reason for his being in an area and provides opportunities to express faith through work. Both face dangers— the first that of not making work a testimony and the second that of letting work monopolize available time. Tentmakers include business and medical personnel and teachers.

A number of *organizations* have already arisen *to aid tentmakers*. Information gathering on available jobs is done by Ruth Siemens and Don Hamilton of the Overseas Counselling Service and also to a certain extent by Intercristo. Interdenominational mission boards like the Bible and Medical Missionary Fellowship and denominational boards like the Southern Baptists have offices devoted to this ministry. At least one employment agency in the United States for overseas personnel is primarily concerned with tentmakers. Also there are specialized organizations, such as the International Assistance Mission in Afghanistan and the United Mission to Nepal, that oversee Christians giving cups of cold water in Christ's name.

What are the strengths of tentmaking ministries? First, they give an example of a Christian calling integrated with secular vocation as Paul did. Secondly, they provide ways of meeting secular people as equals. Thirdly, they can provide personal and financial aid to local congregations naturally, without its being forced as in many church-mission relationships. Fourthly, they correct misconceptions such as the belief that God is interested only in church ministries. Fifthly, it is increasingly expensive to support regular missionaries. Sixthly, these ministries are a means of entering otherwise closed lands like Saudi Arabia and Afghanistan. Seventhly, they avoid the stigma attached to missionaries of being paid propagandists. Finally, tentmakers meet a different and higher level of society than most missionaries do.

There are weaknesses as well. First, there is usually a lack of time for language study and discipling. Secondly, it is hard to serve two masters, especially when your earthly one does not want the local people or government to be upset. Thirdly, most tours are limited to about two years, hardly enough time to accomplish much. Fourthly, because there are no supporting churches, there is normally lack of adequate prayer backing. Fifthly, tentmakers are often isolated in foreign compounds and so do not have contact with the local people. Sixthly, they may lack Christian fellowship. Seventhly, orientation is normally minimal. Eighthly, they lack the stimulus of accountability for their work for Christ. Finally, they may be locked into an unresponsive area because they are not guided by church planning and coordination.

Guidelines for tentmakers should be given in two areas. Every effort should be made to keep a low profile. This means that mission agencies should adopt a secular name for any department dealing with tentmaking ministries. Mission letterheads and return addresses should not be used. Mission organizations should not advertise tentmaking agencies by name and should avoid publicity—especially in print. The latter led to the curtailment of work in Afghanistan on at least one occasion. Muslims have been using Christian publications to gather information on tentmaking activities (Sulaiman 1981; von Denferr n.d.).

Complementary guidelines are needed for some ethical questions. Although the author has suggested that tentmakers keep a low profile, our integrity is part of our witness. We should not do secretly anything we have agreed not to do, no matter how noble the goal. Tentmakers have various responsibilities. The first is to God. However, in indicating that we should obey God rather than men,

Peter is not suggesting that we can obey God by breaking our word to men. Furthermore, he and the other apostles were citizens of their land. They had not agreed to avoid preaching publicly in order to enter the land. Therefore, we need to be aware of and abide by any agreements we have made to the civil authorities or our employer in order to enter the country. Finally, we have responsibilities to the church—especially any local expressions of it—that we do not unnecessarily complicate things for them.

The potential for tentmaking ministries coupled with their present weaknesses suggest a strategy that includes an interagency office and specialized agencies or departments affiliated with missions or denominations. These would be specifically for tentmaking ministries. An interagency office would gather information on jobs (as Ruth Siemens and Intercristo are doing), recruit personnel for these jobs, and provide orientation for them. The office could then help the tentmakers locate other Christians in the area, provide edification through conferences and seminars, and publish materials that would help them be more effective. They not only could correspond with those on the field, but could send roving delegates to help them. Once back in the United States, tentmakers could be debriefed and the information made available to those who follow. Financial aid could be given for tentmakers to take time out for language study and, where necessary, to supplement their salaries and provide schooling for their children. Most will make such large salaries that they can give regularly to the program so that it is self-supporting.

Specialized agencies or departments affiliated with missions or denominations can do what a few are already doing and more. They can appoint tentmakers as "fieldpartners" or "overseas associates." The fieldpartners would then do deputation to encourage prayer support even if they do not need financial support, and they would be mentioned in the yearbook of prayer with any details that should not be known more broadly left out. They would be given orientation, included in meetings with missionaries, and their prayer letters would be circulated by the mission.

While recognizing that God's ways may not be our ways, we must carry on research concerning what kinds of people are best suited to reach different target groups. For example, although there are thousands of dynamic Korean Christians in Saudi Arabia, Saudis look down on them and are not willing to learn from them. In saying this, we recognize that "God has chosen the things of low estate to confound the wise." Another area for study is how to use all the legal channels of witness most effectively. Learning local proverbs such as "A donkey that has been to Mecca is still a donkey" can be used to explain concepts such as sin. Still another area for study is the best people to whom to witness. Local counterparts, partners, and facilitators for government business seem to be the most natural contacts. They are seen privately and regularly, and they are the heads of families.

Third World Missions

A second major movement in the world is the rise of Third World missions. *Time* Magazine says that Protestant churches in the Third World are now sending out 15,000 missionaries of their own, including some to the West (1982:57). They also are sending out tentmakers such as the Korean and Indian workers to Saudi Arabia. Marlin L. Nelson has compiled an annotated bibliography of over 300 titles on the subject besides contributing two books of his own (Nelson 1976; Nelson 1976a:250-84).

The challenge is how to work out our evangelistic methods together, share the work of evangelizing, and develop structures that help us cooperate rather than conflict with each other. The outworking of these can be quite delicate, as the case of the People's Republic of China shows. There the church has been growing behind the bamboo curtain under repressive conditions. Now that there is a crack in the curtain, Western missions and Third World missions, especially Chinese ones, are anxious to help but can set the work back by not cooperating and by being insensitive to the desires of the local church.

First, let us see what Third World missions have to offer. They help to counteract the impression that Christianity is a Western faith. They share many traditional values with those they serve and therefore can often fit into situations without as much shock to themselves and others. They have experience with many of the problems their target group faces—poverty, suffering, sometimes repressive governments, and the spirit world and the occult. Furthermore, they do not tend to develop expensive institutions that are hard to indigenize. On the other hand, they often lack training and experience in missions and do not have adequate finances.

Specific evangelistic methods involving Western and Third World missions must be worked out jointly. Nevertheless, on the basis of what each has to offer and each lacks, a few suggestions concerning joint activity can be given. Third World missionaries can guide us in dealing with the spirit world and the occult and with power encounters involving such things as healings. Our experience and historical theology—especially in Reformed circles—have not prepared us for this. How do we determine if there is real spirit possession? What do we do if there is? How do we practice a gift of healing without tempting God? The Chinese can also teach us how to multiply through house churches, how to feed the sheep with lay leaders, and how to render what is due to Caesar and to God while building the church under government repression.

We in turn have lessons to share on the danger of developing indigenous churches rather than missionary-minded churches. Don Richardson developed a method to help his tribal people be witnesses and support themselves. He trained them to be retail merchants in jungle outposts (Winter 1979:47). This method was practiced by Nestorian merchants centuries before, but a Westerner saw the need to refurbish it.

Data Gathering and Processing

The phenomenal growth of computer capability has provided a useful new tool to locate needs and meet them in a systematic way. Two interdenominational projects have already been great aids in these areas. The first, Intercristo, was organized in Seattle in 1967 to provide computerized personnel information to match potential missionaries with specific mission agency personnel needs. Thousands of candidates have found mission service by this means, especially on occasions such as the Inter-Varsity Christian Fellowship Missionary Conventions at Urbana. Many students feel called to mission service but do not know of sending agencies with needs for personnel of their background, skills, and gifts.

A second major project is the computerized Unreached People file at the Missions Advanced Research and Communication Center (MARC). The continually updated contents of this file have been published since 1979 in the annual *Unreached Peoples* series. Here the unreached are indexed according to name, receptivity, religion, language, and country. In addition each volume has a special focus—Muslim peoples in 1980, Asia in 1981, urban areas in 1982, refugees in 1983, and African peoples for 1984.

These materials are supplemented by information on the forces for evangelism found in the *World Christianity* series published by MARC and the *World Christian Encyclopedia* published by David B. Barrett (1982). The wealth of new information available is being used to motivate Christians and develop new stategies. In the fall of 1979 leaders of the Evangelical Foreign Missions Association (EFMA) met in Kansas City and planned the number of people groups each agency could begin to evangelize in the next decade. The availability of data has also let the agencies of the Interdenominational Foreign Missions Association (IFMA) and other denominational agencies carry on the same systematic planning to meet the challenge.

Other specialized organizations are gathering data to develop strategies for specific areas or people. Among these is ISSACHAR, a Seattle-based research organization that focuses on the Soviet Union, Soviet Eastern Europe, and Inner Asia. Their data acquisition methods include interviews with former residents of these areas, screening of literature, and visits to the areas by data-gathering teams. The results are then put into Challenge Reports (currently on Israel, Yugoslavia, and Outer Mongolia) and training manuals (currently on the U.S.S.R.). These include specific suggestions for strategies.

Information relevant to Muslim evangelization is being gathered by the Samuel Zwemer Institute in Pasadena, which is acquiring a computer for this. A resource pool of literature and other forms of media for Muslim evangelism is being made by the Fellowship of Faith for Muslims in Toronto. If materials like these could be integrated into library computer devices like OCLC, Inc., or DIALOG for immediate location of resources throughout North America, mission preparation and service would be greatly aided.

MARC has set up Systems, Hardware and Research for Evangelization (SHARE) for the exchange of data on mission activity. Those participating in SHARE have access to the services of the Ministry Information Exchange (MIX), a communication base in Chicago. MIX will set up a list of organizations who want to exchange information and then copy and distribute any document that a member wishes circulated.

SHARE also facilitates the exchange of information electronically. Participants subscribe to a commercial computer network known as the "Source," a subsidiary of Reader's Digest. This nationwide electronic mail system transmits information to the computer terminals of participants almost instantly. Selected participants can set up sub-networks within the system for the exchange of information of more restricted interest. Teleconferences can be set up for certain days or weeks, greatly reducing the time necessary for interactive communication.

A number of developments greatly enhance the use of computers for evangelistic purposes. Microcomputers are coming into the price range of families. Satellites are increasing the range that information can be transmitted. Touch-tone telephones can now give homes access to the facilities of larger computers. This means that the evangelist has tremendous sources of information. Also inquirers in restrictive societies could get information and answers to perplexing questions and even take Bible study courses in the privacy of their own homes.

Obviously there are problems with high technology methods. These facilities are least available where the most unreached people live. Western tools convey their own messages, which are not the best for building indigenous churches. Most importantly, they limit personal contact—a significant ingredient of most evangelism. Nevertheless, as a means of gathering and processing information for the development of strategies, computer technology is a major new means of carrying out the Great Commission.

Student Responsiveness

In the 50 years following the inception of the Student Volunteer Movement in the 1880s, it was instrumental in sending out 20,500 missionaries (Kane 1978:103). An even greater potential exists among students today. John E.

Kyle, Missions Director of the Inter-Varsity Christian Fellowship, estimates that there are at least 250,000 committed Christian students on secular and Christian college campuses in North America today (Wilson 1980:17).

During the 1960s the percentage of students at the IVCF Missions Conventions who signed cards of their willingness to become missionaries declined. But in the 1970s the percentage increased from 8 percent in 1970 to 50 percent by 1976 (Winter 1980:5). By 1979 there were 16,500 delegates with many more turned away, and 8,000 or 48 percent signed cards to explore God's will concerning their serving as missionaries. Of these, 2,000 indicated they would actually take steps going overseas with a mission agency. At the same time, 7,000 European students were attending a missionary conference in Lausanne, Switzerland (Wilson 1980:15).

In addition to the International Fellowship of Evangelical Students of which Inter-Varsity is a part, other organizations are also involved in motivating and training students. Campus Crusade for Christ with its Agape Movement has a large training program. The U.S. Center for World Mission, along with the William Carey International University, sponsors student conferences on world evangelization and the Institute of International Studies. Also active are the Navigators, Youth with a Mission, and Youth for Christ.

Continued contact with students who have been challenged through Urbana Conventions is maintained through "Urbana Onward." The special emphasis on unreached peoples is maintained by the Frontier Fellowship and the National Students Mission Coalition at the U.S. Center for World Mission and the Theological Students for Frontier Missions. Publications include the *Student Frontier Fellowship Daily Prayer Guide* and *World Christian Magazine*.

The tremendous potential of college students for world evangelization was recognized in April, 1979, when 20 major mission sending agencies held a consultation on College Students and World Missions and projected extensive growth in recruitment. This growth has been made possible by the enormous and unexpected increase of students in the last decade who are willing to serve in Christian mission.

A special group of students with tremendous potential for reaching the unreached is that of foreign students in North America. They may be considered a major new means because they are coming in unprecedented numbers. According to the Institute of International Education, there were 34,232 foreign students in American colleges and universities in the academic year 1954–55. This figure has grown to 326,000 in 1981–82—an increase of 950 percent. Another 23,000 are attending English language programs. International Students Inc. (ISI) estimates that another 400,000 are here for business or training (*Doorways* 1983:10-11).

The potential for reaching the unreached is evident when we note the countries from which they come. There are 47,555 students from Iran, which *Unreached Peoples '83* lists as having 45 unreached people groups. Another 17,350 are from Nigeria, which has 271 unreached groups according to the '83 annual. Another 10,440 come from Saudi Arabia, which does not have a single indigenous church. They come from major areas of unreached peoples: 30.4 percent from South and East Asia, 37.2 percent from the Middle East, 16 percent from Latin America, and 12.2 percent from Africa.

ISI has a staff of 200 and an annual budget of $2,500,000 devoted to this ministry, but other groups like IVCF also devote personnel and resources to international students. Increasingly local churches near university and college campuses are becoming involved. Currently twenty churches in Dallas have launched a city-wide outreach to the 6,000 internationals there.

Two significant developments show promise for reaching the unreached of closed areas. The People's Republic of China, with 57 unreached people groups, began sending students in the late 1970s. Secondly, until the 1970s only one in ten foreign students was from OPEC countries. Now about one third are, and they are largely from Muslim lands.

Another promising area of outreach involving students is North American students studying in overseas universities. Christian programs like ISI's AC-ROSS (Americans and Canadians Residing Overseas for Study and Service) and the International Studies Program were involved in encouraging this in the past in a modest way. But ACROSS hopes to expand their participants by 50 percent this year. More specialized organizations like the Institute of Slavic Studies in Wheaton are helping Christian students from the West study in Eastern European universities like Moscow's Pushkin University. The opening of the People's Republic of China to North American students is one of the most exciting challenges today.

Despite the obvious potential of students for reaching the unreached, they do have certain drawbacks. Most unreached people are in underdeveloped areas and have a minimum of formal education. Students, particularly at the university level, are usually educated away from relevance to the common people. Often the education is structured according to Western models. Furthermore, there is often a reluctance on the part of those who have escaped "backward" areas and gotten formal education to return to the place of their childhood. Nevertheless, the Lord who left glory to identify with common people can transform others to follow in His steps.

Women's Liberation

One of the significant phenomena of our day has been various forms of women's liberation that have profound implications both for mission agencies and those to whom they minister. Women have played a significant role in world evangelization throughout history. For example, the turning of King Clovis the Frank, and King Ethelbert of Kent to Christian faith in the Dark Ages seems to have been largely through their wives. The earliest faith missions in England and the United States were for single women—the Zenana and Medical Missionary Fellowship organized in 1852 in England and the Woman's Missionary Society organized in 1860 in the United States. Both are now part of the Bible and Medical Missionary Fellowship, which is no longer exclusively for women.

There have, however, been restrictions on their full utilization for missions. The first foreign mission board founded in the United States, the American Board of Commissioners for Foreign Missions, did not accept single women. Thus women like Narcissa Prentiss, who felt called to minister among the American Indians of the West, could not go until they got married. The list of outstanding single women is long—Amy Carmichael of India, Mary Slessor of Africa, Lottie Moon of China, and Mother Teresa of Calcutta to name a few. But frequently they have been relegated to supporting roles like secretaries, bookkeepers, and hostesses. They have been routinely passed over for executive roles even in groups comprised largely of women. Here is a wealth of talent that we are only beginning to tap.

There are dangers inherent in single ministries. The loneliness one feels can lead to self-centeredness. The frustrations of natural drives and desire for intimacy can lead to preoccupation. Without encouragement and constructive criticism of those close enough to do so, people normally do not reach their full potential. Furthermore, there are all the awkward situations that can arise in cultures that try to restrict the activities of women. For example, among the Marri Baluch of western Pakistan, for a woman to eat with a man may suggest an illicit love affair (Rosman and Rubel 1981:27).

Nevertheless, the advantages of utilizing single women are considerable. Without the preoccupation of a family and all the belongings families collect, the single woman is free to concentrate on her work and live a simple lifestyle if she desires. This freedom can give flexibility and mobility as needs and opportunities arise. Likewise, she often can enter more fully into the family and community life of the nationals.

The increased freedom that women are experiencing in much of the world not only gives the single woman missionary more flexibility and mobility in ministry but also gives more freedom for women to hear the gospel. For example, fruitful Bible studies have been held among upper class ladies of Quito, Ecuador (Lausanne Occasional Papers 1980a:27).   In India high priority is given to ministries among Hindu women because they are considered the custodians of the faith (Lausanne Occasional Papers 1980:17-18). There are 500,000 members of the women's movement of one of the Presbyterian denominations in Korea, and the Korean churches are among the most missionary minded in the world. The potential for women's ministries is great.

New Awareness of the Spirit's Activity

Significant phenomena of our day have been the charismatic movement and the signs and wonders associated with church growth in various parts of the world. These have not been confined to fringe churches but have found expression in mainline Protestant ones too. We are challenged to explore what God may be trying to teach us.

It is clear in the New Testament that the coming of the kingdom was attested by signs and wonders (Heb. 2:4) and that healing and exorcism continued in the apostolic period even through those who were not apostles (e.g., Philip in Acts 8:7 and apparently the Galatians in Gal. 3:5). Christians were given evidential gifts by the Spirit (I Cor. 12:8). The Great Commission, which we understand as applying to our day too, includes "teaching them to observe all that I have commanded you" (Matt. 28:19-20). There is no indication that this did not include such works as healing as in the previous commissions (e.g., Luke 9:2; 10:9).

Although there are reports of signs and wonders throughout church history, these are less frequent between the fourth and eighteenth centuries. However, even Luther, who for a time argued against the gift of healing for his day, reportedly changed his mind after seeing men like Melanchthon healed through prayer (*Christian Life* 1982:24-26). Pentecostalism arose in the United States at the turn of the present century, and the charismatic movement appeared in mainline Protestant denominations in the 1950s and in the Roman Catholic Church in the 1960s.

Meanwhile Karl Barth was not the only one to point out that the historic Western theologies had not sufficiently developed the doctrine of the Holy Spirit. Reformed missionaries like Richard DeRidder discovered that traditional Reformed theology did not speak sufficiently to the real needs that people encountered on the mission field. They were concerned with Satan, demons, and charms, all part of the spiritual realm with which they were surrounded in animism. They needed to see the victory of Christ over these powers (DeRidder 1975:222, n.51).

Obviously there is need for guidance concerning the functioning and gifts of the Holy Spirit today, particularly in relationship to the spiritual forces that are so evident in animistic areas of the mission field (though also in occult activities in North America). The Christian Reformed Synod of 1973 concluded:

> The Scriptures do not restrict the *charismata* spoken of by the apostolic witness to the apostolic age. Let the church be open to an acknowledgement of the full spectrum of the gifts of the Spirit.

We urge the churches within thier communal fellowshp to provide for the free exercise of all genuine gifts of the Spirt, so long as they are done "unto edifying" and in "good order" (*Acts of Synod* 1973:481-82).

Because of the need to understand the work of the Holy Spirit today in building the church, the School of World Mission at Fuller Theological Seminary offered the course, "Signs, Wonders and Church Growth." The desire for this was evidenced by a record enrollment of 279 students, many of whom are already praying for the sick and seeing God answer. The entire issue of *Christian Life* magazine for October, 1982, is devoted to this course and related topics. A major portion reports on the spectacular manifestations of the Spirit around the world today (*Christian Life* 1982:50-62). Donald McGavran, who comes from a church background that tends to be critical of healing ministries of this type, has found that where people are healed in Christ's name many are converted (*Christian Life* 1982:39). The same is true of Reformed missions too. Fred Stock, a Presbyterian missionary in Pakistan, reports on the healings and conversions experienced there.

Since God is manifesting Himself in signs and wonders today as He builds His church, we as Reformed Christians must be open to learn from Him even as we test everything by the Word of God. We need to be open to how, when, and where God chooses to work. Even while we shy away from exhibitionism and divisiveness, we must not fall into dead orthodoxy and lack of power. As we look at places like Latin America, we can see that the power of the Holy Spirit evident in spectacular ways is the means by which many unreached are being reached today. May we receive the blessing and privilege of being part of this work.

Methods Whose Time Has Come

David Barrett has given a very full listing of evangelistic methods in the *World Christian Encyclopedia*. Edward R. Dayton and David A. Fraser have discussed means and methods of evangelism in general in *Planning Strategies for World Evangelization* (1980:257-306). Here we are only concerned with those that are new or whose time has come in a special way.

Merriam-Webster defines a method as "a procedure or process for obtaining an object." This reminds us that our first object is to determine our goal—in this case, to be used by God to lead certain unreached people to faith in Jesus Christ as Lord and Savior and to incorporation into a fellowship of Christians. Our goals should be determined by Scripture, but our methods are conditioned by culture, time, and psychology. As the apostle Paul moved from one culture to another, he was "all things to all men." What is effective at one time in history may not be at another. The felt needs of different people suggest different approaches.

McGavran has illustrated how different methods bear fruit in different circumstances by giving examples of church growth from various parts of the world throughout history. He points out different growth factors in each situation that lend themselves to different methods. One method that we might not sanction today was used in Iceland in A.D. 1000. A champion of the Christians met a champion of the non-Christians in combat—as David met Goliath—in what could be called a "power encounter" (McGavran 1981:8-17).

If different methods can be used in different circumstances, what criteria should we use to evaluate them? The present writer's view is that we can be pragmatic as long as we do not depart from biblical principles. Obviously any techniques that are unethical or manipulative are ruled out. To the extent possible we should show a unity of word and deed. Although our focus in these studies is on the unreached, we also need to be concerned in our methods for relationships with the existing church.

According to McGavran experience has shown that church growth is greater the more the methods lead to independence from the missionary, the more people experience group conversion, the greater the speed of their conversion, and the more indigenousness they develop (McGavran 1981:20). Furthermore, he says that methods become less important when either resistance or receptivity to the gospel is high, since people tend to resist or receive the gospel at those times despite the method. He thus believes that good methods are most important for those in between (McGavran 1981:261). In any event our methods should change as people, such as the Chinese today, move from a resistant time to a more receptive time.

Various factors determine which methods are best in each situation. These include the concentration of radio and television receivers in the population, the percentage of adult literacy, the percentage of children in school, the population density, and the amount of social disturbance in recent years. Other factors include the attitude of the state toward evangelism, whether there is a state religion, and, if so, what kind it is. If they are antagonistic, do they jam radios and censor mail? With these criteria in mind we shall look at some contemporary methods under three headings.

Methods Involving Modern Technology

Television is a new way to reach some of the unreached. There are 250 million television sets in the world (Johnstone 1980:42). But they are not concentrated in some of the areas of the unreached. For example, India has only one set per 10,000 people (Barrett 1982:370). However, it can be an increasingly effective medium where it is used. The average high school graduate in North America has watched 15,000 to 16,000 hours of television as opposed to being in class only 12,000 hours and, if he goes to church, being there less than

1,000 hours (Lausanne Occasional Papers 1980:28). Furthermore, television viewers do not normally listen to the radio except when driving in a car. And Third World people are following our lead as they are able to do so.

Television lacks the incarnational aspect of Christian witness and requires creative programing to compete with secular programs. But it has been used effectively in the Third World, and satellites are greatly increasing its range. A cult in Columbia presented a program on the problems, solutions, and adventures of a family. The situations were relevant to real life, and spiritual applications were added. Then teams visited homes to discuss the program with those that watched it (Lausanne Occasional Papers 1980a:32). Such a method provides the personal touch so important to Christian witness. Video cassetts have also been used effectively in places like Egypt and Saudi Arabia.

Radio is not new and lacks personal contact but continues to be perhaps the best way to get the verbal content of the gospel into closed or resistant lands. And communication satellites are increasing its range, while microtechnology has made possible powerful shortwave receivers that fit into the palm of one's hand. Research has shown that radio is best for creating an awareness of the gospel, not leading to a personal commitment to Christ (Dayton and Frazer 1980:277). In order to add personal contact and follow up, broadcasters such as those in the Arabic programing of the Back to God Hour are trying to put local Christians in contact with their listeners.

Modern technology continues to enhance audio-visual possibilities. Computers make it easy to generate simple graphics like cartoons. Gospel Resource and Program Exchange uses the Apple computer to draw figures ("sprites") for telling Bible stories. Previously Gospel Recordings Incorporated provided manually operated record players. Now moderately priced solar chargers can be used to operate cassette recorders where there is no electrical supply. The potential power of a tape ministry can be seen in the rise of Khomeini, who made it a major medium for arousing followers in Iran while he was in exile in France.

The telephone is being used as a method of witness to Muslims and others in Brussels. The Gospel Missionary Union recently printed 30,000 flyers to let local residents know they could hear the good news by telephone in Arabic, Turkish, French, and Flemish. Where people are reluctant to be seen meeting with a Christian to discuss spiritual matters, the telephone provides an alternate means. The telephone book is being used by Friends of Turkey as a source of names and addresses. Each person listed is sent a letter advertising a Bible correspondence course.

Methods Involving Contextualization

Attempts at contextualization have been made over the centuries. Origen, in a letter written about A.D. 230 to Gregory Thaumaturgus, tells him to extract from the philosophy of the Greeks that which will prepare the people for Christianity (DuBose 1979:201-5). Don Richardson has recently developed this approach in his search for redemptive analogies in the book, *Eternity in Their Hearts* (1981).

Adopting the dress and lifestyle of local holy men was practiced by missionaries such as Robert de Nobili (1577–1656) in India and has been reintroduced with satisfactory results by Roman Catholic priests in India and by Phil Parshall in Bangladesh.

A creative group in Pasadena called Fellowship of Artists for Cultural Evangelism (FACE) is involved in developing ethnic art researchers to help in mission strategy. This involves music, drama, story telling, and graphic art, all traditional forms of communication. This builds on methods used by Thomas Stephens (1549–1619), who wrote Christian puranas in India, and Norwegian bards who used ballads in the time of Olof Haroldsön (995–1030).

New attempts are being made to express Christian meanings in indigenous forms such as those by the Messianic Jewish Movement and Phil Parshall's *New Paths in Muslim Evangelization* (1981). Actually, the latter approach is largely the reborrowing of old Jewish and Christian forms back from Islam. All these attempts have their roots in history and run the risk of syncretism. But they are being developed in a detail that was not characteristic of the more ethnocentric missionary movement of recent years. Others are trying to retranslate the Bible using words that are common in local religions. For example, Vic Olsen and others have made a translation of New Testament into Muslim Bengali, and David Owen is preparing a life of Christ in Muslim Arabic.

Closely related to contextualization is the trend toward designating special homogeneous target groups for evangelization. This is the rationale behind the identification of the 16,750 unreached peoples discussed above. Space will, of course, not permit the mention of the methods that have been developed for different groups.

Methods Involving Various Structures for Personal Contact

With Third World governments taking care of their own educational needs and the handing over of mission institutions to local churches, the Western type of institutions that were originally founded as structures of Christian witness are losing much of their evangelistic effectiveness. Various other structures have developed. Saturation evangelism has been widely used, although C. Peter Wagner has indicated that it is not as productive as imagined. The same effort focused on responsive segments of the society could be more fruitful (Wagner 1971:122-60).

Methods are being developed to help great-campaign evangelism be combined with hospitality evangelism. Before Leighton Ford came to Wichita, Kansas, couples were encouraged to invite six to eight neighbors and friends who were not Christians to a social evening in their home and later to invite them to come and watch a telecast of Leighton Ford who, after an evangelistic presentation, answered telephone calls to the television station (Lausanne Occasional Papers 1980:26). This type of approach could be adapted to other countries with unreached segments of the society. House church evangelism is a promising method, and we have much to learn from the Chinese as to how they used it to communicate Christian love and support to non-Christians in trials. The house approach of St. Andrew's Fellowship in Lahore, Pakistan, has been helpful in Muslim evangelization.

There are also structures that use mobility. Groups like Operation Mobilization have passed out Christian literature with visiting teams of young people for years. Now they have "God's Navy" in the ships MV Logos and MV Doulos, which move from port to port as bases of Christian outreach. Though they lack the continued identification with people that is part of the gospel, North African Mission personnel, isolated in places like Tunisia, have felt the visits to be helpful, for they created a new awareness of the gospel.

Another form of visitation evangelism follows in the steps of Marco Polo and his uncles, who, if they can be trusted, brought back an invitation from China for missionaries to come. Now that tourists are allowed into the People's Republic of China, some in a limited way have been able to bring Bibles and share their faith. This has been a supplement to the ministry of the Far East Broadcasting Co. and the witness of local Christians. This can, however, cause problems to local Christians if not done discreetly and does not allow the continued contact normally necessary in evangelism and nurture.

Then there are professional contacts that can be made through the United Nations, UNESCO, the World Health Organization, and other diplomatic, cultural, scientific, athletic, or business contacts on the international level. A few Christians meet quietly with world leaders for prayer and devotional sharing. Though the results wisely are not publicized, they are finding responsiveness as these people realize their need for divine help and sense a bond with deeply spiritual Christians.

As we look over the contemporary means of reaching the unreached, we can see God's hand in the movements and phenomena of our day. We can derive comfort from His words, "I shall build my church." He will build it through our methods and, at times, despite them.

Chapter 10
Restructuring Mission Boards
Paul E. McKaughan

As one studies in a cursory fashion the major waves of modern missions, one is struck with the fact that to meet the existential challenge of each new wave, new structures were formed. The great new societies of the Carey era gave way to the inland movements of the 1880s (when China Inland Mission and Africa Inland Mission were formed). The specialized structures of post-World War II missions filled the need as they reacted to a more technologically specialized environment. These were responses to a changing environment for world evangelization, and older structures could not or would not make the necessary adjustments. These lost much of the initiative and were relegated to a secondary plane of influence and importance in the world evangelization enterprise.

Today we are seeing a similar emergence of new structures to reach un-reached and hidden peoples. These structures have begun to emerge and are represented by organizations such as Operation Mobilization, Youth with a Mission, Campus Crusade for Christ International, the U.S. Center for World Mission, and many others that now comprise one half of all evangelicals serving overseas in missionary endeavors. They are committed, all of them, to the completion of the task of world evangelization as they themselves have defined it. And in attempting to reach their goals, they have redefined the work environment in which we have lived so comfortably for so long.

My subject is not how to form new societies, but rather how to restructure mission societies and mission boards to reach the unreached. A July, 1982, working paper of the Evangelical Foreign Missions Association defines an unreached people as "a people group among which there is no indigenous community of believing Christians with adequate numbers and resources to evangelize this people group without outside (cross-cultural) assistance."

A mission board can be defined as a voluntary society that has been formed (within or outside a denominational structure) to transform our resources (people, dollars, or money) into qualitative and quantitative church growth in another geopolitical or cultural reality.

What is involved in restructuring? Restructuring implies that there exists in our mind's eye an organizational future significantly different from what we presently know. It implies that we as missions have succeeded in accomplishing certain tasks that have made us organizationally viable. We have, under God, been successful. But we recognize that where we are now is no longer the place we desire to be. Reaching unreached peoples as defined by the EFMA study commission is not our present primary thrust or involvement, but we wish to make it so—not just in verbal communication, but also in fact—fact that can be observed objectively.

Presuppositions

Let me lay before you six presuppositions upon which I will build.

Presupposition 1. Others in this book are dealing with the theological and missiological implications of reaching the unreached. While I realize that every aspect of our lives must come under the discipline of Scripture, I also know that my own area of expertise, if indeed I have one, is in missions management. Therefore, I will try to focus my comments on those aspects of reaching the unreached which pertain to working mission organization.

Presupposition 2. We have in mission structure a dynamic that is not present in the secular world. In our organizations, which Ralph Winter has called sodalities, we have the leadership and power of the Holy Spirit, which enables us to function with resources that an ordinary organization does not have. However, there also exist many ways of behavior and operating that constantly testify to our humanity. Most observable behaviors are present in both mission organizations and structures devised to accomplish merely temporal goals. Many lessons can be learned from an observation of human organizations when passed through the discipline of Scripture.

Presupposition 3. All voluntary societies are in a sense parachurch. The church is not a voluntary association. The church is the eternal fountainhead to which we all belong and from which our societies and boards flow. They participate in the same life and are under the same authority, Jesus Christ. These societies are a part of the church in its wider sense. But the church as the gathered worshiping community is the only body that in God's Word has been promised permanence. It is central and guaranteed continuity in its basic form.

Many times this gathered community works through other structures which are much more limited in nature. The church is preoccupied with "being," and this quest spawns a constantly changing kaleidoscope of structures to meet the existential challenge and "doing" it faces. The church is multidimensional; it defies specific focus. It has been charged with proclaiming and living out the whole counsel of God.

All unidirectional or focused organizations are parachurch—less than the church, yet a part of it. The executive action arm is almost always single-dimensional in its focus. These parachurch organizations are voluntary societies to accomplish a specific God-given task. For this task they are mandated by the church (through personnel and dollars designated to the support of the ministry), thus determining a measure of control.

Presupposition 4. Generalizations and distillations are helpful in understanding the complex issues even though they may lack precision. Some time ago I encountered in a publication of the American Medical Association an article on corporate planning entitled, "Skyhooks and Walking Sticks." It stated that "skyhooks" are our idealized and internalized world views, or perceptions of reality. We could not imagine looking at the world any other way. "Walking sticks" are powerful conceptual simplifications that bridge the gap between the crude, large boundaries of our skyhooks and where we are right now in terms of our known experience. These generalizations, while crude, can be helpful in defining the problem and encouraging solutions. I will be applying these principles to the subject of reorganizing missions to reach the unreached.

Presupposition 5. The task of restructuring a board or agency is not drawing a new organizational chart or merely drafting a new purpose statement. It isn't even changing the chief executive officer or reshuffling the pieces of our organizational puzzle. Any or all of these things may be necessary. But all can be changed and still not radically affect the organizational purpose, the people and how they relate structurally (organizationally), and their impact on reaching unreached peoples. This calls not just for restructuring, but for organizational renewal. This is what I hope this chapter is all about.

I will be discussing the problems a mission board faces when it attempts to focus on reaching the unreached and some potential solutions to those problem areas. We will cover three major areas:

1. Vision (purpose).
2. People.
3. Organizational structures and their implications.

We will conclude with some suggestions that we can take back to our own organizations.

Vision

Vision is a world-and-life view, a skyhook, a mental vision of the future taking place. It is the frame that limits the sphere of activity to the canvas upon which God wants us to paint.

Vision is personal. That is, vision always comes to a group through a person and then is embraced by the group selectively. Vision comes before anything else. We learn in communications theory that even at the most rudimentary level no communication is initiated without a mental picture of the desired response. This in a limited sense is vision.

The vision that can shape reform or redefine an organization is usually not incremental. It tends to be a flash of insight. It is what Allan Thompson calls a strategic concept, "an applied biblical principle relating to God's biblical purposes whose time has come and will completely renew or redirect an organization or methods." It is the driving force in planning, as well as the realization of that plan.

The vision in effect jumps from where we want to be and where we believe God wants us to be back to the present. And therein lies its power. True vision redefines the context of our existence since it is focused on the future rather than tied to a series of regular but often insignificant changes from the past. Vision is a frame separating the truly relevant from all other activities, good though they may be.

Stanley Davis, in his article, "Transforming Organizations: The Key to Strategy Is Context," has said:

> "Visualizing the completed act" means, first, that the breakthrough quality of the plan lies in its totality. It cannot be appreciated and implemented fully—any more than it could have been conceived—if it is approached incrementally. "The component actions," the steps individuals will take in carrying out the plan, will be suboptimal unless each individual first apprehends the completed totality (1982:74).

Vision comes from an existential reaction to our environment and what God says about it in His Word. But vision is not bringing something out of nothing, especially for the Christian organization. Our vision already exists in the future, in God's plan. So for the Christian, both individually and corporately, the business of vision is one of discovery, not invention.

The concept of hidden peoples redefined our concept of the mission world in which we live; it turned our attention to a job we knew we needed to do but somehow expected to happen automatically as new churches emerged. This shift was drastic. It caused us to ask questions we have never asked. We found out a lot about hidden peoples that we didn't know before because before we weren't asking questions. We didn't even know we didn't know.

Once again, vision comes from God. It comes from knowing His Word and His revealed plan for mankind. It comes from knowing the condition of man, the world in which we live. It is not mere human invention. It is spiritually illuminated discovery.

The restructuring problem arises when in a single organization you have two visions, one new and one old. At first, this tension is not recognized. Only the implications or overt behavior or outworking (implementatation) are seen. And they seem ordinary, even mundane. The visions behind the actions remains hidden for a time.

The clash between visions or world views becomes especially ardent when different world views are competing for our limited resources of manpower, time, and money. An illustration of a clash in paradigms (the vision by which we define our context) was the reaction of those who were familiar with wind sailing to the advent of steam-driven boats. Closer to home, we can look at the tension generated between Ralph Winter of the U.S. Center for World Mission and the more established mission boards as he began to promote the idea of hidden peoples through media. He brought out of academia a new vision of mission that was out of sync with the more traditional view. We could call this a shift from a church relations paradigm to an unreached peoples world view.

In such situations crisis tends to be valuable. In fact, it is almost imperative for the emergence of new visions or world views because it breaks the old stereotypes that are inadequate for the crisis. But people don't give up their vision without a fight. It isn't a question of logic, because people always argue on the basis of their perception of the world in which they live. How often we have seen biblical proof-text battles. Often people not only see things differently; they feel they live in completely different worlds. For example, in missions we can see at least two views. One says we must nurture the emerging church until it becomes involved in reaching unreached peoples because it is the church that is central to God's plan. The other says that we missionaries have a primary responsibility to reach unreached peoples no matter what the emerging church does, and that is our reason for existence as missionaries.

The lack of vision or even an outdated vision (paradigm or world view) often comes from isolation. It comes from being shut up in ourselves rather than immersed in the environment. Vision comes when we focus upon needs and opportunities and what God has to say about them rather than becoming bogged down in resources and their management. If our thinking is concentrated on resources, it can only lead us to incremental growth, not to rebirth or reorganization or a new vision. As we just manage existing resources, we focus on the past. What is necessary is conversion, not gradualism. There must be a willingness to let go of one vision and give oneself to accept another.

To summarize, the driving force in a mission is vision or a dream. This is not a mystical experience, but rather a mental picture of a future event taking place. In that sense, it's personal, and it comes from personal interaction between the Word of God and the people of God as they apply that Word to the environment and context in which they live. This type of driving vision is the first step toward organizational renewal and a shift of purpose.

People

In *The Self-Renewing Society,* John Gardner makes the point that renewal always comes from the radical fringe and that if we are to be a self-renewing society, we must protect those elements at all costs.

Others have stated that the artists, because of their heightened awareness of our environment through the world of sight, sounds, and sensations, are the forerunners of the future among us. Renewal comes through people.

Richard Roeber, in *The Organization in a Changing Environment,* says:

> If we knew where to look, we would find the future in our midst.
>
> We cannot see them because at an early stage of development they reveal little of themselves, and what they do reveal is disguised by a habit of growth within existing systems. Moreover, we are certain to misinterpret what we see: our perceptions are formed by experience and for this purpose the past is always out of date. . . .
>
> However, while change is more rapid than in the past, it is still continuous. But the changes in our perception—or rather in the models against which we judge reality—are discontinuous. The new systems break through the surface of our perceptions in ways that appear to be discontinuous, although they have been gathering strength in our midst all the time (1973:154-55).

The new systems he speaks of are comprised of people. Some have called them change agents.

If the future is among us, it is found in our people. And they are people who for whatever reason are in touch with an environmental reality that has not touched us or the mainstream of our organization. They are able to find, as they apply God's Word to that reality, a future that we have not seen.

As mission boards we have tended more and more to take people into our structures only after long periods of acculturation, after we are sure that their world view (vision) is identical to ours. Through the educational processes of our Bible institutes and seminaries, and by experience in traditional forms of ministry, we have effectively weeded out those individuals who would hold to or might be susceptible to another vision or world view. This truncates our ability to make the jump to a new future reality, and the raw material for renewal is often simply not in our midst.

Donald McGavran has made an outstanding contribution in missions literature with his church growth emphasis, itself a new vision or paradigm in missions. It was a great experience for me, as a young missionary, to be exposed for the first time to his book, *Bridges of God,* and to recognize that a new convert in Brazil could lead me and my small struggling church into renewal, new growth, a new market area for the gospel. I learned that as one who was seeking to communicate the gospel, I should cherish this new convert as God's bridge to another people group. My contention is that we must bring that same kind of thinking to the problem of restructuring our missions to reach the unreached. We can't mechanically reorganize our way to that end. We must cherish those individuals within our organization who have a vision, a world view, a paradigm for the future, as in fact the bridges of renewal. They are the foundation stones of a restructuring of our mission to reach the unreached.

People bring renewal. Therefore, the refocusing of the mission may be more readily accomplished by incorporating significant numbers of men and women whose vision coincides with the focus of discipling unreached peoples. It is in the recruiting process that we have one of the most potent tools for restructuring. This mandates a growth mentality on the part of the board and leadership.

Organizationally we don't operate in a vacuum. People participate in a given organization because it meets their needs, not just to earn bread to put on the table (though that's part of it). Their work is a means of identification with a vision of world view. People teach in schools for far less money than they could earn in industry, given similar educational prerequisites. This visionary selectiveness is especially true as people identify with mission organizations. We can renew our organization by recruiting people with a new and different vision. Once we have them, we as leaders must nurture them and protect them from the organizationally hostile environment, recognizing that they are the bridges to future relevance. At this point, leadership is really stewardship. It is husbanding those people, the resources for renewal brought to us by God.

Sometimes we will have to make hard choices in terms of sifting the relevant and the irrelevant vision. It will be difficult to allow competing divisions or groups within the organization to develop and generate significant organizational disharmony because of the clash of values. The challenge for the Christian mission leader is to keep the differences from being personal and acrimonious and to insist that all operate within the biblical norms that govern relationships, making the Bible the effective arbiter and standard of conduct.

To review, vision is the driving force of mission. It comes as a discovery of God's will for the future, perceived through the interaction of His Word and our environment. It comes to perceptive individuals, more often than not out of the mission establishment mainstream. We may be able to refocus as we bring into the organization significant numbers of people who share a common vision for the future, even though that vision may be different from the core of our organization.

"God has no grandchildren" was a statement made by Vance Havner, and it is true. Each generation must have its own vision, because vision is for a specific context and time. Vision is given to people, never to organizational machinery. It is people that renew organizations. Organizations can stifle people of vision, but these same people will go out and form new organizations. Isn't this what has happened? It is the mission management's responsibility to protect the visionaries, the ones on the cutting edge, the radical fringe, and seek ways to implement their visions.

141

Organizational Structures and Their Implications

We have seen that meaningful organizational renewal comes from conversion to a new world view, and that people are the bridges to seeing that new vision accomplished.

Lastly, we must recognize that we are a structural reality, and that structure influences our ability to retool, to adapt to the change in environment, and to make the future a reality.

"Doing" always demands structure if we are to extend action beyond the individual's own ability and include other men and women who buy into the vision. The ability to create and work within a variety of structures is a God-given response to our humanness. We need to work in relation to other beings. Organizational structure may not be an essential part of the nature of the church, but organizations structured for a specific action will always be less than the fullest manifestation of the church. The more narrow the focus of the organization, the more "parachurch" is the tendency. But also the more outward a dynamic is generated if the organization is in fact in vital contact with environmental reality and what God's Word says about it.

Organizational structures are adaptable to small, incremental, predictable changes. They have a natural tendency for fine-tuning themselves, and staying more or less in balance when the shock isn't too great. In a stable organization, the prevailing vision and its organizational purveyor become the end rather than the means to the end. Protecting the organization at any cost becomes more important than its impact on the world, because harmony is primary if balance is to be maintained. They do not adapt well to a major shift. The shock of new visions and people is magnified by the rapidity and intensity of environmental change in our world today, and crisis is often the result.

This organizational crisis in not always bad. In fact, Professor Bo Hedberg, in his article, "How Companies Can Learn to Handle Change," says,

> You need crises once in a while. Companies place a premium on achieving cooperative and contented employees. But too much harmony, too much happiness is harmful in the long run. Success makes companies insensitive to change. Conflict, crises and cash shortages are essential for long-term survival (1979:33).

How do we know when we've reached the stage where maintaining the status quo becomes our primary focus? Hedberg gives the following progression of stagnation:

1. Things are developing nicely. Then come radical changes in patterns of competition and new technology. Markets disappear, the rules of the game change. The first thing we see is that organizations don't believe these changes are happening. They deny that signals that are different

from the normal path are real.

2. They say, "We're not trying hard enough. Let's do more of what used to be successful." They thus reinforce behavior that was successful in the past. This is often the wrong thing to do.
3. Then they say, "It's probably a temporary phenomenon. We'll weather the storm, postpone recruitment and major investments, change cash flow to get more money in." All this time, they're selling off necessary slack.
4. Ultimately they accept the fact that changes are not going away. But by then it's too late.

This describes various missions we all know, perhaps even our own. The mere articulation of a new, or even adjusted, vision, is enough to start a major organizational crisis. When a mission gets into crisis or finds it is increasingly irrelevant, the reaction is often to reinforce the maintenance of law and order and increase activity by working harder. This makes for feelings of security, especially for us leaders.

Organizations comprise people, and groups of people presuppose culture. Culture is made up of the formal and informal rules and sanctions which govern how we relate with each other and with our environment. This is true of organizations as well as cultures in a wider societal sense. In restructuring the tendency is to reform the structure to protect our present organizational "culture" and make things run more smoothly, efficiently, and peacefully.

One of the reasons change is such an organizational threat is that it affects the balance of power as well as the culture of the organizational environment. This is especially true when there is a confrontation of vision or world view, such as the radical shift from the traditional missionary approach of nurture to the concept of reaching unreached people. Organizational tension is created as different skills are needed and different relationships demanded. We are seeing this tension in our seminary graduates and traditional missionaries as we ask them to plant churches in urban centers where there is no parish to serve, no traditional sermons to preach, nor even parishioners to visit and nurture. A whole different set of skills is necessary, skills that seem to be more basic and simple, almost demeaning to a "religious professional."

In spite of the organization's natural tendency, the status quo is not our goal. To reach the unreached is. A restructured organization that meets the requirement of the future, known for sure only by God but glimpsed by faith in our mind's eye, is our quest.

In missions we have tended to two extremes in reaction to the clash of vision, perhaps even caused by a desire to reach the unreached. We have structured our organizations and then sought to define our vision of the future and our strategy for accomplishing it. The structure thus becomes the limiter, the prison, and the

143

organizational chart becomes the map to some as yet undefined future. On the other extreme, we have denied our present organizational reality and attempted to start from scratch as though the task was the only reality of our organization's existence. The first extreme leads to self-satisfied stagnation and irrelevance, while one result of the latter can only be likened to the paralysis induced by surgical intervention with procedures too radical for the condition of the patient. Debilitating shock and sometimes even death result.

Organizationally we must joyfully accept the fact that we are a reality. That fact is testimony to our having done many things right. To operate with any other conclusion would be to deny the fruitfulness of the most productive enterprise for positive change in human history—foreign mission organizations. God has in fact blessed our efforts.

How, then, can we begin to restructure our organizations so that they can meet the challenge of reaching unreached peoples? Let me propose some suggestions.

The first step is the recognition that we don't exist for ourselves. We exist for others, for reaching the unreached. Organizational productivity can only be validated outside its own system. The first step often comes when we shift our primary awareness from ourselves to our environment.

Nothing succeeds like success. It is very important that we as mission leaders define organizational success not merely in terms of effectively reaching unreached peoples. And this definition must be stated in such a way that the individuals in the various departments and divisions know what they are striving for and will be able to ascertain when they have reached it.

Much of the recent emphasis on management in missions comes from a desire to manage (that is, plan, organize, and control) present resources in order to further a vision past its prime. We need to make a shift to managing from the future, not from the past.

Stanley Davis, in the article previously cited, states that we leaders must operate in the future present. Strategy is rooted in the future. Organizations usually reflect at best the present, and all too often the need for control or lack of it is felt in the past. This orientation often makes the organization irrelevant, out of step even with the informal systems we face today. This is why many of our new visions and people often suffer. In restructuring your organization, project yourself into that future reality of the new vision. Orient your organization to the future present, not the past present. Start restructuring with a mental picture of your vision and then adjust it to meet present needs. It's not inventing a new structure so much as discovering the natural organizational forms growing out of the future reality in your mind's eye.

In assessing the risk factor of organizational development, Peter Drucker has defined three kinds of risks. There are risks we can afford to take; there are risks we can't afford to take; and there are risks we can't afford not to take. This is very applicable as we speak of restructuring to reach the unreached.

I stated previously that we are an organizational reality, and the fact that we do exist testifies to God's blessing and the good things that have come out of our organizations. It is important as we restructure that we avoid placing our organizations in jeopardy to the extent that failure would put us out of business. We can't afford that kind of risk, and there are at least two dangers of which we must beware.

The first is the risk of alienation of our people within the organization (our missionary staff) by trying to impose, top-down, a new vision (ours) and a new structure (also ours) that is seen to be in conflict with their image of the "heart of the mission." Missionaries and staff in missions come to the organization because they identify with the organizational vision and administrative style of the past. If radical change comes from the top down, it is inevitable that much field staff leadership will be lost. People will be threatened. And people who are threatened are liable to reinforce the old in an attempt to gain security from it rather than take a blind leap of faith to the new.

This also holds true for supporters of a mission. Though supporters may be more open to change since their vested interest and informational base are less entrenched, no one wants to feel that the organization they have been supporting was inadequate, and thus the program irrelevant. The facts of successful ministry in the past and present must be highlighted in order to maintain the trust and confidence of the supporter. That trust must be cherished, but as stewards/managers we must seek to guarantee not just past investment but also future viability.

The second danger is the risk of irrelevance, holding on to a past dream for its own sake. Eventually the facts will get out, but only after a time because of an organization's ability to perpetuate itself. This is especially true of non-profit organizations, which deal not in concrete, value-added production, but rather in promises and the abstract.

Irrelevance and organizational alienation of staff and supporters are losses we can't afford.

The risk that we "can't afford not to take" is equipping or restructuring our organizations to reach the unreached, for they comprise that overwhelming percentage of the world which must be faced with the gospel of Jesus Christ. We dare not just concentrate on the Christian minority and leave three-quarters of the world's population to fend for itself. That would be an overt refusal to obey Christ's command. It would be embracing, and being suffocated by, organizational self-absorption rather than risking renewal in order to complete the task.

How, then, do we assume affordable risks in the process of restructuring our missions? And how do we break the risk we "can't afford not to take" into affordable parts? One of the best methods is what Peter Drucker calls "the strategy for abandonment." He states that an organization's renewal ought to be built on the discontinuance of an old program every time a new one is added. This will assure a constant flow of new vision and new structures. It will also assure an adequate resource base for those new organizational entities to flourish.

Whenever people are working together, structures are emerging. The task and strategy will determine our organizational structure if we let it, if we are oriented in the future rather than merely rooted in the past.

If the trauma of lopping off and pruning programs that still have life in them will be too painful to the organization, perhaps a natural death is better than execution. This is often far kinder but sometimes too costly. If the leadership refuses nurture and support for a division or project, it will eventually wither up and die. But it may take fifty years, and that may be too late for the emerging organization of the future.

Perhaps a good test question is, When was the last time you discontinued a program? If some programs are not discontinued, new programs constantly have to fight for viability and available resources. This "strategy for abandonment" is a good way to avoid the wholesale overhauling of an organization. It can be done gradually, taking the most obviously outmoded programs and cutting them off as new ones are added. But it will not be easy because all programs have a constituency base.

Communication for the growth or demise of programs is where educating the constituency to the new vision and strategy for reaching the unreached becomes critical. We all know there is a tremendous communications gap. Our constituency's image of missions is sadly out of date because of the lack of information. But where there is so little information, the opportunity to change and redefine organizational purposes and structures may be most fertile. The challenge of reaching the unreached will have ready advocates who will in turn apply pressure to older organizational units that may not be in step with it, if we but educate them.

This has been the strength of at least two organizations that have turned up some good healthy heat on all of us: the Association of Church Missions Committees (ACMC) and the U.S. Center for World Mission and her related tentacles. They have in a short time gained influence by reeducating a large and vocal mission constituency. They have redefined for our constituencies the job of missions according to their own vision. We must use this effective tool of communications to build up new programs and allow others to wither and die. It requires tact and God's divine wisdom to know the "risk you can afford to take," for in the process you can not only educate, but also alienate. Know your people, but educate them, don't pander to them. They too should be included in the process of organizational renewal.

Another strategy that is often helpful is the strategy of adhocracy. We can use this through the creation of task forces, pulling together on a temporary, ad hoc basis key individuals from various divisions to attempt a particular project with unreached peoples. Once an ad hoc organization has functioned successfully for a couple of years, it becomes entrenched with its own constituency and takes its place in the organizational structure. Adhocracy also allows us to experiment with new structures such as matrix types of organization until the most efficacious one emerges.

We are working in unstable environments that are constantly changing. Our organizational structure should reflect this fact by granting greater autonomy to our operational units and allowing them to develop those plans and methodologies which are most effective in reaching the unreached, the focus of our activities. We will also be providing an organizational climate in which creative people with vision can be developing new ideas and new approaches that will bring successful innovation into the main body. We can reduce bureaucratic controls because of the information and communication explosion, which insures more immediate feedback between field and headquarters or between units on the same field. We must allow greater autonomy in determining operational and planning options in our field units while increasing the insistence upon accountability through the use of technology. We do this to insure that we will not be condemning people of vision, our organizations, and the church to an era in which a plethora of new emerging structures will be vying for the support of the church, thus creating more confusion and waste.

Summary

In order to restructure to reach the unreached, we must invest our time and dollars into the future, not in organizationally fine-tuning the past. If we don't, we won't have an organizational future. If we as leaders do not create a verdant organizational environment by recruiting creative people of vision into our organizations, by nurturing them, and by allowing and planning for creative structural alternatives that will enable them to fulfill their God-given vision, we will look back twenty years from now and find that the unreached are still unreached and the percentages will have changed, and that to our detriment.

Let me quote John Naisbitt in his bestseller, *Megatrends:*

> We are living in a *time of parenthesis,* a time between eras. It is as though we have bracketed off the present from both the past and the future, for we are neither here nor there. We have not quite left behind the either/or

America of the past—centralized, industrialized, and economically self-contained . . . we have approached problems with an eye toward the high-tech, short-term solutions.

But we have not embraced the future either. We have done the human thing: We are clinging to the known past in fear of the unknown future. . . . Those who are willing to handle the ambiguity of this in-between period and to anticipate the new era will be a quantum leap ahead of those who hold on to the past. The time of the parenthesis is a time of change and questioning.

. . . This newly evolving world will require its own structure. We are beginning to abandon the hierarchies that worked well in the centralized, industrial era. In their place, we are substituting the network model of organization and communication, which has its roots in the natural, egalitarian, and spontaneous formation of groups among like-minded people. Networks restructure the power and communication flow within an organization from vertical to horizontal (1982:251).

I have read few paragraphs that were more descriptive of us as mission organizations facing the challenge of a changing environment and a refocusing of vision to reach unreached peoples. Let me share the final paragraphs of that book.

Such is the time of parenthesis, its challenges, its possibilities, and its questions.

Although the time between eras is uncertain, it is a great and yeasty time, filled with opportunity. If we can learn to make uncertainty our friend, we can achieve much more than in stable eras.

In stable eras, everything has a name and everything knows its place, and we can leverage very little.

But in the time of the parenthesis we have extraordinary leverage and influence—individually, professionally, and institutionally—if we can only get a clear sense, a clear conception, a clear vision, of the road ahead.

My God, what a fantastic time to be alive! (1982:252).

Amen. We bring to this kaleidoscope of change the flexibility and freedom of response that comes only from having the unchanging revelation of God and His plan (the Word) and the unchanging destiny of serving the King, the one supreme ruler over all the universe for all time. Let us boldly restructure our organizations and do what is necessary to fulfill His mandate to disciple the nations by reaching the unreached.

Chapter 11
Mobilizing the Seminaries
Addison P. Soltau

Introduction

Within the broader discussion of reaching the unreached the topic of mobilizing our church institutions for theological education for this task must also be included. In doing so, however, we touch an issue that lies near the heart of the problem of reaching the unreached. More than fifteen years ago this problem was pointed out in an address delivered by Dr. James F. Hopewell of the Theological Fund. His topic was "Preparing the Candidate for Mission." And in that address he spoke of the existence of a worldwide problem, that of a need for ministers who could lead their congregations in active outreach into the world beyond the boundaries of the institutions of the church. The problem, he said, is that "surprisingly few candidates are prepared to engage in that mission with any consistency or accuracy. And while this fault may be attributed to most any aspect of modern church structure, it seems particularly encouraged by the pattern of theological education now practiced in most seminaries around the world" (Winter 1969:38). Dr. Hopewell's charge focuses on the very issue before us, that is, not merely the preparation of candidates to minister outside their own church boundaries, but to lead their congregations to do so.

The problem is more complex, however. A wider dimension has to do with the effectiveness of the seminary as a training instrument. Some are raising the question as to whether the seminary is the best place to train people for the pastoral ministry. "We are at a stage in history where education is being attacked from every angle. The church is being forced to re-evaluate. Theological education is one of the favorite targets" (Rowen 1977:1). While attempting to maintain certain distinctives in its theological institutions, theological education has been shaped by forces at work in the entire field of education. The scope of this study will not allow detailed discussion of these issues. We will try instead to limit ourselves to pointing to some of the major forces at work in the church especially in the understanding of its mission, how these have affected the preparation and training for mission, and lastly how seminaries can be more responsive to the task of reaching the unreached and thereby become more effective.

A discussion of theological education and its shortcomings leads inevitably to the church since the church and its teaching ministries are inextricably intertwined. Those charged with preparing candidates for ministry have traditionally received that charge from the church. In general, the seminary has reflected the church's broader understanding of ministry. That discussion we must, because of space, leave aside.

The Wider Context: The Church and Missions

In his opening remarks on the history of the expansion of Christianity, J. H. Bavinck makes some startling statements. "We see in [the history] the continuous wrestling of God with his church, a struggle which seeks to put the church on the proper footing, on the path that God would have it follow" (Bavinck 1960:275). God wrestles with His church, Bavinck suggests, because of its long-standing unwillingness to be involved in His cause, His mission. Two of the major ingredients of this attitude he identifies as fear of the unknown and spiritual blindness otherwise termed theological misunderstanding. Added to these two is a third, perhaps of a more subtle nature. Bavinck writes about the ever-present inclination "to keep the status quo, to remain undisturbed, a tendency which he says always plagues the church" (1960:276). The church loves to be occupied with its own problems. It also loves peace and calm and is deadly afraid of anything that can shake it up and bring unrest.

If Bavinck correctly identifies some of the basic attitudes within the church community, there is great likelihood that these same attitudes have been carried over into church institutions, including those committed to theological education. To identify more clearly the genesis of these attitudes we turn to a brief historical overview of the expansion of Christianity.

Historians point to the first three centuries of Christianity and its expansion as a time when missions was understood by the church as the task of ordinary Christians and of congregations acting together. Mission was a total act which involved preaching, teaching, baptism, personal witness, and service. The church was thoroughly missionary in its outlook and the question of special missionary activity never came up for discussion. The first three-hundred-year period has been characterized therefore as one of spontaneous growth, a time in which the news of the gospel spread over the empire by the spontaneous witness of every church member.

Significant changes took place following the emperor Constantine's decree which made Christianity the recognized religion of the state. There was a shift in the way the church understood itself and its mission. Mission now came to be understood in a geographic sense. The unbeliever who needed to be evangelized was no longer one's neighbor, but the barbarian who lived on the borders of the empire. In a comparatively short time missions changed from being an activity of the local congregation and became a task carried on by special agents in remote areas. Unbelievers were no longer within reach of the daily witness of the ordinary believer.

This new understanding of mission dominated the thinking of the church from then on. From the fourth century missions was thought of as something distinct from the mainstream of the church's life. Of greater significance is that this understanding has persisted up to the present time. In starkest terms the church, as an institution, lost its missionary nature during those sixteen centuries. Only in the last fifty years or less has the church once again begun to see its true nature as missionary, its very calling to mission constituting one of its essential elements.

This is one part of the story. History also brings to light the fact that, despite the loss of its missionary nature and its preoccupation with itself, God did not abandon His church or cease to wrestle with it to bring it back to the understanding of its true nature. God has never allowed the church's reluctance to thwart His purposes. Even when the church establishment has shown itself unable and/or unwilling to stir itself to take the gospel to the ends of the earth, God has provided others outside the established structures to undertake this task. Monks and martyrs in ancient past, missionary orders in medieval years, and more recently the Pietists assumed the task that rightfully belongs to the church. We are thankful to God that He has forgotten neither those upon whom He has willed to place His grace, nor His body, the church, which He has chosen to be the instrument to bring His grace. We may also be thankful to all the "miserable enthusiasts" who responded to what they believed was God's call to mission, and gave their lives to reach the unreached, despite the obstacles the established church may have put in their way.

One of the more enduring lessons to be learned from the various periods of history, especially the modern one, is the failure of those involved in missionary activity to challenge the theology of their day or to be challenged by it. The Pietist movement is only one example of this. Those involved in the spread of the gospel were content to do the work of missions rather than seek a broad theological base for what they believed to be God's clear and unmistakable purpose. On the one hand the church utilized theology to serve its own ends, to excuse its unwillingness to participate in missions. But on the other hand, while the Pietists remained steadfast in their pursuit, they did so without much recourse to theology. In short, the modern missionary movement was primarily a non-theological one.

As an added feature they were convinced that missions could best be conducted not by the church itself, but through corporations or societies. Thus on both philosophic and pragmatic grounds the church was perceived as being uninvolved, unresponsive, and unwieldy for the cause of missions.

Partly due to its own indifference and partly due to the indifference of those who loved the church but were content to missionize without the church's blessing, the church was allowed to disassociate itself from one of its major tasks throughout a large portion of its history.

Directly related to the above and to the topic before us was the resulting perception of the role of theology in missions. While Pietism was responsible for unleashing a new missionary élan, the movement was not based upon a missionary theology, at least not a very clearly articulated one. In fact, there was a kind of suspicion about church-articulated theology with its preoccupation with many issues other than the missionary one. Theology, it was thought, had its place, but not in the producing of missionaries, or of a missionary sending church.

This disassociation of the church institution and its missionary responsibilities has persisted through the years and is one of the facts of our time. Today this is evidenced in all the parachurch movements and all those who demonstrate such extraordinary missionary purpose. They continue to reach out aggressively to the unreached, but they do so apart from the direction of, or accountability to, the church. The majority of the evangelists and missionaries of our day bypass the training offered by theological seminaries, believing it to be unrelated to their calling at best, and possibly a hindrance at worst. In a related way those who have attended and graduated from seminary are often looked upon as being hopelessly trapped in theological games and controversy detached from the world and disinterested in bringing the lost to Christ. At best, seminaries are looked upon as institutions to prepare for the parish ministry, rarely for missions and evangelism. As Michael Green says in the foreword of his book, *Evangelism and the Early Church*, "Most evangelists are not very interested in theology: most theologians are not very interested in evangelism" (Green 1970:7).

The Narrower Context: Theological Education

Where was theological education in all of this? It was obviously part of the problem, not only in what it included or failed to include in the curriculum, but in the way the classical subjects of theology were taught. For a closer look we turn first to treatment of missiology in the theological curriculum. We will also need to mention other sectors of theological education that have had impact upon our missionary understanding.

Missiology in Theological Education

"The teaching of world missions has not, except in periods of a popular missionary tide, been a subject of great popularity with theologians and seminary students" (Danker and Kang 1971:153). This fact was documented in greater detail twenty-five years ago in a two-volume work by O. G. Myklebust and more recently in other brief articles (cf. Scherer, Bosch, Verkuyl, and others). As a subject taught in seminary, missions has been a comparative newcomer to theological education. And coupled with this is the notion that it has no rightful place alongside the established disciplines.

Princeton Seminary was the first to make plans to "found a nursery for missionaries" (Myklebust 1955:146). This occurred in 1811. The decisive year of breakthrough on a broader scale, however, did not come until 1867, when a variety of lecture series on missions was begun in several American seminaries, along with a move to establish cadres of missions in German universities. A report of the Ecumenical Missionary Conference in New York in 1900 reported, "The study of missions is slowly rising to the rank of a theological discipline" (1900:100). It would be twenty to thirty years before most American schools added full or part time professorships in world missions and required at least one course in missions.

Not only was the subject of world missions introduced very recently, but it had to be forced upon the institutions through pressures from outside the seminary proper. The Student Volunteer Movement encouraged a fresh concern for the evangelization of the world among college students, and it was they who entered seminary to prepare for service abroad. The introduction of mission courses came about partly in answer to their requests. Then, in the 1920s, when there was a noticeable decrease in the number of volunteers for missionary service, some mission agencies brought pressure to bear on seminaries to establish chairs of missions in hopes of keeping the movement alive. Mission courses thus introduced into the seminary programs reflected less a new theological understanding, but more an adjustment on the part of the seminaries to growing pressure from those who had vested interests.

A third perspective, related to the other two, is that while courses were offered in missions and chairs of mission established, there was little consensus as to where these courses belonged in the theological encyclopedia. Traditionally theology has been subdivided into biblical, systematic, historical, and practical disciplines. Within this division missions was most often treated as a subdivision of practical theology. In certain instances it was incorporated under church history or dogmatic theology. At other times missions courses were given an independent status, not so much on philosophic, but on pragmatic grounds. In American seminaries "the motivational and promotional aspects of missionary education clearly took precedence over the scholarly scientific aspects" (Danker and Kang 1971:146).

Missiology entered the curriculum as a theological orphan to be treated generally as an addendum and looked to as a means of providing instruction in technique rather than a theology of mission. As one writer put it, "It was a science of the missionary, for the missionary" (Glazik 1968:459). It lacked antiquity, many felt, because it did not appear in the classical encyclopedia. Still others thought missions to be superfluous, for its major concerns were dealt with by the other major theological disciplines. Finally and most recently it was felt to be anachronistic because the missionary movement in the West was clearly on its way out. Such was its treatment in theological education up to the time of World War II.

How did missions fare after the war? By the year 1967 the number of university chairs of missions in America was declining and missions courses in mainline denominational seminaries were being absorbed into courses on ecumenics or history of religions. Theological declension, ecumenism and religious tolerance, decolonization, and oft-repeated charges of theological imperialism contributed to the phasing out of missions programs and courses in some major quarters of the church.

In marked contrast, a renaissance among evangelical churches in America began to produce increased student enrollment in theological seminaries, a growing interest in missionary studies and a noticeable increase in the number of lectureships in missiology at evangelical seminaries. A decline in theological certitude produced a matching decline in those engaged in the mission of the church in mainline churches. The new surge in evangelicalism brought about a new missionary impulse in the church, the seminary, and missionary candidates.

While we should be greatly encouraged by this new surge of missionary interest, we may not overlook some less apparent concerns. Commenting on this, David Bosch writes, "Since most evangelical missionary work is considerably younger than that of the Roman Catholic and so-called ecumenical churches the evangelicals may face problems in the future similar to those of other churches, particularly as what they now call missions increasingly becomes interchurch relations" (Bosch 1982:14). Unrelated to mainline denominations and their counterparts in the Third World, evangelical missionaries work with Christian groups often still in formative stages, groups which have not raised some of the major questions faced by the Western churches.

The second comment regarding the evangelical resurgence in missions relates to Bosch's warning. Behind his caution lies the deeper question regarding this new impulse in missionary outreach. Does it reflect a restoration of theological values, a reordering of theological priorities which the church has lacked for so many years? In the present state of a new missionary élan, does the evidence point to a church that has finally gotten its theological head straight with school and training centers for preparing missionaries who formulate theology that will move the church along on its mission?

Sad to say, there is some disquieting news that this is not the case and that rather than theology, studies in the social and behavioral sciences are expected to provide the new insights needed to reach people with the gospel. There appears to be an impatience in certain circles with those who wish to turn to the Scriptures again. Behind the impatience is the assumption that further theological reflection is not the need of the hour. Instead, concentration should be given to new strategies to reach the unreached. This type of thinking reflects the continuation of a very old idea in the minds of many, which is that theology as such is not directly related to the mission of the church and has not been productive in the past. The perceived need for the new day is not a new theology, or a theology reworked, but a new strategy. The new strategy is derived not from the Scriptures but by perceiving what "God is doing in the world."

Two conclusions are noted here. Missiology still seeks a secure place in theological education. And the church needs a more clearly defined and articulated theology of itself and its missionary task.

The Seminary as a Training Ground for Missions

What about the seminary itself as an institution in which to train for reaching the unreached? Are the graduates motivated for this task? Are the seminaries producing a goodly number of well-qualified graduates to enter into the mainstream of the church's mission, some into cross-cultural ministries and others into ministry in their own culture to guide the people they serve to reach the lost in their own communities?

Before we attempt an answer to these questions, listen again to Dr. Hopewell's comments about the seminary model: "I would like to contend, at least for the purpose of argument, that most of these factors that comprise our understanding of typical theological education have been unconsciously designed to avoid, and thereby hinder the basic Christian intention of mission. . . . In a time when our understanding of the ministry more and more implies its dynamic, missionary function, we continue to rely upon a system of preparation which at its roots is essentially static and isolationist" (Winter 1969:38-39). While we may be tempted to dismiss these remarks as harsh and Dr. Hopewell as a harping critic, we would do well to remember that he is not only a well-trained and keen observer with mission field experience of his own; he has traveled farther and visited more theological institutions on the face of the earth than any other man.

The issue before us, if we may believe that Dr. Hopewell has assessed the state of theological education with any accuracy, has to do with the system of education he calls static and isolationist. Similar comments are made by others who view the present seminary model as unfit for preparing people to serve any people but their own. I place their comments alongside those of Dr. Hopewell for comparison:

Like the churches they serve, seminaries are powerfully bound to tradition and slow to change. This is particularly true among the more conservative seminaries where curriculum experimentation and change are often resisted as steps toward liberalism. Their faculty members, usually the product of long years of academic training in elite institutions, are locked into cushioned academic and professional life-styles and cut off from the real suffering and life-styles of urban inhabitants. The students are often the product of very narrow experiences. They are likely to have been carefully sheltered and nurtured in the church and its activities, are likely to have gone to a denominational college, and reflect in many ways the efforts made to shield them from urban culture and its problems. Many seminary students grew up in middle-class homes (or, if not, are well on their way to establishing one) and lack understanding of other, specially lower classes.

Finally, churches and denominational officials often bring forces to bear that prevent the seminary from developing in ways that would enable him to minister effectively in the urban context. He is subtly discouraged from creative experimentation and is pressured to be "success" and "growth" conscious rather than "mission" oriented (Ellison 1974:114).

The criticism of these writers centers on one or two major foci.

The first and foremost touches on the way the seminary community is isolated from the world with which it has to do. It is charged with being static, isolationist, and slow to change. Part of the problem lies in the fact that the seminary model is derived from the monastery, in which the principle of withdrawal and concentration was primary, and more recently on a model from the 1900s.

More important, however, is our theological understanding of ourselves and the world in which we live. "Still circling within the orbit of a Corpus Christianum mentality, the church of the Reformation creeds is a static, rather quiet corner of the world. It is busy, to be sure, with its own housecleaning but it has little concept of inviting in the neighbors to gossip the gospel" (Conn 1982:35). Few wish to deny that the creeds are lacking in explicit missionary theology. But it remains true that these historic Reformed confessions lack an adequate expression of the teaching of the Scriptures concerning the apostolic task of the church. So lacking are they, in fact, that there are those within our communities who feel that the Reformed tradition is threatened by too great a missionary emphasis. Neither the creeds nor the theology they reflect help us to see the world realistically.

Our myopic state is further laid bare in the manner in which we have universalized these creeds. "We in the West wait for the churches in the Third World to accept as their statements of faith those shaped by a Western church three centuries before in a *corpus christianum*" (Conn 1983:17). What was good for our European forefathers is not only good for us, but the rest of the world as well.

Our theological isolation is buttressed by our cultural setting. The seminary faculty and the student body represent one class of people. Both come from a church or churches that have historically been aligned with one class, the middle class of America. Middle class orientation and thinking does little to prepare people for lifelong and serious exposure to the great masses of the world who live differently than we.

Finally, the isolationistic mentality of both our theology and our culture leads to a concept of training for ministry understood almost exclusively as pastoral care of established Christian congregations. The classroom model and preaching emphasis strongly suggest a gathered people. Communication is oriented to the insider, not the outsider. Furthermore, the institution "is gift-oriented, not gift-receiver or gift-giver oriented" (Conn 1982:13). During seminary experience, energies are primarily directed to learning about the gift. Less time is spent on learning how to communicate that gift. We are taught that the truth of the gospel, if communicated verbally in an accurate form, will be so convincing that the results will be assured. The gift-orientation focuses our attention on the package and what we know, less on what we are, and to whom we speak. Ted Ward refers to this as "intellectual meritocracy" (Conn 1982:93).

Other forces are at work, one of which Eugene Nida refers to as informal education. Its importance can hardly be minimized (Nida 1981:103). The seminary itself may or may not contribute directly to this kind of education. More important, however, is whether or not it recognizes its presence in the culture, and takes steps to minimize its effects within the seminary community. For example, North American society has created enormous rewards for success and equally severe penalties for failure. The seminary student is often taught both in and out of the classroom to be success and growth conscious, not necessarily mission conscious.

In the light of these charges made against the seminary model as we know it, how effective can it be in preparing candidates for the church's mission? Are there other, better models that can be substituted for the one we use now?

The answer to these and other questions lies first of all, not in the seminary itself, but in a redefining of the church and its mission. That discussion is not my designated theme, but allow me a remark or two to set the stage.

There is a body of convincing evidence that points to the fact that traditional definitions of the church have said too little about its mission. While the church's preoccupation with itself has been one of the chief obstacles to mission, the attitude has not been sufficiently challenged by its theology. Those who have engaged in mission have been content to ignore prevailing theology, unconsciously sensing that it did little to move the church on its mission.

157

It is now more than time for the church to begin to understand itself anew, according to its biblical description. As Stephen Neill wrote over thirty years ago, ". . . what we need is a true theology of the church. All our ecclesiologies are inadequate and out of date. Nearly all of them have been constructed in the light of a static concept of the church as something given, something which already exists. Much attention has been concentrated on external 'marks of the church' " (Neill 1959:112)!

The validity of defining and concentrating on the external marks of the church is not the issue. What is missing, and too often ignored, is the necessity of setting these marks within the framework of the church's mission. Richard DeRidder points out "that in Acts 2:42 the teaching, fellowship, breaking of bread, and prayers of the newly-formed Spirit-filled and Spirit-enlarged disciple fellowship [is] described within the missionary context of the Pentecost story from which it cannot be extracted" (DeRidder 1975:213). When the marks are seen in any other way, the invariable tendency is to revert to a static concept of the church, and once again the church begins to turn in upon itself.

To set the marks of the church clearly and decisively within the context of mission should serve as an important corrective to the church's longstanding problem of introversion, that of seeking its own good even to the point of forgetting its nature. As long as the problem of the church and its mission is ignored, any discussion of theological education is useless. A redefining of the church and missiology should begin to open the way for further reflection on how the church can prepare its people for its mission.

It is at this point that we find the contribution of Hans-Werner Gensichen very helpful for this discussion. He draws the distinction between missionary intention and dimension. The church's entire nature, he asserts, is characterized by missionary dimension (Bosch 1982:25). This is supported by our previous assertions, that everything the church is and does must be seen in the context of mission, although a specific missionary intention is not necessarily implied. This being the case, the church carries out the basic and continuing tasks of worship, fellowship, nurture, and service, each one having a missionary dimension although not necessarily an explicit missionary intention. The church has always existed to praise God by word, deed, prayer, and worship. This doxological task is so central and all-controlling that it should constitute the very core of the life of the church. History shows that, even with the best of intentions, when the missionary dimension is forgotten or lacking, worship very quickly turns in upon itself and begins to lose its true meaning.

The church is not only called to praise God; it is also called to be concerned with itself. It makes the Word of God known to each generation, it perseveres in the service of God, and exercises loving care of the souls belonging to it. Fellowship and nurture lie at the heart of the church's existence but, with worship, must also be seen in the context of mission, having a missionary dimension. The church may not forget its Head, or itself. It may not forget the world either. The missionary dimension of the body of Christ means that fellowship and nurture exercised within the body may not happen at the expense of those outside the body. The witness of the members of the early church had definite and specific impact on those who observed their conduct. The expression, "See how they love one another," spoken about believers, by those outside the church, said something about the level of that love exercised among Christian people. It also said much about the impact this had on those who could observe the quality of that love and measure it against the lack of that same commodity in their own lives and community.

The missionary dimension of the church's fellowship was not overlooked by those early Christian believers or lost as a witness to the unbelieving community. Believers who wish to remain quiet to brood about God and their souls' needs find themselves confronted by a biblical ecclesiology. The missionary dimension of the church is primary. Unless the church is brought face to face with the fact that it is missionary through and through, that it is missionary by its very nature, and that the missionary task belongs to the entire body, missionary work very quickly becomes the activity of specialists carried on in unknown places of no great interest to the main body. More importantly, however, the message of the church becomes twisted in the process and, instead of the gospel, it begins communicating mere propaganda. Its efforts become primarily directed to producing exact copies of itself.

If the missionary dimension/intention motif is properly understood, how might it aid the seminary to reach the unreached? Does the motif offer hope that the institution can function in a more significant way in preparing people for mission? Can the models under present use be structured for both missionary dimension and intention.

The seminary model in the institutions we represent is the classical one. Emphasis is given to accreditation of the course of study, a classical theological curriculum taught through the classroom structure. The majority of course offerings are required and the material covered represents what is thought to be the basic minimum required for ministry. The more self-consciously Reformed the institution, the more carefully the pattern Calvin established is imitated, i.e., the ability to read the Scriptures in the original languages, a thorough knowledge of the Scriptures, and a knowledge of theology.

No significant change has been suggested to alter that pattern. Each department in the seminary guards its assigned portion of the curriculum, and curriculum experimentation is often rejected outright. Those of us who belong to confessional churches, who self-consciously follow a theological tradition and view change with some suspicion are hereby faced with our greatest dilemma. On the one hand, the culturally pluralistic society in which we live forces us to believe that the gospel is directed to all people, not just white, Anglo-Saxon suburban dwellers. If the church is called to witness to the world, nothing less than the world can be its vision. We are confronted throughout the world with the issues of population explosion, nuclear war, widespread poverty, and hunger. We are daily faced with those issues, plus the staggering fact that there are 2.8 billion people all around us who do not know Christ. In spite of all this, however, missiology occupies a miniscule portion of the theological curriculum and we continue to do what we have always done, in the same way.

The greatest hope for change lies in the utilization of the dimension/intention motif. Rather than trying to decide where and how missiology fits best in the course of studies, we might wish to start first with the concept suggested earlier—that of seeing missiology as a dimension of all theology. David Bosch writes, "Missiology should provoke theology as a whole to discover anew that mission is not simply a more or less neglected department of the church's life which only enters the picture when a specialist from outside appears on the scene or when a collection is taken. Missiology is not simply yet another subject, but a dimension of theology as a whole, an indispensable dimension which must preserve the church from parochialism and provincialism" (Bosch 1982:26). It should serve as a "gadfly in the house of theology" (Conn 1983:19). As gadfly, it is there to expose, act as irritant, seek to bring back to proper biblical focus lectures and studies that fail to relate to the world of people. It sits on the front row of the classroom, insisting that the lecture guide the student in applying the gospel to the outsider, be he or she the Hare Krishna who looks for people to talk to in the airports of the world, or the family on welfare in one of our American cities.

As a dimension of theology missiology is interested in all the disciplines of theological education, the way the courses are taught, how worship is conducted, even in student and faculty conversation in the lunchroom. It is there to confront provincialism wherever it is discovered, to help people gain a greater vision of the world, to point them to the Scriptures again for a fresh understanding of God's concern for the peoples of the world. If the marks of the church are to be seen in the context of mission, if the nature of the church is truly mission oriented, the critical function of missiology should serve to keep this before the Christian community, especially in theological education. The seminary theologian must not be allowed to forget that the early Christian mission was the progenitor of theology; that the church was by circumstances forced to theologize; that theology, biblically understood, has no reason to exist other than critically to accompany the church in its mission to the world. "In the words of Martin Kahler, theology is a companion of the Christian mission" (Bosch 1982:27).

Missiology directs questions, points fingers, persuades, rebukes, reminds. "Its presence among other disciplines will be dialogical and attentive, provocative, and responsive. . . . It should strive to be the most charismatic of all disciplines, at once confident of its own validity and urgency, but flexible and humble enough to learn from all" (Danker and Kang 1971:151).

If missiology can serve in this way to stimulate renewed thinking regarding God's desire for the world and the mission upon which He would send His church, if it can serve as a catalyst within the theological curriculum to cause the seminary instructors to relate their respective disciplines to the world, if it can prompt faculty and student alike to move beyond background and training to see the richness of God's grace in His church around the world and in other cultures, then missiology will have begun to fulfill one of its major tasks. "Missiology must exert itself in and out of season to help theology—especially Western theology—find its way back down from the upper regions of the towers of academia to the ground floor of human reality" (Gort 1980:46).

All the above is academic if we have failed to find ways to introduce this missiological dimension into the life of the seminary. For further discussion I suggest the following areas to center our attention.

First, I would like to call attention to what I believe is the first level of possible influence leading to change. While the chick and egg analogy might be appropriate for this issue, and we could debate whether a beginning of a shift might begin first in the church or the seminary, I would plead that the place to begin first is in the seminary and with those most likely to influence others, the members of the administration and faculty. It also may appear to be an oversimplification, but I would further argue that a conference of this kind supplies the best forum for discussion. Missiologists and mission agency directors have gathered by themselves too often without involving seminary personnel directly with the missiological agendas of the church. When we meet for mission consultations I have yet to find very many teachers of theology, church history, or the exegetical studies meeting with us. How is it that we do not invite them? Failing to do this, do we not continue to perpetuate the divorce of mission and theology, which has dogged the church's footsteps these many years? We may be glad that recent conferences on theology and mission that Trinity Evangelical Divinity Seminary of Deerfield, Illinois, has hosted have avoided the dichotomy to the mutual benefit of theology and missiology. I would further submit that if we cannot find areas of commonality and integration, we must go back to the Scriptures again for new guidance.

It is also important that deans of faculty and seminary presidents be included in these mission consultations. These two administrators are responsible for the selection of faculty candidates. Their efforts to screen and bring to their respective faculties those who are committed to the missionary dimension makes their presence at such gatherings vital.

I wish to shift the emphasis now to how the mission sending agencies can be useful in establishing this missions dimension. First and most important, how much have we looked to the seminary to provide the theological base and undergirding for missionary theory and practice? Have mission committees and boards actively sought this kind of help? Following this, have they further sought to include the seminary in strategy discussions, and the on-going theological dimensions of the task? Secondly, have mission agencies utilized the seminary faculties as theological resources for the solutions to questions such as mission-church relations, polygyny, idol worship, etc., as these issues have been raised in the various sectors of mission activity? Finally, do our mission agencies actively see the seminary as a place to recruit personnel and further, as a place to advertise specific needs such as those involved in the evangelization of Muslims, etc.? Mutuality and reciprocity between our church committees and agencies must be the norm. And only as mission administrators seek the help of the seminaries will the latter begin to sense their involvement at this level.

The other area that can have great bearing on the mission dimension of seminary life is that of biblical attitudes to be modeled within the seminary community. Despite being one of the essential factors in creating and sustaining a missionary dimension, it can also be easily overlooked in the academic atmosphere. J. H. Bavinck deals with this subject in a chapter entitled, "The Broader Approach" (Bavinck 1960:90-120). He discusses what the missionary is and does as he or she lives among people of another culture and how, in many ways, the missionary preaches literally hundreds of sermons before opening one's mouth to preach a formal one. The Scriptures, Bavinck asserts, are never concerned with preaching alone, but with all the other elements constituting the environment in which preaching takes place. Thus when we think of the way the seminary can be mobilized for reaching the unreached, specifically the missionary dimension, I submit that the modeling of Pauline types of attitudes and responses are essential. David Bosch's small booklet entitled, *A Spirituality of the Road* (1979), makes a significant contribution to this discussion. The studies in this book are based on Paul's second letter to the Corinthians and their focus is on the missionary spirituality. In place of the Pilgrim's Progress model on the one hand, or the Jonah model on the other, Bosch, following Paul, unequivocally advocates as a third model that of the cross, which is sensitive to both the misery of people and the glory of God.

Those who teach in a seminary need constantly to ask, How are firm convictions about Jesus Christ and the Bible built and strengthened in the seminary context without at the same time creating a spirit of arrogance and boasting? Bosch points to the answer from the life and ministry of Paul.

On the basis of the centrality of the cross Paul's ministry is characterized by modesty. Such modesty does not, however, in any way exclude conviction, which is a difficult lesson for us missionaries to learn. We seem to think that modesty, nonagression, being considerate and tolerant in our ministry imply a degree of haziness and even indulgence on our part. Conversely, if we believe that we can only proclaim the gospel on the basis of a clear conviction that it is the only saving message, we tend to go about in an arrogant and uncompromising way, even to the point of imposing ourselves and our message upon others. In 2 Corinthians Paul shows us a third way. Although going about in a humble modest and unassuming way, he leaves no doubt about his conviction that the message he proclaims involves a matter of life and death. . . . The apostolic ministry, however modest and weak, does not remain without effect. Nobody remains neutral; salvation is at stake here (Bosch 1979:82-83).

This is but one illustration from Paul's life that is instructive for every Christian concerned for faithfulness, especially for that one who ministers the gospel across cultures. Paul follows the path of true servanthood, a word that occupies a key place in his letter. He finds the delicate balance, Bosch explains, "being in his Father's house where he presumably has certain rights, yet nevertheless being a stranger in that house, without rights or claims" (1979:65).

The seminary is to be one of the primary areas where the student can become acquainted with and practice this kind of attitude. In fact, the daily expression of such an attitude will accomplish much in the broader area of the missionary dimension and can create an atmosphere in which a deep concern for the world's lost can be fostered.

Finally, in the discussion of enhancing the missionary dimension of the seminary, if we believe that the church discovers her true nature only as she moves from one world to another, when she crosses frontiers (whether they be geographic, ethnic, or linguistic), we must determine to increase the international character of the seminary community. Theology teaches that the church is a brotherhood that overcomes all socio-cultural barriers. For this truth to become a reality we are to actively include those who are not ordinarily a part of our race or class and confront the isolationist mentality found on many of our campuses.

Missiology is concerned, however, not only with the missionary dimension, but also and very directly with the missionary intention. When we speak of this in the context of theological education, we have in mind the introduction of specific programs and disciplines into the curriculum through which the missionary intention can be clearly seen. This includes the areas of communicating the gospel in other cultures, the meaning of contextualizing the gospel, the study and evaluation of non-Christian religions as well as missionary anthropology. The practical implications of the church's crossing particular frontiers needs to be discussed within the context of the classroom.

What must be included with the classroom experience is the matter of "doing" theology. "Theologies are formed in specific contexts" and certain major lessons about the task can be learned only in these situations, in cross-cultural ministry. Internships, and other opportunities for ministry during the seminary years, serve to heighten the understanding of the task. Intellectual propositions in the classroom must be judged over against the human situation. Neither correct life nor correct doctrine is possible without experiential knowing.

A word of caution needs to be spoken here. Reactions to the suggestion to add more courses in the curriculum will be varied. Negative ones will point to the fact that the curriculum load simply cannot be stretched to include more courses, and the most effective way to deal with these courses is to establish a program for those who wish to specialize in missions. The same may be said for intern or fieldwork programs, which bring seminary students into contact with people from other cultures and economic strata.

It is this kind of suggestion that I wish to oppose. When we speak of the missionary intention in the seminary, I am suggesting that the curriculum reflect this intention, instead of characterizing missiology courses as "electives" brought in for the "specialists." Courses in missiology are not designed primarily for the candidate for overseas ministry. By including courses of a missiological nature within the required course work of theological education, a strong statement is being made that this training is essential for ministry, however that ministry develops. Consistent pressure must be brought to bear to undermine the age-long concept that the routine business of the church is unrelated to mission, and the church's missionary outreach is limited to specialists. The missionary intention of the seminary will be strengthened with the addition of courses and programs in which students are made aware of not only the world-wide mission of the church, but their place in it.

In conclusion, I wish to affirm again that by treating missionary dimension and intention as complementary, yet independent themes, missiology becomes an indispensable ingredient of the theological curriculum. This must be stated again and again. And it is just at this point that I wish to add a corrective to what I believe both Bosch and Scherer have stated incorrectly. In Bosch's concluding remarks on the topic of missiology in the theological curriculum he states, "The church cannot expect missiology to yield results which, according to its very nature and being, it cannot produce. . . . In other words, it is not theology but the Lord of the church who grants the church faith, vision, fervor and perseverance" (Bosch 1982:31). James Scherer curiously enough reaches the same conclusion. "Theology, in short, can serve as a corrective to missionary arbitrariness and onesidedness. But it cannot, in the nature of the case, motivate to missionary action" (Danker and Kang 1971:149). None of these writers takes the trouble to inform their readers just why theology, "from the nature of the case," cannot motivate. In contrast I wish to reaffirm that it is the Word of God found in the Holy Scriptures from which we derive our motivation and missionary fervor. Our theological reflection, if it is true to the Scriptures, should provide motivation and fervor, and those who thus hear the Word of God will be motivated to examine their own lives in the light of Holy Writ regarding their own calling. They should also be stimulated by the same Scriptures to bring this message to others to whom they have been called to take the gospel. True, it is the "Lord of the church who grants the church faith, vision, fervor and perseverance," but it is this same Lord who speaks through His Word. As we faithfully speak that word, in the pulpit and in the podium, we may rely on the Holy Spirit of God to bring that Word to the hearts of all those who hear and desire to obey. May God move through our seminary communities to bring about His desired end, that the unreached may be reached with the good news.

Contributors

Harvie M. Conn, former missionary to Korea for 12 years, now serves as professor of missions at Westminster Theological Seminary, Philadelphia. He also directs that institution's urban missions program, a collaborative effort in association with the Center for Urban Theological Studies. His latest book is *Evangelism: Doing Justice and Preaching Grace* (Zondervan, 1982).

Roger S. Greenway is associate professor of missions at Westminster Theological Seminary, Philadelphia. He came to the post in 1982 after 12 years' experience as a missionary in Sri Lanka and in Mexico and six years as Latin American secretary of the Board for World Missions, Christian Reformed Church. He has pastored an urban church in North America and is author/editor of eight books. He is the editor of the new periodical, *Urban Mission.*

Paul B. Long brings 27 years of overseas experience to his current position as associate professor of missions at Reformed Theological Seminary, Jackson, Mississippi. He served in the (then) Belgian Congo until 1960. Subsequently he was re-assigned with his family to Brazil, where they spent 17 years helping start churches along the 1500-mile Brasilia-Belem highway.

Paul E. McKaughan serves as coordinator of Mission to the World, the foreign mission arm of the Presbyterian Church in America. He supervises the work and ministry of 330 missionaries in 30 countries, making his agency the largest Presbyterian mission force in the world. Before his present task, he served in Brazil with Overseas Crusades.

James W. Reapsome has been managing editor of the *Evangelical Missions Quarterly* since its inception in 1964. From 1979 to 1982 he served in a similar role for *Christianity Today.* His journalistic career has included service as a public relations director for Inter-Varsity Christian Fellowship and a professorship in religion and journalism at Malone College.

Robert D. Recker is associate professor of missions at Calvin Theological Seminary, Grand Rapids, Michigan. He joined the faculty in 1969 after 15 years of service with the Christian Reformed Church in Nigeria.

Paul G. Schrotenboer has served as full-time general secretary of the Reformed Ecumenical Synod since 1964. The synod was organized in 1946 by three churches of the Calvinist tradition. Its constituency, by 1980, totalled 38 denominations representing a membership of over five million. Schrotenboer retains his ministerial credentials in the Christian Reformed Church of North America.

Addison P. Soltau is currently associate professor of missions and dean of student life, Covenant Theological Seminary, St. Louis, Missouri. He came to that institution in 1977 after five years on the staff of Reformed Bible College, Grand Rapids, and 17 years as a missionary in Japan under the Reformed Presbyterian Church, Evangelical Synod.

Ralph D. Winter is the founder and now general director of the U.S. Center for World Mission, Pasadena, California. The center is a cooperative effort focused on people groups with no culturally relevant church. During his ten years as a missionary of the United Presbyterian Church in the U.S.A. in Guatemala, he was instrumental in the formation of the movement called Theological Education by Extension. Following his ministry in Central America, he spent ten years as a professor of missiology at the School of World Mission, Fuller Theological Seminary, Pasadena.

J. Dudley Woodberry currently serves on the staff of the Samuel Zwemer Institute, Altadena, California. The institute serves as a "nerve center," a research and training program for Muslim evangelization. He comes to the program after years of experience and academic background in the Muslim world of the Middle East.

Bibliography and References Cited

Abbott, Walter M., ed.
  1966. *The Documents of Vatican II*. Baltimore: America Press and Geoffrey Chapman.
Acts of Synod
  1973. Grand Rapids: Board of Publications of the Christian Reformed Church.
Anderson, Gerald H., ed.
  1961. *The Theology of the Christian Mission*. New York: McGraw-Hill Book Company.
  1982. *Witnessing to the Kingdom*. Maryknoll: Orbis Books.
Barrett, David B.
  1968. *Schism and Renewal in Africa: An Analysis of Six Thousand Contemporary Religious Movements*. Nairobi: Oxford University Press.
  1982. *World Christian Encyclopedia: A Comparative Study of Churches and Religions in the Modern World, AD 1900-2000*. New York: Oxford University Press.
Bavinck, J. H.
  1960. *An Introduction to the Science of Missions*. Philadelphia: Presbyterian and Reformed Publishing Company.
Beaver, R. Pierce, ed.
  1966. *Pioneers in Mission: A Source Book on the Rise of American Missions*. Grand Rapids: William B. Eerdmans Publishing Company.
  1967. *To Advance the Gospel: Selections from the Writings of Rufus Anderson*. Grand Rapids: William B. Eerdmans Publishing Company.
  1973. *The Gospel and Frontier Peoples. A Report of a Consultation, December, 1972*. South Pasadena: William Carey Library.
Berkouwer, G. C.
  1976. *The Church*. Grand Rapids: William B. Eerdmans Publishing Company.
Bosch, David J.
  1979. *A Spirituality of the Road*. Scottdale, Pa.: Herald Press.

1981. "In Search of Mission: Reflections on 'Melbourne' and 'Pattaya,' "
Missionalia 9 (April): 3-18.

1982. "Theological Education in Missionary Perspective." *Missiology* 10
(January): 13-34.

Chaney, Charles L.

1976. *The Birth of Missions in America.* South Pasadena: William Carey
Library.

Chauncy, Charles.

1762. "All Nations of the Earth Blessed in Christ, the Seed of Abraham."
In *Pioneers in Mission: A Source Book on the Rise of American
Missions,* edited by R. Pierce Beaver. (Grand Rapids: William B.
Eerdmans Publishing Company, 1966, pp. 190-209.

Conn, Harvie M., ed.

1976. *Theological Perspectives on Church Growth.* Nutley, N.J.: Presbyterian and Reformed Publishing Company.

Conn, Harvie M.

1982. *Evangelism: Doing Justice and Preaching Grace.* Grand Rapids:
Zondervan Publishing House.

1983. "The Missionary Task of Theology: A Love/Hate Relationship?"
Westminster Theological Journal 45 (Spring): 1-21.

Cook, Harold R.

1971. *Historic Patterns of Church Growth: A Study of Five Churches.*
Chicago: Moody Press.

Danker, William J., and Kang, Wi-jo, eds.

1971. *The Future of the Christian World Mission.* Grand Rapids: William
B. Eerdmans Publishing Company.

Davis, Stanley M.

1982. "Transforming Organizations: The Key to Strategy Is Context."
Organizational Dynamics 10 (Winter): 64-80.

Dayton, Edward R.

1980. *That Everyone May Hear: Reaching the Unreached.* Monrovia:
MARC.

Dayton, Edward R., and Fraser, David A.

1980. *Planning Strategies for World Evangelization.* Grand Rapids: William B. Eerdmans Publishing Company.

Dayton, Edward R., and Wilson, Samuel, eds.

1982. *Unreached Peoples '82. The Challenge of the Church's Unfinished
Business. Focus on Urban Peoples.* Elgin, Ill.: David C. Cook
Publishing Company.

1983. *The Refugees Among Us. Unreached Peoples '83.* Monrovia, Calif.:
MARC.

Denferr, Ahmad von

n.d. *Christian Presence in the Gulf Region.* n.p.: The Islamic Foundation.

DeRidder, Richard R.

1975. *Discipling the Nations.* Grand Rapids: Baker Book House.

Doorways

1983. "Did You Know?" *Doorways* 9 (Spring): 10-11.

Douglas, J. D., ed.

1975. *Let the Earth Hear His Voice.* Minneapolis: World Wide Publications.

Drafts for Section Uppsala 1968

n.d. Geneva: World Council of Churches

DuBose, Francis M., ed.

1979. *Classics of Christian Missions.* Nashville: Broadman Press.

Ecumenical Missionary Conference, New York 1900.

1900. Vols. 1-2. New York: American Tract Society.

Ellis, William T.

1909. *Men and Missions.* Philadelphia: The Sunday School Times Company.

Ellison, Craig, ed.

1974. *The Urban Mission.* Grand Rapids: William B. Eerdmans Publishing Company.

Engel, James F., and Norton, H. Wilbert.

1975. *What's Gone Wrong with the Harvest? A Communication Strategy for the Church and World Evangelism.* Grand Rapids: Zondervan Publishing House.

Evangelical Foreign Missions Association.

1982. "Reaching Unreached Peoples: Guidelines and Definitions for Those Concerned with World Evangelization." Unpublished working draft.

Filius, Jan.

1982. *Bij Weijze van Verslag: Raadvoor die Zending.* Oegstgeest, Netherlands: de Hervoormde Kerk.

Flatt, Donald C.

1973. "An Ethnological Approach to Mission: Bruno Gutmann in Kilimanjaro," in *The Gospel and Frontier Missions. A Report of a Consultation, December, 1972,* edited by R. Pierce Beaver. South Pasadena: William Carey Library, 1973, pp. 139-153.

Gerber, Vergil, ed.

1971. *Missions in Creative Tension.* South Pasadena: William Carey Library.

Glasser, Arthur F., et al.

1976. *Crucial Dimensions in World Evangelization.* South Pasadena: William Carey Library.

Glasser, Arthur F., and McGavran, Donald A.
1983. *Contemporary Theologies of Mission.* Grand Rapids: Baker Book House.

Glazik, Joseph.
1968. "The Meaning and the Place of Missiology Today." *International Review of Missions* 57 (October): 459-67.

Goodall, Norman, ed.
1968. *The Uppsala Report 1968. Official Report of the Fourth Assembly of the World Council of Churches. Uppsala, July 4-20, 1968.* Geneva: World Council of Churches.

Gort, Jerald D.
1980. "The Contours of the Reformed Understanding of Christian Mission: An Attempt at Definition." *Calvin Theological Journal* 15 (November): 47-60.

Green, Michael.
1970. *Evangelism in the Early Church.* Grand Rapids: William B. Eerdmans Publishing Company.

Hassing, Per.
1979. "Bruno Gutmann of Kilimanjaro: Setting the Record Straight." *Missiology* 7 (October): 423-33.

Hedberg, Bo.
1979. "How Companies Can Learn to Handle Change." *International Management* 34 (April): 33-36.

Henry, Carl F. H., and Mooneyham, W. Stanley, eds.
1967. *One Race, One Gospel, One Task.* Vols. I-II. Minneapolis: World Wide Publications.

Hesselgrave, David J., ed.
1979. *New Horizons in World Missions: Evangelicals and the Christian Mission in the 1980s.* Grand Rapids: Baker Book House.

Hoekendijk, J. C.
1948. *Kerk en Volk in de Dultse Zendingswetenschap.* Amsterdam: Kampert and Helm.

Hoekstra, Harvey T.
1979. *The World Council of Churches and the Demise of Evangelism.* Wheaton, Ill.: Tyndale House.

Johnston, Arthur.
1978. *The Battle for World Evangelism.* Wheaton, Ill.: Tyndale House.

Johnstone, P. J.
1980. *Operation World.* 2nd edition. Bromley, Kent: STL Publications.

Kane, J. Herbert.
    1978. *A Concise History of the Christian World Mission.* Grand Rapids: Baker Book House.

Keysser, Christian.
    1924. "Mission Work Among Primitive Peoples in New Guinea." *International Review of Missions* 13 (July): 426-35.
    1980. *A People Reborn.* Translated by Alfred Allin and John Kuder. Pasadena: William Carey Library.

Kraemer, Hendrik.
    1938. *The Christian Message in a Non-Christian World.* 3rd ed. Grand Rapids: Kregel Publications.

Kraft, Charles H.
    1979. *Christianity in Culture: A Study in Dynamic Biblical Theologizing in Cross-Cultural Perspective.* Maryknoll: Orbis Books.

Lindsell, Harold, ed.
    1966. *The Church's Worldwide Mission.* Waco, Texas: Word Books.

Lara-Braud, Jorge.
    1983. "The Role of North Americans in the Future of the Missionary Enterprise." *International Bulletin of Missionary Research* 7 (January): 2-5.

Latourette, Kenneth Scott.
    1936. *Missions Tomorrow.* New York: Harper and Brothers.

Lausanne Occasional Papers.
    1978. *No. 1: The Pasadena Consultation on the Homogeneous Unit Principle.* Wheaton, Ill.: Lausanne Committee for World Evangelization.
    1978a. *No. 2: The Willowbank Report — Gospel and Culture.* Wheaton, Ill.: Lausanne Committee for World Evangelization.
    1980. *No. 8: Thailand Report — Christian Witness to Secularized People.* Wheaton, Ill.: Lausanne Committee for World Evangelization.
    1980a. *No. 10: Thailand Report — Christian Witness to Nominal Christians among Roman Catholics.* Wheaton, Ill.: Lausanne Committee for World Evangelization.
    1980b. *No. 14: Thailand Report — Christian Witness to Hindus.* Wheaton, Ill.: Lausanne Committee for World Evangelization.
    1982. *No. 21: Grand Rapids Report — Evangelism and Social Responsibility, An Evangelical Commitment.* Wheaton, Ill.: Lausanne Committee for World Evangelization and the World Evangelical Fellowship.

McGavran, Donald A., ed.
    1936. *Church Growth and Group Conversion.* Reprinted in 1973. South Pasadena: William Carey Library.

McGavran, Donald A.

  1955. *The Bridges of God*. London: World Dominion Press.

  1955a. "New Methods for a New Age in Missions." *International Review of Missions* 44 (October): 394-403.

  1956. "The People Movement Point of View," *Church Growth and Groups Conversion*. J. W. Pickett, A. L. Warnshuis, G. H. Singh, and D. A. McGavran. Lucknow, India: Lucknow Publishing House, pp. 1-7.

  1959. *How Churches Grow*. New York: Friendship Press.

McGavran, Donald A., ed.

  1972. *Crucial Issues in Missions Tomorrow*. Chicago: Moody Press.

McGavran, Donald A.

  1979. *Ethnic Realities and the Church: Lessons from India*. South Pasadena: William Carey Library.

  1981. *Understanding Church Growth*. Revised edition. Grand Rapids: William B. Eerdmans Publishing Company.

  1982. *The Challenge of the Unreached Peoples*. Pasadena: William Carey Library.

  1983. "The Priority of Ethnicity." *Evangelical Missions Quarterly* 19 (January): 14-23.

McQuilkin, J. Robertson.

  1973. *How Biblical Is the Church Growth Movement?* Chicago: Moody Press.

  1983. "Looking at the Task Six Ways." *Evangelical Missions Quarterly* 19 (January): 4-12.

Marshall, Peter, and Manuel, David.

  1977. *The Light and the Glory*. Old Tappan, N.J.: Fleming H. Revell Company.

MARC

  1974. *Unreached Peoples Directory*. Monrovia, Calif.: MARC.

Maury, Philippe, et al.

  1960. *History's Lessons for Tomorrow's Mission: Milestones in the History of Missionary Thinking*. Geneva: World Student Christian Federation.

Metzger, Bruce M.

  1971. *A Textual Commentary on the Greek New Testament*. New York: United Bible Societies.

Michaelson, Johanna.

  1982. *The Beautiful Side of Evil*. Eugene, Oregon: Harvest House Publishers.

"Miracles Through the Ages."

  1982. *Christian Life* 44 (October): 24-26.

"Mission and Evangelism—Ecumenical Affirmation."

1982. *International Review of Mission* 71 (October): 427-51.

Montgomery, James H., and McGavran, Donald A.

1980. *The Discipling of a Nation*. Santa Clara, Calif.: Global Church Growth Bulletin.

Murray, John.

1976. *The Claims of Truth. Collected Writings of John Murray*, vol. 1. Edinburgh: The Banner of Truth Trust.

Myklebust, O. G.

1955,

1957 *The Study of Missions in Theological Education*, vols. 1-2. Oslo: Egede Instituttet.

Naisbitt, John.

1982. *Megatrends: Ten New Directions Transforming Our Lives*. New York: Warner Books.

Neill, Stephen C.

1959. *Creative Tension*. London: Edinburgh House Press.

1964. *A History of Christian Missions*. Grand Rapids: William B. Eerdmans Publishing Company.

Neill, Stephen, Anderson, Gerald H., and Goodwin, John, eds.

1970. *Concise Dictionary of the Christian World Mission*. London: Lutterworth Press.

Nelson, Marlin.

1976. *The How and Why of Third World Missions*. Pasadena: William Carey Library.

Nelson, Marlin, ed.

1976a. *Readings in Third World Missions*. Pasadena: William Carey Library.

Nida, Eugene A.

1981. " 'Why Are Foreigners So Queer?' A Socioanthropological Approach to Cultural Pluralism." *International Bulletin of Missionary Research* 5 (July): 102-6.

Niles, D. T.

1962. *Upon the Earth: The Mission of God and the Missionary Enterprise of the Churches*. New York: McGraw-Hill Book Company.

Parshall, Phil.

1981. *New Paths in Muslim Evangelism*. Grand Rapids: Baker Book House.

Partners.

1983. "Why Is the Church in China So Alive?" *Partners* 41 (Jan./Feb./Mar.): 12-15.

Pentecost, Edward C.

1974. *Reaching the Unreached. An Introductory Study on Developing an*

Overall Strategy for World Evangelization. South Pasadena: William Carey Library.

Pickett, J. Waskom.
1933. *Christian Mass Movements in India*. Lucknow, India: Lucknow Publishing House.
1938. *Christ's Way to India's Heart*. Lucknow, India: Lucknow Publishing House.
1963. *The Dynamics of Church Growth*. New York: Abingdon Press.

Reapsome, James W.
1983. "Church Planting and 'the New Man's' Lifestyle." *Evangelical Missions Quarterly* 19 (January): 68-71.

Richardson, Don.
1981. *Eternity in Their Hearts*. Ventura, Calif.: Regal Books.

Roeber, Richard J. C.
1973. *The Organization in a Changing Environment*. Reading, Mass.: Addison-Wesley Publishing Company.

Rosman, Abraham, and Rubel, Paula G.
1981. *The Tapestry of Culture*. Glenview, Ill.: Scott, Foresman and Company.

Rowen, Samuel F.
1977. "The Future of Theological Education." *Issues for Christian Leaders. Briefs from Westminster Theological Seminary* (November/December): 1-3.

Samuel, George.
1978. "Unreached Peoples: An Indian Perspective." In *Unreached Peoples '79. The Challenge of the Church's Unfinished Business*. Edited by C. Peter Wagner and Edward R. Dayton. Elgin, Ill.: David C. Cook Publishing Company, pp. 79-94.

Sanborn, Peter.
1815. "The Extent and Perpetuity of the Abrahamic Covenant: A Motive to Missionary Exertion." A sermon preached before the Massachusetts Missionary Society at their annual meeting, May 30, 1815. On file in the archives of Northern Baptist Seminary.

Sheldon, Alan.
1980. "Organizational Paradigms: A Theory of Organizational Change." *Organizational Dynamics* 8 (Winter): 61-80.

Starling, Allan, ed.
1981. *Seeds of Promise: World Consultation on Frontier Missions, Edinburgh '80*. Pasadena: William Carey Library.

Sulaiman, Ahmad Abu.
1981. "Enter the 'Tentmaker.'" *Impact International* (June 26–July 9, 1981).

Taber, Charles R.

1973. "Evangelizing the Unreached Peoples: What to Do and How to Do It." In *The Gospel and Frontier Peoples. A Report of a Consultation, December, 1972*, edited by R. Pierce Beaver. South Pasadena: William Carey Library, 1973, pp. 118-35.

Taylor, John V.

1966. *For All the World: The Christian Mission in the Modern World*. Philadelphia: Westminster Press.

Tippett, Alan R.

1967. *Solomon Islands Christianity*. London: Lutterworth Press.

1970. *Church Growth and the Word of God*. Grand Rapids: William B. Eerdmans Publishing Company.

1971. *People Movements in Southern Polynesia*. Chicago: Moody Press.

Verkuyl, Johannes.

1973. *Break Down the Walls: A Christian Cry for Racial Justice*. Grand Rapids: William B. Eerdmans Publishing Company.

1978 *Contemporary Missiology: An Introduction*. Grand Rapids: William B. Eerdmans Publishing Company.

1978a. *De Onvoltooide Taak der Wereldzending*. Kampen: J. H. Kok.

Vicedom, George.

1965. *The Mission of God*. St. Louis: Concordia Publishing House.

Wagner, C. Peter.

1971. *Frontiers in Mission Strategy*. Chicago: Moody Press.

1979. *Your Spiritual Gifts Can Help the Church Grow*. Glendale, Calif.: Regal Books.

Wagner, C. Peter, and Dayton, Edward R., eds.

1978. *Unreached Peoples '79. The Challenge of the Church's Unfinished Business*. Elgin, Ill.: David C. Cook Publishing Company.

1980. *Unreached People '80. The Challenge of the Church's Unfinished Business*. Elgin, Ill.: David C. Cook Publishing Company.

1981. *Unreached Peoples '81. The Challenge of the Church's Unfinished Business with Special Section on the Peoples of Asia*. Elgin, Ill.: David C. Cook Publishing Company.

Ward, Ted.

1982. "Metaphors of Spiritual Reality. Part 1: Biblical Metaphors of Purpose." *Bibliotheca Sacra* 139 (April–June): 99-110.

Warneck, Gustav.

1901. *Outline of a History of Protestant Missions from the Reformation to the Present Time*. London: Oliphant, Anderson and Ferrier.

Warren, Max, ed.

1971. *To Apply the Gospels: Selections from the Writings of Henry Venn*.

Grand Rapids: William B. Eerdmans Publishing Company.

Weigle, Luther A.

1928. *The Pageant of America*. New Haven: Yale University Press.

Willis, Avery T., Jr.

1979. *The Biblical Basis of Missions*. Nashville: Convention Press.

Wilson, J. Christy, Jr.

1981. *Today's Tentmakers*. Wheaton, Ill.: Tyndale House.

Wilson, Samuel, ed.

1980. *Mission Handbook: North American Protestant Ministries Overseas*. 12th edition. Monrovia, Calif.: MARC.

Winter, Ralph D., ed.

1967. *The Evangelical Response to Bangkok*. South Pasadena: William Carey Library.

1969. *Theological Education by Extension*. South Pasadena: William Carey Library.

Winter, Ralph D.

1970. *The Twenty-Five Unbelievable Years, 1945–1969*. South Pasadena: William Carey Library.

1970a. *Say 'Yes' to Mission*. South Pasadena: William Carey Library and InterVarsity Press.

1974. "Seeing the Task Graphically." *Evangelical Missions Quarterly* 10 (January): 11-24.

1977. "The Grounds for a New Thrust in World Mission." *Evangelical Missions Tomorrow*, edited by Wade T. Coggins and Edwin L. Frizen. South Pasadena: William Carey Library, pp. 1-26.

1978. *Penetrating the Last Frontiers*. Pasadena: William Carey Library.

1979. "The Future of the Church: The Essential Components of World Evangelization." *An Evangelical Agenda: 1984 and Beyond*. Pasadena: William Carey Library, pp. 135-63.

1982. National Student Missions Coalition January 1982 Newsletter.

266.5
C753

71818

LINCOLN CHRISTIAN COLLEGE